P9-CRO-568

A

Introduction

XCELL+ is a computer application package that enables you to build a "logical model" of a manufacturing process. A model you build using XCELL+ can simulate the operation of a factory so that you can estimate its production capacity and study alternative ways to improve its performance.

The simulation of manufacturing processes been used with considerable success for many years. But until recently, the effort required to build such models was so great that the technique was not as widely used as it could have been. Moreover, simulation required substantial expertise in a specialized programming language, and the investment in time to reach a reasonable level of competence meant that simulation was generally practiced by technical specialists, rather than by the engineers and managers who were faced with the problem.

Now that is rapidly changing. XCELL+ is one of a growing number of simulation packages that are much easier to learn and to use than the conventional simulation programming languages. These new packages permit engineers and managers to build their own models in many cases, and to call on simulation specialists only when a high level of detail or complexity in the model is required.

To some extent, these packages represent a "spreadsheet approach" to simulation. Like the modern computer spreadsheet, the new simulation packages do nothing that could not have been done a decade ago. However, by reducing the necessary effort by several orders of magnitude, the spreadsheet made it possible for ordinary mortals -- that is, non-programmers -- to use this method of financial projection, and the result was a tremendous increase in the number of users. Similarly, a substantial reduction in the effort required to construct a simulation model should result in a rapid increase in the number of people who use this technique.

For example, in the past, although many schools have had specialized courses devoted to the technique of simulation, there was relatively little actual "hands-on" use of the technique in laboratories in manufacturing engineering or operations management courses. Such courses cannot, in general, assume that the students have had a prerequisite course in simulation, and cannot spare the time to teach a conventional simulation language. Now however, with packages like XCELL+, it is entirely practical to make routine assignments that require the construction and operation of a simulation model, even in a course where neither the instructor nor the students have previous training in simulation. Our students at Cornell are now literally accomplishing, in routine assignments, tasks that would have reasonably represented a master's thesis a few years ago.

Most of these new simulation packages run on a personal computer and, although this certainly contributes to their appeal, it is not the key element of their contribution -- XCELL+ could be operated just as effectively using a terminal connected to a time-shared mainframe computer as it does on an independent personal computer. The significant difference in these new systems is the <u>character of the user interface.</u> These packages are not programming languages, in the usual sense of that term. They can be characterized as "menu-driven systems". That means that at each point in their use, the user is presented with a menu of choices -- the actions that are available in that context. There are many different ways of implementing menu-driven systems -- some very effective and pleasant to use, and others much less so. Of course, computer users have been proven to be amazingly tolerant. They learn to put up with remarkably clumsy applications, but in this case even the worst of the new menu-driven simulation systems is still significantly easier to learn to use than a conventional programming language.

On the other hand, the price of simplicity in these simulation packages is unquestionably some loss of both generality and power. Most of the new packages, XCELL+ included, are tailored to a particular area of application, and model other types of system poorly, if at all. This is in sharp contrast to the conventional simulation languages which are, in fact, universal programming languages and are capable of modeling anything that can be modeled. There is also inevitably some loss of detail in the models readily constructed with the new packages. They are sometimes characterized as "quick and dirty" systems, meaning "quick and with a limited level of detail", but that is not necessarily a bad thing. Simulation modelers often include more detail than is really necessary just because it is possible, and if the new packages inhibit that tendency it will be advantageous for many problems.

The analogy with spreadsheets can easily be overstated. Simulation modeling is inherently not a trivial process, and hence not one that will ever be as widely used as financial projection. The best that can be expected from packages like XCELL+ is that they will reduce the mechanics of constructing a simulation model to the point where more attention can be given to the important conceptual aspects of modeling.

A common characteristic of the new simulation packages is their use of computer graphics. For example, Figure A-1 shows an example of a factory model in XCELL+. Although some packages use graphics primarily as a means of displaying results, others like XCELL+ go one step farther and use graphics during the <u>construction of the model.</u> XCELL+ is inherently a graphical system, and relies heavily on a schematic graphical representation to guide the construction of the model, as well as to illustrate the way in which it works. XCELL+ resorts to tabular displays and lists only as supplements to the graphical displays.

As is apparent in Figure A-1, XCELL+ uses <u>symbolic graphics</u> rather than realistic pictorial graphics. That is, there is no attempt to make the elements of an XCELL+ model look like their real counterparts. Some other contemporary simulation systems use much more elaborate three-dimensional graphics, and produce elegant pictorial representations. However, the price for such graphical elegance is exacted in the additional computer hardware required, in slower execution of the model, and in increased difficulty of constructing a model. The XCELL+ graphics were designed to be an effective compromise between the presentation of the logical relationships in a factory model and the costs incurred by that presentation.

XCELL+ uses color to increase the amount of information than can be displayed effectively at one time, but the cost of color plates for this User's Guide was prohibitive. Consequently, all the figures in the User's Guide are photographs using a monochrome computer system that automatically substitutes different shaded patterns for different colors. The actual color displays are much more effective than these black-and-white pictures.

Figure A-1

Example of an XCELL+ factory model

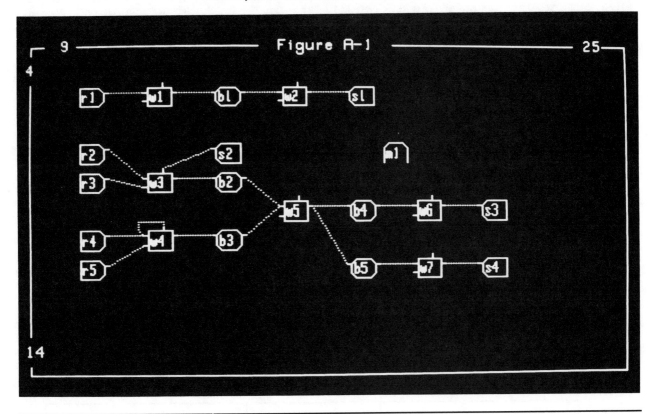

A.1 Loading XCELL+; Getting Started

XCELL+ runs on PC-compatible computers with EGA-compatible graphics. The details of the hardware and operating system requirements are given in Appendix 4.

Before it can be used, XCELL+ must be "installed" on your computer. General procedures for installation are given in Appendix 4; specific details of installation accompany the disks on which XCELL+ is supplied.

To use XCELL+ on a computer in which it has already been installed you must first select the disk, and possibly the directory, where XCELL+ resides. Assuming your computer has a hard disk, and that you have just turned the computer on, chances are good that the appropriate disk selection has been made automatically. If so, to load XCELL+ from the disk to the computer's main memory you simply give the command

                    XLP

to the MSDOS operating system. That is, you should type the letters XLP and then press the <return> key. If this results in an "improper command" message, the proper disk selection has not been made and you will have to get local instructions as to where XCELL+ resides in the disk storage system.

If the disk selection is correct, and the operating system can find XCELL+, it will take a few seconds to load the program. Loading is complete when

the XCELL+ logo appears on the display screen. From that point on, you are
in the   completely self-contained "XCELL+ environment", and you   need know
nothing more about the MSDOS operating system.   You are in this XCELL+
environment until you press the <QUIT> key in XCELL+, at which point you are
returned to MSDOS. (If you exceed one of the dimensional limits of XCELL+,
as described in Appendix 1, you are automatically returned to MSDOS.)

The files containing factory models are distinct from the XCELL+ program
file, and can be stored on floppy disks or on a hard disk.   The files are
managed by the XCELL+ **file manager**, described in Section F.

A.2 The Control of XCELL+ Menus _____

XCELL+ presents the menu of choices available to you in a row of eight boxes
across the bottom of the screen. These boxes describe the role that is
currently assigned to each of the eight "special-function keys" that XCELL+
uses. The boxes on the screen represent keys F1 to F8, from left to right.
When a box at the bottom of the screen is unlabeled the corresponding
function key has no assigned role at that point.

There are, of course, many more than eight choices you must make in using
XCELL+, but only eight at a time can be displayed and assigned to function
keys. To use XCELL+ you need to understand how these menus are managed.

XCELL+ actions, or choices, are grouped into sets called "menus". Each menu
can have as many as eight choices, shown in the eight boxes at the bottom of
the screen. (Not every menu needs the full eight choices, so in some menus
some boxes are empty.) For example, when you first enter XCELL+ you are
automatically in **main** menu and the row of boxes looks like the following:

HELP			new factory		file manager		QUIT
F1			**F4**		**F6**		**F8**

KEYS >>

This means that the only choices available to you at that point are:

    <HELP> -- to view a "help screen" with introductory information
        about XCELL+

    <new factory> -- to begin the construction of a new factory model

    <file mgr> -- to use the built-in **file manager**, presumably to retrieve
        from disk storage a factory model you (or someone) had
        previously built and stored

    <QUIT> -- to leave the XCELL+ package and return to the operating
        system.

The other boxes are empty; the corresponding keys have no current role, and
pressing any of them would only cause the system to beep in warning.

The **file manager** is another menu, and pressing key F6 moves you from **main**
menu to **file manager** menu. A message on the screen reports that you are now
in this different menu, and the row of key-label boxes on the screen changes
to present the choices available in this menu:

HELP	merge factory	assign disk	erase file	list files	retrieve factory		back to main
F1	**F2**	**F3**	**F4**	**F5**	**F6**		**F8**

KEYS >>

At this point, the actions you may take consist of:

  <HELP> -- to view a "help screen" concerning file manager actions

  <merge factory> -- to merge a stored factory model with the model in
                      the workspace. (In this case, since there is no
                      workspace model, <merge> is equivalent to
                      <retrieve>.)
  <assign disk> -- to change the choice of disk drive

  <erase file> -- to delete a factory model from disk

  <list files> -- to list the factory models stored on disk
                      (List all files with a ".XL4" suffix.)
  <retrieve factory> -- to retrieve one of the stored factory models

  <return> -- to leave **file manager** menu (and return to **main**)

Later, key F7 will be <store factory> to store the workspace model onto
disk, but at this point there is not yet a model in the workspace.

Suppose that you use F5 to list the names of the models available, and then
F6 to retrieve one of those models, copying it from disk into the XCELL+
workspace (which will hold exactly one model). This terminates your
immediate need for the **file manager** so you press F8 to return to **main**.

Now that there is a factory model in the workspace, the **main** menu offers
additional choices:

HELP	change display	analysis	new factory	design	file manager	run	QUIT
F1	**F2**	**F3**	**F4**	**F5**	**F6**	**F7**	**F8**

KEYS ››

All of the choices that were available before, when you initially entered
XCELL+, are still available, but now that there is a factory model in the
workspace you can also choose:

  <change display> -- to change the form of the display of the model

  <analysis> -- to **analyze** the structure and flow potential of the model

  <design> -- to modify the characteristics (**design**) of the model

  <run> -- to **run** the model

Change display, **analysis**, **design**, and **run** are different menus, and pressing
the corresponding key causes you to leave **main** and enter one of these menus,
just as you entered the **file manager** in the previous example.

The convention employed in the User's Guide is to use boldface type to
denote a menu, and <...> to denote the key associated with a particular
label shown in a box at the bottom of the screen. For example, we will
write "press <file manager> to enter **file manager** menu". It is never
necessary for you to remember that <file manager> happens to be assigned to
key F6 since that is always obvious from the labeled boxes at the bottom of
the screen. The key label and the menu name are not always exactly
identical. For example, <change cell> is the key used to move you to
WorkCenter design menu. In some cases, the actual key-label box on the
screen will be an abbreviation of the form shown here in the User's Guide,
since only a limited number of characters fit in the key-label box. For
example, <new factory> actually appears as <new factry> on the screen.

XCELL+ will rarely tempt you with an action that you cannot really choose.
For example, this is why the <change display>, <analysis>, <design>, and

<run> choices were not offered in the initial **main** menu. Since there was no factory model in the workspace at that point, none of these choices could be used at that time.

The key assignments are made consistently throughout XCELL+. For example, key F8 is always reserved for the purpose of leaving the current menu to return to the previous menu. As another example, in those contexts where a HELP screen is available, key F1 is always used to display the HELP screen. Keys F2 to F7 sometimes represent a change of menu, for example, <file manager> in **main**, but at other times represent a direct action in the current menu, for example, <list files> in **file manager** menu.

It may help you to understand the movement from menu to menu to know that the menus are arranged in a hierarchical structure called a "tree". **Main** is the trunk of the tree; **file manager**, **analysis**, **change display**, **design**, and **run** are the principal branches that emerge from the trunk.

─────────────────────────── **Figure A-2** ───────────────────────────

The base of the menu-tree

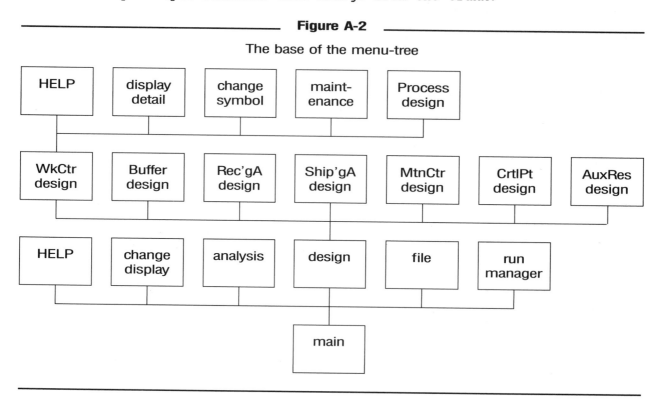

You should think of key <u>F8</u> <u>as</u> <u>causing</u> <u>a</u> <u>move</u> <u>down</u> in this menu tree -- that is, closer to the **main** trunk. The other keys that change menu cause an upward move in the menu-tree. The direct-action keys that do not change menu, of course cause no move in the menu-tree.

Even the <HELP> key in XCELL+ causes a change of menu, moving up to the **HELP** menu in which a screen of textual information is displayed. The **HELP** menu is always the same -- there is only <return>, assigned to F8, to move back down to the previous menu.

Note that you can only move up and down and never sideways in the mode-tree. For example, the only way of moving from design to run is to first move down from design to main, and then up from main to run.

Although it is not labeled on the screen (like keys F1 to F8), key F10 also has a special role. From any point in the menu-tree key F10 causes an <u>direct</u> <u>jump</u> to **design** menu. That is, if you are in one of the menus above **design** in the menu-tree, F10 is equivalent to enough F8s to get you down to **design**. If you are in a menu that is not above **design**, F10 is equivalent to enough F8s to get you down to **main**, and then a single <design> to move up to

design. **Design** menu enjoys the privilege of this direct jump key simply because of the high frequency with which you need to return to **design**. Although, you never <u>need</u> to use this direct jump, you will find it very convenient -- particularly when you are using the more complex options in XCELL+ that take you to high levels in the menu-tree. (On keyboards with only eight special-function keys, key F1 serves as this direct jump whenever it does not have some other role.)

A complete description of the menu-tree is given in Appendix 2.

A.2.1 The Use of a Mouse with XCELL+

A Microsoft-compatible Mouse can be used in place of some of the directional and function keys. The Mouse must first be installed according to the directions in the Microsoft Mouse User's Guide. In particular, the MENU.COM program should be reviewed. XCELL+ provides the necessary specifications in a file named XLPMOUSE.MNU. Once the Mouse is installed, it can be activated by giving the command

                    MENU XLPMOUSE

prior to invoking XCELL+. Then the Mouse operates as follows:

1. Mouse movement (left/right/up/down) moves the cursor for cell selection
2. the left Mouse button is equivalent to F7 (usually meaning <select>)
3. the right Mouse buttton is equivalent to F8 (usually meaning <cancel> or <return to previous menu>)
4. both Mouse buttoms pressed simultaneously is equivalent to F10 (meaning <direct jump to **design**>)

A.3 The Cellular Grid of the Factory Floor _____

A distinctive and fundamental characteristic of XCELL+ is the use of a <u>uniform</u> <u>rectangular</u> <u>grid</u> for the factory floor. That is, the factory is represented as a uniform grid of "cells", and each element of the factory occupies exactly one of these cells. Essentially, to construct an XCELL+ model you choose elements (from the basic types described in Section A.4) and position each element in some cell of the factory floor. (Unfortunately, today the word "cell" is often used in manufacturing to denote an integrated group of machines. In XCELL+, a cell is just a particular area of the factory floor.)

Note that since each element in an XCELL+ model occupies exactly one cell, all factory elements are necessarily represented as having the same size. If the elements of the real factory actually have significant differences in size, then the XCELL+ model will to some extent be geometrically distorted. It will then not accurately reflect the relative sizes of elements, nor will the relative positions on the factory floor be exactly represented. XCELL+ is intended to represent only the logical relationships between elements, and it uses geometric representation only as a tool. Although in most cases an XCELL+ factory model is recognizably similar to a scaled drawing, XCELL+ is not intended to be a "factory layout tool".

In many contexts in the use of XCELL+, in particular in **design** menu, you need to select one particular cell. Whenever XCELL+ is inviting you to select a cell a distinctive "cell-cursor" will appear on the screen. You can move this curser about with the ordinary cursor keys: <up>, <down>, <left>, <right>. Each stroke of one of these keys <u>moves</u> <u>the</u> <u>cursor</u> <u>one</u> <u>cell</u> in the indicated direction.

For example, when you are in **design** menu you can position the cell-cursor on an empty cell to indicate where you would like to create a new element, or on a full cell to indicate which cell you would like to change (or move, or remove). When you return from **design** to **main**, the cell-cursor disappears since there is nothing you can do to individual cells in **main** menu. On the other hand, suppose you move to **WorkCenter design** menu from **design**, by pressing <add WorkCenter> when the cell-cursor is positioned on an empty cell, or <change cell> when the cell-cursor is positioned on an existing WorkCenter. The cell-cursor then changes form to indicate that you are (temporarily) committed to the design of that particular cell, and are not at the moment free to move the cell-cursor around the floor.

A.4 The Basic XCELL+ Building Blocks

Much of the simplicity of using XCELL+ rests on the fact that there are only a very small number of different types of elements used to construct a factory model. The types of element that occupy a cell are the following:

    -- <u>WorkCenters</u>, where Processes are run to perform work

    -- <u>ReceivingAreas</u>, where material is received from the outside
                  world

    -- <u>ShippingAreas</u>, from which finished material is shipped
                  to the outside world

    -- <u>Buffers</u>, where work-in-process inventory is stored

    -- <u>MaintenanceCenters</u>, from which service teams are sent to
              repair or provide scheduled maintenance for WorkCenters

    -- <u>ControlPoints,</u> intersections of Paths and traffic control
             points in an asynchronous materials handling system

---

Figure A-3

Graphical symbols for five basic cell types

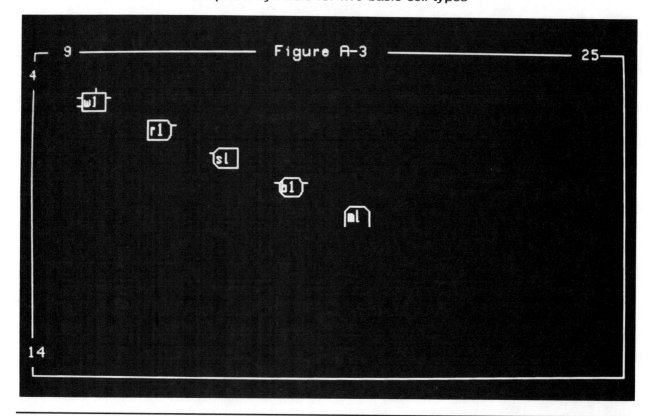

> -- <u>AuxiliaryResources,</u> sites from which Resources are supplied to perform Processes
>
> -- <u>PathSegments,</u> connecting two ControlPoints, over which Carriers can transport material

The model in Figure A-1 included examples of each of the different types of element. The graphic symbol for each type is shown in Figure A-3, in the order listed above. That is, "W1" is a WorkCenter, "R1" is a Receiving-Area, etc. (The names shown are the default names assigned automatically by the system. You can rename the elements with more meaningful names.)

Figure A-3b shows a model in which a network of Paths and ControlPoints allows Carriers to transport material from a ReceivingArea to a bank of four WorkCenters, and another network allows Carriers to move material from those WorkCenters to a ShippingArea.

In addition to these eight types of elements that occupy cells,   there are three other important design elements:

> -- <u>Processes,</u> that describe the work done at a WorkCenter
>   (A particular WorkCenter can have many Processes,
>   but only one can be active at a time.)
>
> -- <u>Links,</u> that describe the material flow to and from a Process
>   (A link can be regarded as an infinitely fast
>   conveyor with no storage capacity.)
>
> -- <u>Carriers,</u> moving elements, superimposed on PathSegments or
>   ControlPoints, to carry loads over a materials
>   handling network

Figure A-3b

Example of model with asynchronous materials handling

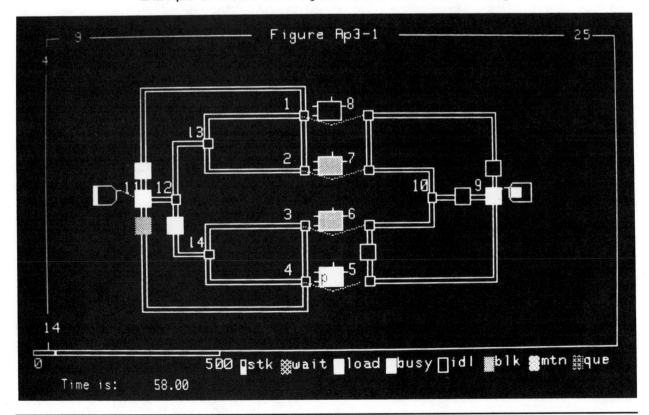

Figure A-4

A portion of the menu-tree above WorkCenter design

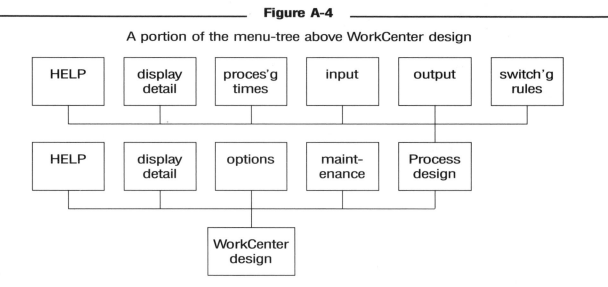

Links appear as direct cell-to-cell lines, as shown in Figure A-1. (As will be explained in Section B, the point at which a link connects to a particular cell conveys information about the characteristics of that particular cell and that link.)

The Processes are the key elements of an XCELL+ model, since these are the elements that actually do the work. ReceivingAreas, ShippingAreas, and Buffers exist only to manage and measure the material flow to and from Processes (along links). WorkCenters provide physical hosts for Processes and in doing so provide a mechanism by which Processes can be made mutually exclusive. (Processes at different WorkCenters can operate simultaneously, but Processes at the same WorkCenter can only operate one at a time.)

Processes are necessarily the most complicated elements of the model to specify. In addition to the links that specify material flow to and from the Process, you must also specify the rules that control <u>which Process is active</u> at any point in time. All of the options involved in specifying a Process are grouped in menus such as **switch Process**, **processing times**, **input**, and **output** that are accessible from **Process design**, which is accessible from **WorkCenter design**, as shown in Figure A-4.

A.5 A Keystroke Script for Exploration of XCELL+ _____

For your very first exposure to XCELL+, you might try the following sequence of keystrokes, which will retrieve a factory model from disk and run that model:

    <file manager>   to move from main to the file manager

        (press the key corresponding to the disk drive where the factory
                        model is stored)
    <list files>   to see the names of the available factory models
                        (sample models are supplied with XCELL+)
    <retrieve factory>   reply to the prompt with the name of some factory
                        model
    <back to main>   to return to main

    <run>   to move from main to run menu

    <begin run>   to begin running the model (If the model was stored
        or   after it had been run, time will not be 0, and
      <resume run>   the key will be labelled <resume run>.)

<auto run>   to let the model run automatically, at full speed.
                       Alternatively, press <one step> repeatedly to
                              "step" the model along manually.
                       Vary the running speed with <slower> and
                              <faster>.
<pause>   to momentarily pause the running of the model; you
                       can <resume run> and <pause> repeatedly

There are many directions you could go from here. For example, you could
experiment with the variety of different ways of viewing the model while it
is running -- try <controls>. Alternatively, you could try changing the
model.   For example:

<back to main>   to leave run and return to main

<design>   to move from main to design menu
    (position the cell-cursor on some WorkCenter)

<copy cell>   to prepare to create a new WorkCenter that is an
                              exact copy (except for name and location) of
                              the WorkCenter designated by the cell-cursor
    (position the cell-cursor on some unoccupied cell)

<select>   to establish the new WorkCenter in the selected
                              cell
<back to main>   to leave design and return to main

<run>   to run the modified model

       ...

The following script, starts from the very beginning to construct a simple,
3-element factory model. It assumes you are in **main** menu to begin with.
(If you have been following the previous script, you may need to press key
F8 one or more times to get back to **main**.)

<new factory>   to clear the workspace and prepare for a new model
                              (If a model is already present, you will be
                              asked whether to store or discard it.)
                       Choose a name for your factory in response to the
                              prompt. That is, type some short name
                              on the keyboard and press <return>.

<design>   to enter **design** mode
    (position the cell-cursor somewhere in the left center of the
                              screen, using the cursor keys)
<add RecA>   to create a new ReceivingArea R1 at the
                              cell-cursor position
                       You are now in **ReceivingArea design** menu.
                       Enter Part-name "P" and press <return> in response
                              to prompt.
<back to design>   to move back to **design**
    (position the cell-cursor somewhere in the right center of the
                              screen)
<add Shipping>   to create a new ShippingArea S1 at the cell-cursor
                              position
                       You are now in **ShippingArea design** menu.

<back to design>   to move back to **design**
    (position the cell-cursor somewhere between the ReceivingArea and
                              the ShippingArea)
<add WorkCenter>   to create a new WorkCenter W1 at the cell-cursor
                              position
                       You are now in **WorkCenter design** menu.

<add/copy Process>   to create a new Process at WorkCenter W1
                            Enter a name, say "P", for the new Process.
                            You are now in **Process design** menu.
<process times>   to change the default (constant 1) processing-time
                            You are now in **processing-times specification** menu.
<change to uniform> to change processing-times to random observations
                                from a uniform distribution (.5, 1.5)
<back to Process>   to move back to **Process design**

<input>   to move to **Process-input** menu

<X-input>   to select one of two possible input links (X and Y)
        (position the link-cursor on top of ReceivingArea R1, using cursor
                            keys)
<select>   to establish the X-input link between R1 and
                                Process P at WorkCenter W1
<back to Process>   to move back to **Process design**

<output>   to move to **Process-output** menu

<normal-output>   to select one of two possible output links
                                (normal and rework)
        (position the link-cursor on top of ShippingArea S1, using cursor
                                keys, or just by typing S1 <return>)
<select>   to establish the normal-output link between Process
                                p at WorkCenter W1 and ShippingArea S1
<back to Process>   to move back to **Process design**

<back to WorkCenter> to move back to **WorkCenter design**

<back to design>   to move back to **design**

<back to main>   to move back to **main**

<run>   to move to **run**

<begin run>   to prepare to run the model

<auto run>   to begin automatic, full-speed run of the model
    ...

<pause>   to interrupt the run

<results>   to move to **display result** menu

<thruput>   to display factory throughput

<costs>   to display fixed and variable model costs

<utilization>   to display WorkCenter utilization
<WkCtr>

<return>
<return>   to move back to **run**

<controls>   to be able to change "run controls"

<re-start run>   for example, to start the run again from the
                                beginning (automatically moves back to **run**)
<begin run>   to begin run (again)
<auto run>

    ...

<pause>   to interrupt the run

At this point, your display screen should look something like the model shown in Figure A-5.

--- **Figure A-5** ---

Simple 3-element factory model

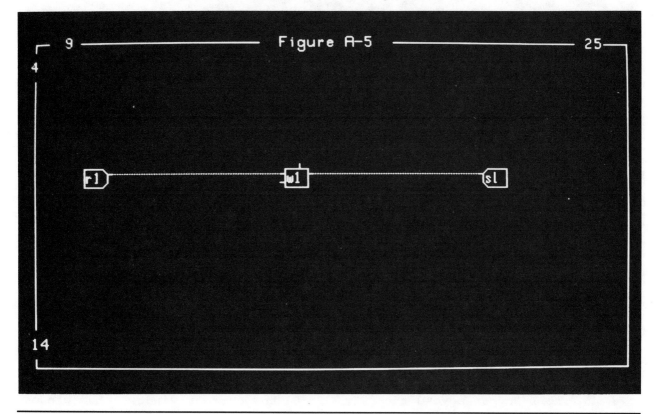

This model is not yet very interesting.   With only a single WorkCenter, and an unlimited supply of material from the ReceivingArea, there is no source of interference between elements and Process P operates happily and continuously. But from this simple starting point, you should be able to imagine many different variations of this model whose behavior would be less obvious, and for which the model would be more interesting and useful. For example, change your model to represent a two-stage production system, such as the one shown in Figure A-6. Even when W1 and W2 have the same distribution of processing-times (say uniform .5, 1.5), the changes in work-in-process inventory in Buffer B1 are very interesting.

A.6 Management of the Display Screen

There is far more information contained in an XCELL+ factory model than can be displayed on the computer screen at one time. To some extent, the choice of which information to display is automatic, depending upon the current mode, but you can also exercise control over the information displayed.

For example, at any point you are viewing the factory floor through a limited "window" -- you cannot see the entire floor at once. You can control:

        -- where to position the display "window" on the factory floor
                (a computer graphics function called "panning")

        -- whether to display the floor in "normal" or "reduced" scale
                (a computer graphics function called "zooming")

Figure A-6

Model of a two-stage production system

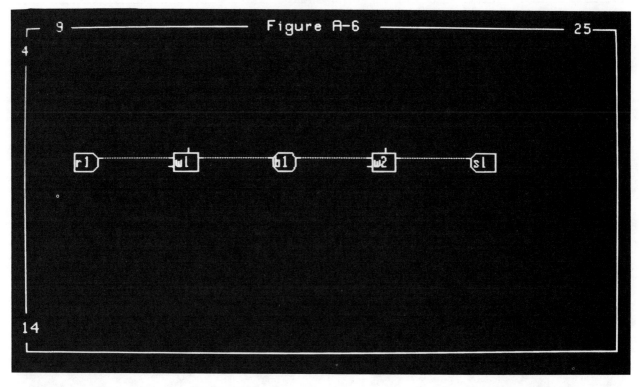

To some extent, the position of the display window is automatic -- if you move the cell-cursor beyond the limits of the current window, the window automatically scrolls left or right, or up or down to a new position. However, you can manually reposition the window in **change display** mode, which is accessible from **main**.

The choice between normal and reduced-scale can only be made in **change display** menu. Your choice of scale is persistent, throughout **design** and **run**, until you return to **change display** and change it. Figure A-7 shows the reduced-scale form of the same factory model shown in normal-scale in Figure A-1. Figure A-8 shows the reduced-scale display of Figure A-7 after the viewing window has been shifted down and to the right.

A <display detail> key is included in many menus, throughout XCELL+, to temporarily devote the entire display screen to a single cell. This moves to the **detail display** menu; press F8 to restore the previous display.

A.6.1 Suppress Display of a Cell

You can optionally suppress the display of individual cells. When display is suppressed, the element appears on the screen only as an unobtrusive dot in the center of the cell, rather than with the usual graphical symbol. This is particularly useful when dummy or auxiliary elements must be used to extend the capability of XCELL+.

Suppression of display is controlled from the **options** menu, which is accessible from the various different design sub-menus -- **WorkCenter design**, **Buffer design**, etc.

Suppression of display of Paths, ControlPoints and Carriers is slightly different. There is a <suppress/resume draw> key in **change Segment** menu -- which causes the display of the entire Path to be suppressed.

Figure A-7

Reduced scale display of the A-1 model

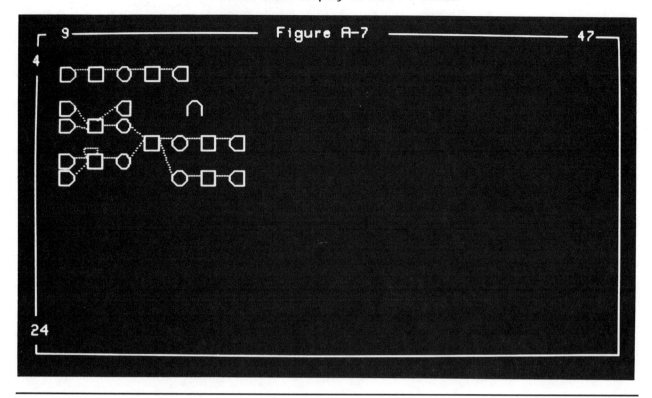

Figure A-8

Shifted view of the A-7 model

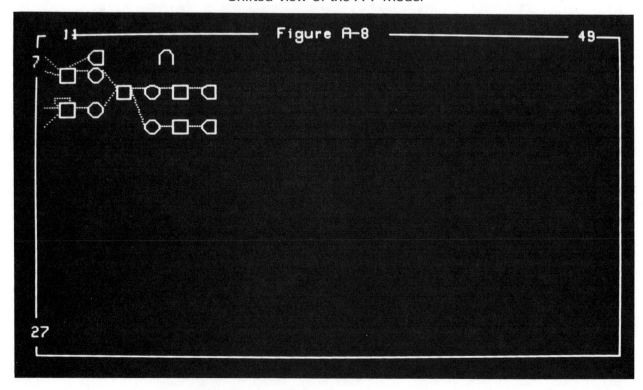

Suppression of display of ControlPoints and Carriers is entirely automatic. The display of a particular ControlPoint is suppressed if the display of all Paths connected to it is suppressed. The display of a particular Carrier is suppressed if it is currently positioned on a PathSegment or ControlPoint that is suppressed.

A.7 Floor Areas _____

To improve the appearance and clarity of the display, different Areas of the model can be identified by using different colored backgrounds. This is done in the **change Areas** menu, which is accessible from **change display** in **main**.

Four colors are available (blue, red, magenta and light blue) in addition to the normal black. Color can be assigned on a cell-by-cell basis. The colored background appears at the **main** menu level, and a colored outline appears on the **run** screen, but Areas do not appear on the **design** screen.

The **change Areas** menu also permits placement of textual labels on the display. The label begins on the cursor-cell and continues to the right as far as necessary. (It is your responsibility not to use labels that run into each other.) These labels appears on all screens when normal-scale display is being used.

Used together, background colors and labels can help to delineate and identify various functional Areas of the model.

B

Design of a Factory Model

B.1 The Design Menu

The **design** menu allows you to make changes in the structure of a factory model. You do this by performing one or more of the following actions:

-- creating new factory elements, in cells of the factory floor that are currently unoccupied

-- changing the characteristics of existing factory elements

-- removing an existing factory elements (clearing the cell)

-- moving an existing factory element from its current cell to another (currently unoccupied) cell

Each of these actions requires you to select a particular cell on the factory floor. You do this by moving the cell-cursor from one cell to another, using the <up>, <down>, <left> and <right> arrow-keys. When you press one of the keys in the **design** menu, the action chosen is performed with respect to the cell currently designated by the cell-cursor.

Since there are different actions that can be performed on an occupied cell from those that can be performed on an unoccupied cell, the **design** menu changes as you move the cell-cursor about on the factory floor. When the cell-cursor is positioned on an unoccupied cell, the **design** menu looks like the following:

add WkCtr	add Buffer	add RecA	add ShipA	add MaintC	add CtrlPt	add AuxRes	back to main

Each of these keys (except <back to main>) creates a new element of the particular type in the cell designated by the cell-cursor. All of the characteristics of the new element have default values. At the same time, you are automatically moved from **design** mode to the corresponding sub-mode of design, so you can change the characteristics of the element you just created. For example, <add WkCtr> creates a new WorkCenter, and moves you from **design** to **WorkCenter design**. You might then, for example, change the breakdown characteristics of the WorkCenter. (The default WorkCenter never breaks down.)

17

On the other hand, when the cell-cursor is positioned on an occupied cell,
the **design** menu looks like the following:

refresh display	display detail	chg all . . .	copy cell	remove cell	move cell	change cell	back to main

<Change cell> causes a move from **design** mode to one of the specific element
sub-modes of design, depending on the type of element in the cell designated
by the cell-cursor. For example, you would move to **WorkCenter design** if the
designated cell is a WorkCenter.   In moving to **WorkCenter design** the form of
the cell-cursor changes to indicate that you are temporarily involved with
this particular cell, and cannot at the moment move the cell-cursor about on
the factory floor.   When you go <back to design> from **WorkCenter design**, the
cell-cursor changes back from its fixed-position form to its movable form.

Note that **WorkCenter design**, for example, works the same way whether you
reach it by pressing the <add WkCtr> key when the cell-cursor is positioned
on an empty cell, or the <change cell> key when the cell-cursor is
positioned on an existing WorkCenter. In other words, **WorkCenter design**
does not know whether it is working on a brand new WorkCenter you just
created, or if you are returning to an existing WorkCenter.   In either case,
it allows you to change any characteristic of that particular WorkCenter.

The <copy cell> key represents an alternative way to create a new element.
When a new element is created by copying an existing element, as far as
possible the characteristics of the new element are the same as the
characteristics of the specified source element.   When it doesn't make sense
to copy the characteristics, the default value is applied.   For example,
since no two elements can have the same name, the name of the source element
cannot be copied to the new element, so a default name is given to the new
element.

B.1.1 The Tabular Editor

In the **design** menu, when the cell-cursor is on an occupied cell, the <change
all> key invokes the Tabular Editor.   This presents a table listing selected
attributes for up to 25 elements of the type selected by the cell-cursor.
You can change these values by positioning the table-cursor and pressing the
<change one> key. You can also change all of the values in a particular
column of the table to agree with the selected value by pressing the <change
all shown> key. The <change all in factory> key changes all attributes to
match the value selected, whether or not those elements are shown in the
table.

When there are more than 25 elements of the particular type, there will be
<next page> and/or <prev page> keys to allow you to see elements other than
those initially shown.   (The initial selection depends upon the particular
element selected and the order in which the elements were created.)

When the element selected by the cell-cursor is included in a special "Floor
Area" (see Section A.7) only other elements in that particular Floor Area
will be included in the table.

B.1.1.1 Default Attributes

The top row of the table in the Tabular Editor shows the default values for
certain attributes of the different types of elements.   These are the values
that are applied to each newly-created element of that type.   Using the
Tabular Editor these default values can be changed, but note that the new

values will be applied only to new elements subsequently created and are not applied retroactively to existing elements.

Choosing appropriate default values will save time in building a model since it will reduce the number of individual changes you must make.   But note that you must create at least one member of each type of element before you can invoke the Tabular Editor (and set new default values) for that type.

B.2 WorkCenter Design

WorkCenters are the hosts for Processes, which are the elements that do the actual work in the factory model.   The other elements -- Buffers, ReceivingAreas, and ShippingAreas -- essentially support the WorkCenters as holding   areas   for   material   not   currently   being   processed. MaintenanceCenters also provide support services for repair and scheduled maintenance of the WorkCenters.

A WorkCenter is capable of performing a variety of different Processes -- but each WorkCenter can perform only one Process at a time. Consequently, the design of a WorkCenter consists primarily of the design of the individual Processes that are performed at that WorkCenter. There is no limit on the number of Processes at a given WorkCenter (although there is a limit on the total number of Processes in the factory model; see Appendix 1).

The only characteristics associated with a WorkCenter directly, as opposed to the characteristics of its Processes, are those involved with maintenance. Both breakdown and scheduled maintenance are characteristics of the WorkCenter, rather than an individual Process. These properties are described in Sections B.2.2 and B.3.

The menu in **WorkCenter design** is the following:

HELP	display detail	options	maint- enance	delete Process	add/copy Process	change Process	back to design

B.2.1 Process Design

A Process is an operation on a particular Part at a particular WorkCenter. The Process name is the same as the name of the Part on which it works. Since a particular Part can be processed at various different WorkCenters, there can be (and usually are) Processes having the same name that are performed at different WorkCenters. (These Processes do not necessarily have any other characteristics in common other than the same name.)

Pressing the <add/copy Process> key in **WorkCenter design** results in a prompt to enter the Process name. If the name you enter is a "new" name (not already the name of a Process at this WorkCenter) then a new Process is created with that name. If you enter the name of a Process that already exists at that WorkCenter then you are invoking the "copy Process" action. There is a second prompt for the name of the new Process, which is a copy (has the same attributes) as the Process first named.

Each Process has the following characteristics:

        -- two input links, called X-input and Y-input

        -- two output links, called normal-output and reject-output

-- a mechanism to control the percentage of output that is
       rejected, included provision to allow the percentage
       to "drift" up or down

-- a mechanism for generating processing-times (time per piece or
       cycle)

-- setup-times (time to changeover the host WorkCenter from one
       Process to another)

-- rules that specify when the Process is invoked, and how long
       it runs before the WorkCenter switches to another
       Process

The characteristics of each Process are completely independent of those of
other Processes on the same WorkCenter -- their only interaction is that
they compete for the services of the Workcenter. Only one Process at a time
can be "active" at a particular WorkCenter.

When you are in **Process design** mode, only the links for that particular
Process are shown on the screen; links for other Processes at the same
WorkCenter are temporarily erased. When you move back from **Process design**
to **WorkCenter design**, the links for all the Processes at that WorkCenter
reappear.

Note that all links connect a Process to some other element, and all links
must be established from their Process end. For example, an input-link from
a Buffer to a Process must be established from **Process design** mode, and not
from **Buffer design** mode. You must establish the link backward from the
Process and not forward from the Buffer.

B.2.1.1 Input to a Process

Input to a Process is supplied along an input-link. Each input-link has one
specific source -- which usually is a ReceivingArea, a Buffer, or the output
of another Process.

Optionally, a Process can also have a second input-link -- but note that
when two inputs are specified, both must be available for the Process to be
performed.   That is, a two-input Process is an assembly operation where one
unit of each type of input is put together to make one unit of output.

The input-links to a Process are arbitrarily called the "X-input" and the
"Y-input" and are shown on the screen as attached to the two stubs on the
left side of the WorkCenter symbol (X-input to the top stub and Y-input to
the bottom stub.) The two input-links are logically equivalent. If a
Process needs only a single input-link, that can just as well be the Y-input
as the X-input.   Examples of different combinations of X-input and Y-input
are shown in Figure B-1.

Although a Process can have at most two direct inputs, it is easy to model
an assembly Process that requires three or more inputs by using a "composite
WorkCenter" -- see Section C.2.3.

Although a multiple-input Process is an assembly operation -- that is, an
"and" function that combines the inputs -- it is also easy to model a
situation where there are alternative inputs, only one of which need supply
a unit to the Process (an "or" function of the inputs).   You simply route
all of the inputs to a Buffer (there is no restriction on the number of
direct inputs to a Buffer, but all must consist of the same part) and then
specify that Buffer as the source of the input-link of the Process. (The
Buffer can have zero capacity, so its presence does not alter the behavior
of the model.   The appearance of this Buffer on the display screen can be
suppressed so that the input-links appear to be directly connected to the
Process.)

The input to a Process need not be a Part with the same name as the Process itself. That is, Process A could have Part B as an input. On the other hand, the input <u>can</u> have the same name -- Process A can have Part A as input. This flexibility means that you can model a sequence of operations on the same Part, performed on different machines, as well as a complicated structure of subassemblies and common-use Parts.

Note that an input-link to a Process cannot be specified until the source element for that link has been created. For example, an input-link that runs from a Buffer to a Process must be established from Process design, but the Buffer must already exist. If the source element for the input-link does not exist, and you <select> an empty cell with the link-cursor, a source element is <u>generated automatically</u>, along with a message warning you that this has occurred. However, the default source element for an input-link is a Buffer, which may or may not be what is required. If you do not create the source element before the Process to be linked to it, and if the default source element is not the right type, it will be necessary for you to leave **Process design**, return to **design** to create the appropriate source element, and then return to **Process design** to specify the input-link.

When an input-link to a Process is the direct output of another Process -- without an intermediate Buffer, the link can be specified from either side. That is, you can specify it as the input-link to the second Process or the output-link from the first Process. In either case, the opposite Process must already exist before you can establish a link to it. That is, you can create the first Process, then the second Process, and then specify an input-link from the second Process back to the first Process, or you can specify the second Process, then the first Process, and then specify an output-link from the first Process forward to the second Process.

The X-input link to a Process (but not the Y-input link) can also be connected to a ControlPoint. However, in this case, if one Process at a WorkCenter draws its X-input from a ControlPoint then all Processes at that same WorkCenter also draw their X-input from the same ControlPoint link. The different Processes at that WorkCenter can (optionally) have different Y-input links, but they all share the same X-input link from the ControlPoint. This X-input link to the Processes is called the "dropoff-link" from the ControlPoint.

When a ControlPoint has a dropoff-link directly to a WorkCenter, a loaded Carrier at that ControlPoint can only dropoff its unit if the name of the Part matches the name of one of the Processes at the WorkCenter. Note that this is different from X-input links from ReceivingAreas or Buffers. For example, if the X-input of Process P comes from a Buffer, you can specify that a unit of Part Q in that Buffer can serve as the X-input. But if the X-input of Process P comes from a ControlPoint, then only a unit of Part P, on a Carrier at that ControlPoint, can serve as the X-input.

Another difference between an X-input link to a ControlPoint, and an X-input link to any other type of cell is that this link can be established <u>from either end</u> -- that is, either as the X-input line from some Process at the WorkCenter, or as the dropoff-link from the ControlPoint. Recall that links that do not involve a ControlPoint must always be established from the end associated with a Process.

Although dropoff directly from a ControlPoint to a WorkCenter is allowed, it is generally advantageous (in both the model and the real factory) to provide a Buffer between the ControlPoint and the WorkCenter. This reduces the time when traffic on Paths through the ControlPoint is blocked by a Carrier waiting to dropoff.

When dropoff from a ControlPoint is directly to a WorkCenter, there is the option of "engaging" the Carrier while the Process involving the unit on the Carrier is performed. When the engagement option is specified, the ControlPoint serves as both the X-input link and the normal-output link (see Section B.2.1.2) for every Process at the WorkCenter. When the engagement option is specified, the Carrier making the dropoff remains at the ControlPoint through dropoff, processing, and pickup, and then departs with the processed unit on-board.

Neither dropoff nor pickup-links can be established to a ControlPoint that is serving as either a HoldingPoint or a ChargingPoint (see Sections B.9.1 and B.9.5).

B.2.1.1.1 Null-Input Processes

Processes are not required to have any input-links. If an input-link is specified, then a unit must be delivered over that link for the Process to be performed, but if neither an X-input link nor a Y-input link is specified, then the Process is considered to not require any external material, and is therefore never idle for lack of material.

This is a convenient alternative to linking a Process to a ReceivingArea that will always have the (default) unlimited arrival mechanism. But note that taking this shortcut deprives you of use of the "tagging" feature by which individual units can be tracked through the factory (since units are tagged at the ReceivingArea where they originate).

More important uses arise when a WorkCenter is being used in some ingenious way to control the timing of other activities, or to otherwise trick XCELL+ into modeling more complex processes than those of its natural domain. For example, consider the examples described in Sections C.2.4, C.6, and C.7. In addition, by using AuxiliaryResources even more ingenious tricks are possible -- and null-input Processes can be even more useful.

─────────────────────────── **Figure B-1** ───────────────────────────

Examples of input-links and output-links

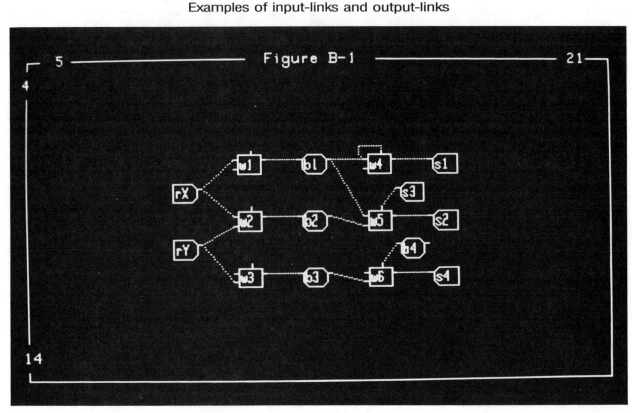

B.2.1.2 Output from a Process

Each Process has a single normal-output-link and, optionally, a single reject-output-link. Each of these links has a specific element as its destination. The output-links are specified in **Process design**, but the destination element must exist before the link can be established.

The normal, or "good", units of output from a Process are delivered over the normal-output-link to a ShippingArea, a Buffer, or as input to another

Process. The normal-output link is shown on the display as attached to the stub on the right side of the symbol for the WorkCenter.

Regardless of the names of the Parts specified as inputs to a Process, the default name of the output from the Process is the same as the Process name itself. That is, Process "A" produces units of Part "A". However, you can specify some other Part name for the output. That is, Process "A" can produce units of Part "B". This is more important than it may seem at first, since it allows a single WorkCenter to have several Processes, with different characteristics, all producing the same Part. One frequent use of this facility is to have a "rework" Process, with different characteristics from those of the original Process, running on the same WorkCenter. See option (3) in Section B.2.1.2.1.

The normal-output link from a Process can also be connected to a ControlPoint (but not to a ControlPoint serving as either a HoldingPoint or a ChargingPoint). When this is done, the same link serves as the normal-output link for <u>all</u> <u>of</u> <u>the</u> <u>Processes</u> at this WorkCenter.

When the normal-output link is directly connected to a ControlPoint, the completed output of the Process can only be disposed of when there is an <u>empty</u> <u>Carrier</u> at the ControlPoint. Unless an empty Carrier is waiting when the Process completes a unit, the Process is blocked until an empty Carrier arrives. The WAIT option in **traffic control** for empty Carriers can reduce the amount of time that WorkCenters are blocked -- but the waiting Carrier can, of course, also block other Carriers.

Although direct connection of the normal-output link of a Process to a ControlPoint is allowed, it is generally advantageous (in both the model and the real factory) to provide a Buffer between the WorkCenter and the ControlPoint. This can reduce the time the WorkCenter is blocked waiting for an empty Carrier, and the time that traffic through the ControlPoint is blocked by an empty Carrier waiting for pickup.

You can also direct the reject-output link of a Process to a ControlPoint -- but it must be the same ControlPoint that receives the normal-output. That is, you cannot direct the reject-output of a Process to a ControlPoint unless the normal-output of that Process is also directed to (the same) ControlPoint. (The normal-output link must be established first.) In order to differentiate between normal and reject units picked up at this ControlPoint, you must assign a different name to the units of normal-output. (The units of reject-output have the same name as the Process itself.)

Another difference between a normal-output link to a ControlPoint, and a normal-output link to any other type of cell is that this link can be established <u>from</u> <u>either</u> <u>end</u> -- that is, either as the normal-output link from some Process at the WorkCenter, or as the pickup-link from the ControlPoint. Recall that links that do not involve a ControlPoint must always be established from the end associated with a Process.

B.2.1.2.1 Reject-Output Units

The default for a Process is perfect yield -- all the output is delivered over the normal-output-link. Optionally, you can specify some percentage of units to be "rejected" after processing. The rejection mechanism is random. You specify the long-run percentage rejected; the probability that each individual unit is rejected is determined by this percentage. This percentage can optionally "drift" up or down, as described below in Section B.2.1.2.2.

There are three alternatives for the disposition of rejected units -- that is, there are three types of destination for the reject-output-link drawn to connect to the stub on the top of the WorkCenter. The alternatives are:

1. The rejected units can be <u>recycled</u> through the same Process. That is, the Process works on the unit repeatedly until it is finally accepted. (Subsequent tries have the same processing time characteristic and the same chance of rejection as the first try.)

2. The rejected units can be <u>scrapped</u>, by directing the reject-output-link to a ShippingArea.

3. The rejected unit can be <u>reworked</u>, by directing the reject-output-link to a Buffer that supplies the input to a rework Process. (The rework Process can be performed on the same WorkCenter as the original Process, or by a Process at some other WorkCenter. If the characteristics of the rework Process are essentially the same as those of the original Process, it is simpler to use the recycle mechanism described above, rather than define another Process specifically for rework.) Note that the reject-output-link for rework must go to a Buffer, and cannot go directly to the input of another Process. You can however, use a zero-capacity Buffer and/or suppress the display of the Buffer, so this is not really a significant restriction.

All three reject-output choices are illustrated in Figure B-2.

Although the terminology of "yield" and "reject" suggests a particular use for the normal/reject partition of the output of a Process, it is possible to use this random partition of Process output for other purposes. However, keep in mind that the partition is <u>probabilistic</u>.   It would not, for example, be appropriate to use this mechanism for a Process that supplies two downstream Processes alternately. Such alternate delivery could be modeled by having two identical Processes at the supplying WorkCenter, each

Figure B-2

Examples with different disposition of reject-output

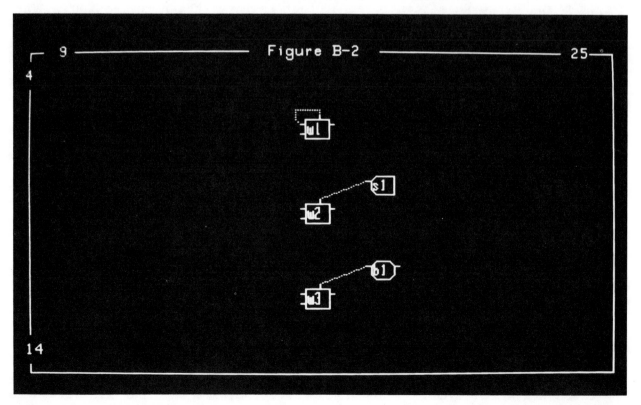

with a batch-size of one (see Section B.2.1.5) and zero setup-time, and each
supplying one of the downstream Processes.

B.2.1.2.2 Drift of Reject-Output

Optionally, the percentage of rejected units of a Process can be made to
change with repetition of the Process. The percentage is said to <u>drift</u>.
There are three components to the specification of reject drift:

1. The <u>initial value</u> I of the reject percentage.

2. The percent <u>change</u> C.

3. The <u>reset limit</u> R.

Let P be the percent of units rejected.   The drift mechanism works as
follows:

1. Initially, P = I, unless you manually set the initial value of
P different from I.

2. If C > 0, then for each unit processed

$$P = P + C*(100-P)/100$$

If C < 0, then for each unit processed

$$P = P + C*P/100$$

Note that when a rejected unit is <u>recycled</u>, P is not changed
by the second and subsequent passes over the same unit.

3. If C > 0 and R is specified, then

If P >= R, then P is reset to I
The time to perform this reset is given by
the "minor setup time" for the Process (see
Section B.2.1.4) and the Process is "in
setup" and not producing for that length of
time (which can, of course, be of length 0)

4. Anytime the Process is setup, whether or not this is caused
by reaching the reset limit R, the value of P is reset to I.

Drift is specified for each Process independently. The default value of I
is P, of C is 0, and R is unspecified. Note that this drift in the
percentage of rejects is a negative exponential function -- the rate of
change diminishes with continued repetition of the Process. Note also that
drift is a function of repetition and not time.

There are a variety of ways of using this drift mechanism. Perhaps the most
obvious, using a positive value of C, is to represent tool wear. However,
with negative values of C, drift can also be used to model different forms
of "learning". A Process can learn in the sense that its yield gradually
improves, or by recycling its reject-output, in the sense that its average
production rate increases.

B.2.1.2.3 Multiple Units of Normal-Output

Optionally, each repetition of a Process can produce multiple units of
output. That is, one cycle, consuming one unit of input (or one unit each
of X-input and Y-input) can produce several units of output. The number of
output units is a constant, the same for each cycle, and all of the output
units are the same kind of part. The default number of output units is 1.

The output units are discharged along the normal-output link of the Process one at a time, and the Process cannot begin its next cycle until the last of the output units from the last cycle has been removed. If there is "capacity" at the other end of the normal-output link to receive all the units, the total discharge takes place in zero time, but there is no automatic internal storage for output within the WorkCenter, and the Process will be <u>blocked</u> until the last unit of output is disposed of -- whether there is one unit of output per cycle or more than one.

Note also that multiple output applies <u>only to the normal-output</u> of the Process. When a unit of output of the Process is rejected, it goes out on the reject-link as a single unit. You should think of the partition of output as something that occurs <u>after the inspection</u> of the result of the cycle, so that only good units are partitioned into multiple units.

B.2.1.2.4 Null-Output Processes

Processes do not have to have a normal-output link. When a normal-output link is specified, it must be free to dispose of a completed unit or the Processes becomes "blocked". However, if no normal-output link is specified, it is assumed that no material output is produced by the Process. No blockage occurs, and the next cycle can begin whenever material (and, optionally, AuxiliaryResources) is available.

As with null-input Processes, there are a variety of uses of this facility. The most obvious is for the convenience of not having to specify an immediate-shipment (default) ShippingArea in situations where disposal of output is not a consideration. More subtle and important uses arise when Processes are used as pseudo-timing devices for which no real output is produced. Again, the price of this convenience is loss of the normal mechanisms associated with a ShippingArea -- the computation of throughput, and (for tagged units) of average flow-time and average waiting time.

A WorkCenter with a single null-input and null-output Process can also be a useful device. Although it is unconnected to the rest of the model in terms of material flow, it can share use of AuxiliaryResources and/or MaintenanceCenters with other WorkCenters, and thus can be used to alter the availability of those resources to the other WorkCenters.

B.2.1.3 Processing-Times

"Processing-time" is the time required to perform the Process on each unit -- that is, the cycle time or operation time. All times are given as undimensioned "timeunits". You can let a timeunit represent any unit of real time you find appropriate. A timeunit could represent a second, an hour, a day, etc. Of course, you must be consistent throughout the model so that timeunits on different Processes have the same interpretation. These timeunits must also be consistent with those used to specify maintenance activities (Section B.2.2), material receiving schedules (Section B.4) and finished-unit shipping schedules (Section B.5).

There are five choices with respect to the method of obtaining individual processing-times. Each Process is independent of the others in this respect, and each can have a different choice of method:

   1. The time can be a <u>constant</u>, the same for each repetition of the operation. This is the default -- unless you specify otherwise, every processing time is a constant 1.00 timeunits.

   2. The time can be a random value from a <u>uniform distribution</u>. You specify the minimum and maximum value, and every value between this minimum and maximum is equally likely to occur.

   3. The time can be a random value from an <u>exponential distribution</u>. This is a highly skewed distribution in which short times are

common, and long times are rare but possible. (While these long times can represent problems with yield or machine break-down, there are other mechanisms to model those phenomena explicitly. See Sections B.2.1.2.1 and B.2.2.)

4. The time can be a random value from a finite approximation to a <u>normal</u> <u>distribution</u>. You specify a minimum and maximum value, and every value in this range is possible, but values close to the mean are much more likely to occur. (This distribution is obtained by averaging six observations from a uniform distribution with the same minimum and maximum.)

5. The time can be a random value from a <u>general</u> <u>distribution</u> modeled as a Ramberg-Schmeiser distribution. This powerful distribution has Exponential, Erlang, Gamma, Uniform, and Log-Normal as special cases. It can also be used to approximate arbitrary distributions derived from actual empirical data. See Appendix 5.

B.2.1.4 Setup-Times

Setup-time is the time required to prepare the WorkCenter to run one Process when it has previously been running another Process. For example, restarting Process A on a particular WorkCenter when the last previous work on that same WorkCenter was also A does not require setup -- even if there has been an interval of idle-time since A last ran. However, if the last Process run on that WorkCenter was B, Process "A" does require setup even if there has been an interval of idle time since B ran.

No units are produced during setup; setup takes place before the processing of the first unit of the new Process. However, material will be present in the WorkCenter during setup. That is, input units will have already been withdrawn from the cells that supply input to the Process and this material will be waiting in the WorkCenter for the completion of setup.

Setup-time is a characteristic of the individual Process. The setup-time for each Process is a constant -- the same each time the WorkCenter must be set up to perform that Process. You can specify the value for each Process; if you do not specify it, the default setup-time for each Process is 10 timeunits.

There are <u>two</u> <u>levels of</u> <u>setup-time</u>, called "major" and "minor" setup. For this purpose, each Process belongs to a particular group of Processes (the default is group "1"). Processes in the same group are presumably similar, but not identical, with respect to setup. Hence, in general, <u>less</u> <u>time</u> <u>would</u> <u>be</u> <u>required</u> to changeover the WorkCenter from one Process to another Process <u>within</u> <u>the</u> <u>same</u> <u>group</u>. The major setup-time is required only when the new Process on a WorkCenter belongs to a different group from the previous Process on the same WorkCenter. The minor setup-time is required when the new Process belongs to the same group as the previous Process. The default values are 10 timeunits for major setup and 5 timeunits for minor setup. While in most real situations, the major setup time would be expected to be greater than the minor setup time, XCELL+ does not require that that be the case. (There may be situations where it will be useful to model the opposite use of the group-major-minor facility.)

If a drift in the percentage of reject-output has been specified for the Process being setup (see Section B.2.1.2.2) the percentage of rejects is automatically reset to its specified initial value each time setup is performed for that Process. Drift specification can also include a "reset limit" which can invoke a minor setup of the Process even when the WorkCenter is not being switched from one Process to another.

B.2.1.5 Process-Switching

The Process-switch menu is invoked by the <switching control> key in Process-design.

Whenever more than one Process is assigned to a WorkCenter, the rules that control switching from one Process to another become important. This is a complicated question in the real factory, and the mechanisms for modeling these decision rules are necessarily somewhat complex.

The default mechanism -- used unless you specify otherwise -- is to let a Process continue to run as long as it can. That is, it will run until it runs out of input material. (For an assembly Process, that means when it cannot find a unit of either X or Y input.) Only then does any other Process have a chance to run.

Once the current Process surrenders claim to the WorkCenter, the Process selected to replace it is the <u>highest priority startable</u> Process. "Startable" means that material is available. You can assign priority values to individual Processes. (By default, each Process has priority 100.) Among Processes of equal priority, there is "round-robin" selection -- they take turns in rotation.

You can specify a <u>fixed batch-size</u> for a Process. In this case, once the Process is started it will retain claim to the WorkCenter until it has produced that required number of units. (If it runs out of input, it will wait for replenishment.) Only when the required batch is completed will the WorkCenter be surrendered to another Process.

B.2.1.5.1 Process Triggers

The most powerful automatic mechanism in XCELL+ for Process-switching is <u>triggering</u>. Each Process can be assigned a "trigger" that will cause (and allow) it to be invoked. A trigger is simply a stock level in some Buffer, batch-mode ReceivingArea or batch-mode ShippingArea.

If you specify a <u>high-trigger</u> for a certain Process, that Process will be invoked whenever the designated stock <u>increases</u> to whatever trigger-level you specify. (The switch will not take place until the active Process at the same WorkCenter surrenders its claim to the WorkCenter.) High-triggers are a means of implementing a "push production" system. That is, production is controlled by pushing material through the WorkCenters. Normally the stock for a high-trigger will be located <u>upstream</u> from the triggered Process (although this is not a requirement built into XCELL+). In fact, the trigger does not have to be part of the stream of the triggered Process at all. For example, Process B could be triggered by a high level of material produced by Process A, in which case the trigger would be downstream from Process A.

If you specify a <u>low-trigger</u> for a certain Process, that Process will be invoked whenever the designated stock <u>decreases</u> to whatever trigger-level you specify. (The switch will not take place until the active Process at the same WorkCenter surrenders its claim to the WorkCenter.) Low-triggers are a means of implementing a "pull production" system and would normally be located <u>downstream</u> from the triggered Process. But again, since the trigger need not be directly in the flow of the triggered Process it could reasonably be an upstream stock for a different Process.

Triggers can also be based on the <u>total contents</u> of a particular Buffer, rather than the stock of a particular Part in the Buffer. (Just <return> an empty line when you are prompted for the Part name when specifying a trigger on a Buffer.)

Note that during the time delay after the trigger for a particular Process is satisfied, and before the Workcenter becomes available to initiate that Process, it is possible that the designated stock will change so that the trigger is no longer satisfied. The Process is no longer considered triggered and will not be invoked.

While each Process is allowed only a single trigger, there is no limit to the number of Processes that can be triggered by changes in the stock-level at a particular Buffer, batch-mode ReceivingArea or batch-mode ShippingArea.

Triggering is a powerful, but complicated mechanism. You would be well-advised to experiment initially with a relatively simple triggering model, to make sure you understand exactly how the mechanism works, before undertaking to build a sophisticated just-in-time production model.

B.2.1.5.2 Detailed Description of Process-Switching

In case you need to know precisely how Process-switching works, the following gives a detailed description of the algorithms used. First, some careful definitions are required:

> The active Process at a particular WorkCenter is the Process currently being performed at the WorkCenter. All other Processes at that WorkCenter are inactive.

> A batch Process is a Process for which you have assigned a fixed batch-size (different from 1).

> A trigger Process is a Process for which you have specified a trigger level of stock at some Buffer, ReceivingArea or ShippingArea.

> A triggered Process is a trigger Process whose trigger condition is currently satisfied.

> The priority of a Process is a measure of relative importance among the Processes at a particular WorkCenter. The default value is 100; you can assign any integer value.

> A startable Process is a Process for which all input is available. If the Process requires both an X-input and a Y-input, it is startable only if both the X-input and the Y-input are available.

> There is one exception to this definition of a startable Process. When both the X-input and the Y-input to a Process come from the same source element, then the Process is startable if either the X-input or the Y-input is available.

The general, overriding rules are the following:

1. No active Process will be interrupted in the middle of processing a single unit -- all Process-switching takes place between units.

2. No batch Process will be interrupted in the middle of processing a batch. Once a batch Process has become the active Process, it will remain the active Process until the last unit of the current batch is completed -- even if this means the WorkCenter must fall idle and wait for the availability of further input to complete the batch.

3. A trigger Process can never become active until it becomes a triggered Process.

4. Priorities are only relevant in choosing between Processes, at a time when a selection must be made. Priorities cannot override any of the three rules above.

The determination of the active Process for a particular WorkCenter is reviewed, each time any one of the following events occurs:

1. An individual unit is completed, if the active Process is not a batch Process.

2. The last unit of the current batch is completed, if the active Process is a batch Process.

3. Input material becomes available for an idle WorkCenter, if the (last) active Process is not a batch Process with an unfinished batch.

At each review time, the following rules are applied, in order:

1. Select the highest-priority, startable triggered Process.

2. If there is no startable triggered Process, select the highest-priority, startable non-trigger Process.

3. If there is no startable non-trigger Process, make no selection (let the WorkCenter fall idle, or remain idle).

If, in either step 1 or step 2 of this rule, there is a tie for the selection of the highest-priority startable Process, the tie is broken in the following way:

Processes are considered in round-robin order, in the opposite order from that in which the Processes were originally defined at the WorkCenter. The first of the tied Processes encountered is the one selected.

The starting point in the round-robin consideration is:
-- the current active Process, if that is a non-batch Process
-- the successor to the current active Process, if the current active Process is a batch Process.

This means that the WorkCenter tends to continue a non-batch Process (since ties among non-batch Processes are resolved in favor of the incumbent Process), and tends to switch among batch Processes (since ties among batch Processes are resolved against the incumbent Process).

B.2.1.6 Use of AuxiliaryResources

An AuxiliaryResource menu, accessible from Process design, permits the optional specification of one or two additional "resources" needed to perform the Process. For example, these could represent an operator for the machine (WorkCenter), or tooling. When this specification is made, the Process cannot be started unless the AuxiliaryResource (or Resources, if two are specified) is available.

If two AuxiliaryResources are specified, they cannot both be of the same type. For example, if each AuxiliaryResource site represents the number of operators in each labor category, you can specify a team of two operators as necessary to perform a particular Process -- but the team must consist of operators from two different categories, and not two of the same category.

For further information on the behavior of AuxiliaryResources, see Section B.8.

B.2.2 WorkCenter Maintenance

The **WorkCenter maintenance** menu is accessible from **WorkCenter design**.

Two alternative maintenance mechanisms are available. The default is no maintenance -- the WorkCenter is continuously available for work. Note that maintenance is associated with the WorkCenter, and not with individual Processes that run on that WorkCenter.

1. <u>Scheduled Maintenance</u> -- where the maintenance comes due at regular, predictable intervals. (If the WorkCenter is busy with an active Process when the maintenance comes due, the start of that maintenance is postponed until the Process completes processing of the current unit.) Each individual WorkCenter can have its own interval between scheduled maintenance periods. The default interval is 50 timeunits, but you can specify any other value.

2. <u>Random Breakdowns</u> -- where the maintenance comes due at random, unpredictable times. (Random breakdowns only occur when a WorkCenter is busy.) The interval between breakdowns is a either a random value from an <u>exponential distribution</u> or from a <u>general</u> (Ramberg-Schmeiser) distribution. The default is exponential with mean time between failures of 50 timeunits, but you can specify any other value.

   In determining the time between random breakdowns, only <u>busy time</u> for the WorkCenter is considered -- idle time does not count. Consequently, a WorkCenter can only suffer failure when it is running.

For either scheduled maintenance or random breakdowns there are three alternative methods of determining the service (repair) time:

1. Service time can be a <u>constant</u>.

2. Service time can be a random value from an <u>exponential distribution.</u> This is the default, with a mean of 5 timeunits, but you can specify any other value.

3. Service time can be a random value from a <u>general</u> (Ramberg-Schmeiser) distribution. See Appendix 5.

Each WorkCenter can have either scheduled maintenance or random breakdowns, but <u>not both kinds</u> of maintenance at the same WorkCenter. However, if you need to model a real situation in which both kinds of activity are associated with the same WorkCenter you can easily do so with a composite WorkCenter (see Section C.5.3). Create a dummy WorkCenter, with a Process having zero processing-time, and connect this to the output side of the "real" WorkCenter. (It can be placed immediately to the right of the real WorkCenter, and the display of the dummy can be suppressed.) Specify random breakdowns for the real WorkCenter, and scheduled maintenance for the dummy. During periods of scheduled maintenance, the dummy will block the flow of material from the real WorkCenter and effectively shut it down just as if it were in fact undergoing the scheduled maintenance. (Note that assigning the scheduled maintenance to the real WorkCenter and the random breakdowns to the dummy will not work, since the time-between-breakdowns depends upon elapsed processing-time.)

Each WorkCenter must be assigned to a particular MaintenanceCenter to provide the "service teams" that perform the maintenance work. The assignment of WorkCenter to MaintenanceCenter is done in **Workcenter design**, but the MaintenanceCenter should already have been created before this assignment can be made (see Section B.3). Any number of WorkCenters can be assigned to a particular MaintenanceCenter. If more WorkCenters are assigned to a particular Center than there are service-teams at that Center, WorkCenters may sometimes have to wait in queue for service.

Although the terminology of "repair" and "service" suggests certain kinds of activity, in fact the MaintenanceCenters are quite general and can be used for purposes that have nothing to do with actual maintenance. "Maintenance" is just a mechanism with which WorkCenters can periodically be withdrawn from service. For example, suppose you are trying to determine how many operators should be assigned to run eight semi-automatic machines.

(Presumably semi-automatic means that an operator is required part of the time -- for loading, unloading, adjustment, etc. -- but not all of the time.) Specify the maintenance at these WorkCenters to represent the time when an operator is required. Assign each of these WorkCenters to the same MaintenanceCenter where the "service-teams" represent the operators of the WorkCenters. Then run an experiment measuring the thruput of the WorkCenters (or their utilization) for different numbers of service teams at the "operator" MaintenanceCenter. Other suggestions of alternative uses of the maintenance mechanism are given in Section C.2.2 and C.5.

B.3   MaintenanceCenter Design

Each MaintenanceCenter provides service to a particular group of WorkCenters. Both the membership in this group, and the specification of the characteristics of the maintenance activity are specified in **WorkCenter design** rather than in **MaintenanceCenter design**. See Section B.2.2.

The only characteristic, apart from the Center name, that is specified in **MaintenanceCenter design** is the number of "service-teams" that are stationed at that Center. The default is a single-team. When one of the assigned WorkCenters requires service, a service-team is dispatched from the MaintenanceCenter if a team is idle at that moment. If all the service-teams at that MaintenanceCenter are already in service, the Workcenter is placed in a first-come-first-served queue to wait for the next available service-team.

In effect, each MaintenanceCenter and the WorkCenters assigned to it represents a completely separate queuing problem. There is no mechanism with which an overloaded MaintenanceCenter can automatically obtain temporary help from an underutilized Facility, or a Workcenter can in any way dynamically choose which Facility should provide service. You can, of course, interrupt a run and return to **MaintenanceCenter design** to reallocate service-teams, or to **WorkCenter design** to reassign WorkCenters to particular MaintenanceCenters.

There is also no direct mechanism with which to model complex maintenance activities that require the action of <u>two</u> <u>or</u> <u>more</u> <u>service-teams</u> <u>at</u> <u>the</u> <u>same</u> <u>time.</u>

The position of a MaintenanceCenter on the factory floor is essentially immaterial -- its position has no effect whatever on the operation of the model. (There is no explicit provision for "travel time" for service-teams between their home MaintenanceCenter and the WorkCenters served.)

Although each WorkCenter can have either random failures or scheduled maintenance, but not both, a particular MaintenanceCenter is not limited to providing either repair of random failures or scheduled maintenance. That is, its service-teams can provide random service to some of the assigned WorkCenters and scheduled service to others.

MaintenanceCenters, like WorkCenters, can be included in the Gantt chart display (see Section E.2.1.3). As MaintenanceCenters are created, they are automatically assigned to lines on the Gantt Chart -- as long as there are open lines available. When you invoke the Chart option you have an opportunity to re-assign MaintenanceCenters to the different lines of the Chart.

B.4   ReceivingArea Design

A ReceivingArea is a source of material from the world outside the system being modeled. Units move from ReceivingAreas to Processes over the input-links of those Processes (which must be established from the Process end), or over the pickup-links of ControlPoints (which must be established from the ControlPoint end). There is no limit to the number of Processes and/or ControlPoints that can be supplied from a particular ReceivingArea.

The same ReceivingArea can supply both the X-input and the Y-input to a particular Process. Presumably this means that two units of the same type of material are combined in this assembly Process to make a single unit of output.

A ReceivingArea cannot be directly linked to a Buffer or a ShippingArea. If you need to model such a linkage, you can do so by interposing a dummy WorkCenter -- one with a Process having zero processing time. The display of the dummy WorkCenter can be suppressed so it appears the link goes directly from the ReceivingArea to the Buffer or ShippingArea.

Your principal option in the design of a ReceivingArea concerns the manner in which material <u>arrives</u> at the ReceivingArea from outside the model. The choices are:

1. The ReceivingArea can represent an <u>unlimited supply</u> of material. This is the default arrival mechanism, assumed for each ReceivingArea unless you specify otherwise. An unlimited-supply ReceivingArea always has a unit immediately available to satisfy the needs of any Process or ControlPoint that is linked directly to it. During **run**, an unlimited-supply ReceivingArea always appears to be "full" --the bar graph at the left side of the symbol for the ReceivingArea is always full to the top.

   An unlimited-supply ReceivingArea can represent a supplier that is so dependable that you can ignore the possibility of material shortages, or alternatively, can represent non-critical material purchased in generous quantity so that the probability of shortage is negligible.

2. Material can arrive at the ReceivingArea in <u>regular batches</u>. A "batch" consists of one or more units arriving at the ReceivingArea at the same instant in time. "Regular" implies that the interval of time between batches is more or less regular, and is generated automatically by an internal probability mechanism.

   The intervals between batch arrivals are drawn at random from a <u>uniform probability distribution</u>. You specify the minimum (shortest interval) and maximum (longest interval) of that distribution; every interval length between that minimum and maximum is equally likely to occur. If you specify a distribution for which the minimum value is the same as the maximum value, that of course means that every interval has exactly the same length. The default distribution for inter-arrival intervals has both minimum and maximum values of 10 timeunits.

   The size of the arriving batch is also drawn at random from a <u>uniform distribution</u> -- but a different distribution from the one that supplies the inter-arrival intervals. Again, you specify the minimum (smallest batch) and maximum (largest batch) of that distribution. If the minimum and maximum are equal, every batch is of exactly the same size. The default distribution for batch size has both minimum and maximum values of 5 units.

3. Arriving <u>batches</u> of material can be <u>manually specified</u>. That is, you will specify both the batch size and time of the arrival of the next batch, for each batch <u>individually</u>, at the time that that batch arrives. Each time a batch arrives, the run pauses and you are asked to specify the size of this particular batch and the arrival time of the next batch. You can, of course, use this mechanism to feed material to the factory model according to an an actual schedule of material arrival.

   4. Arriving <u>batches</u> can be specified individually from a <u>file.</u> (This
      is an XCELL+ option not available in XCELL.) This is logically
      equivalent to manual-batch arrivals, except that each
      specification of batch size and time-of-next-arrival is drawn from
      a stored file rather than requested from the keyboard.
      Instructions for preparing such a file are given in Section F.5.1.

The manner of material arrival at each ReceivingArea is indicated
graphically by the <u>position</u> <u>of</u> <u>the</u> <u>link</u> <u>stub</u> -- the point where Process
input-links or ControlPoint pickup-links are attached to the symbol for the
ReceivingArea.   For example,   in Figure B-3, ReceivingArea R1 is
unlimited-supply, R2 is regular-batch, R3 is manual-batch, and R4 is
file-batch.

When material arrives at a particular ReceivingArea in batches, that
ReceivingArea also has a <u>limited</u> <u>storage-capacity</u> -- that is, it can only
accommodate a fixed number of units.   The default capacity depends upon the
particular arrival mechanism, but you can assign any capacity you choose.
When a ReceivingArea has a limited storage-capacity, an arriving batch can
contain more units than can be accommodated.   The excess unit are
"rejected", and the system automatically keeps track of the quantity
rejected at each ReceivingArea.

When material arrives at a particular ReceivingArea in batches, the stock on
hand at that Area can be used as a "trigger" to invoke Processes at
WorkCenters.   See Section B.2.1.5.2. The stock at a particular ReceivingArea
can trigger any number of different Processes, and each Process can have its
own trigger level and direction.

An option for an unlimited-supply ReceivingArea is to "log" (into a data
file) the times when individual units are requested from the ReceivingArea

---

Figure B-3

Graphical representation of ReceivingAreas with different arrival mechanisms

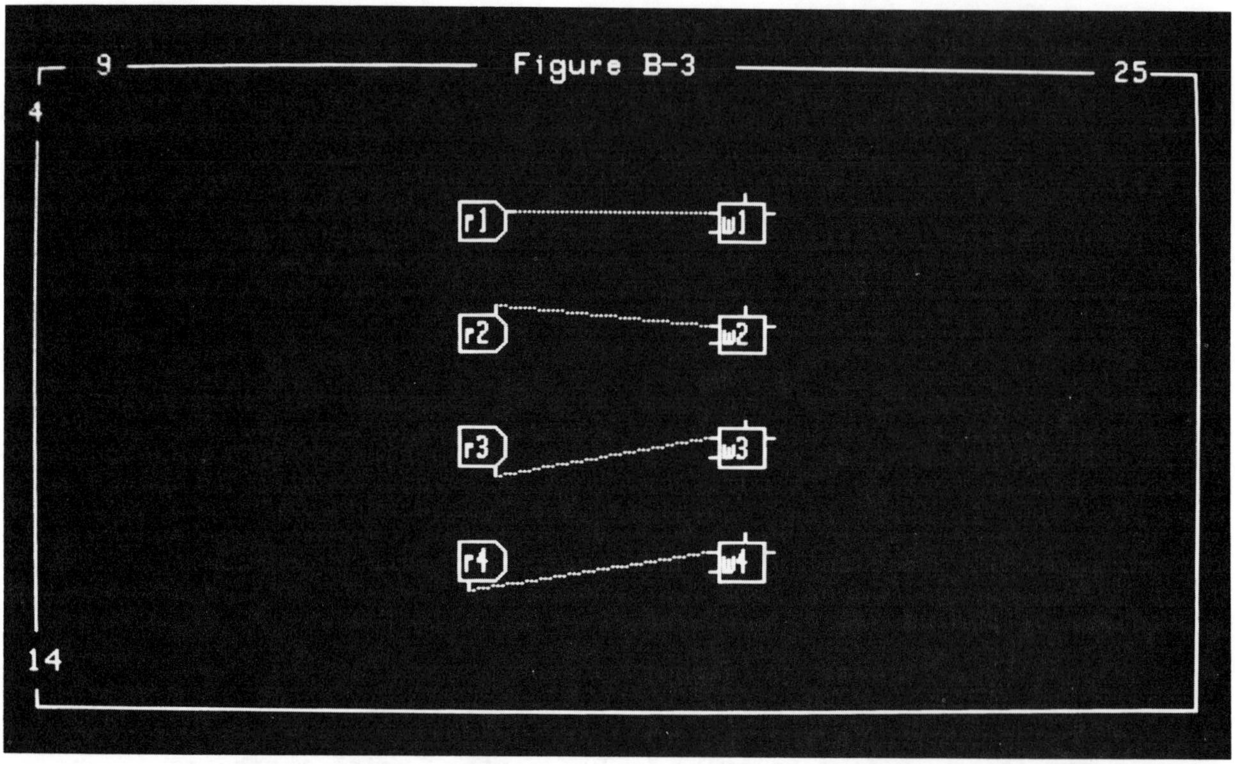

by the factory. This log represents the "natural demand pattern" for the
model, and can be subjected to analysis outside of the XCELL+ package. See
Section F.5.2.

Each ReceivingArea is a source of <u>one</u> <u>particular</u> <u>Part</u>. Several
ReceivingAreas can supply the same Part, but a single ReceivingArea cannot
supply two different Parts. A commitment to a particular Part must be made
immediately as the Receiving Area is created, but it can subsequently be
changed.

This commitment of a ReceivingArea to a particular Part is not a significant
restriction on the links from the ReceivingArea to the X-input or Y-input of
a Process, since Parts of any type can be specified as X-input or Y-input to
the Process, and need not necessarily have the same name as the Process
itself. However, when the pickup-link of a ControlPoint is connected to a
ReceivingArea, then the commitment is important since loads picked-up at the
ControlPoint consist of the Part associated with the ReceivingArea. This is
necessary since every load on a Carrier must be identified as to the
particular Part that it contains.

B.4.1 Tagging Units Released from a ReceivingArea

Optionally, individual units can be "tagged" as they are released from a
ReceivingArea into the factory. The tagging feature is really a **run** mode
option (see Section E.3) but the <u>frequency</u> with which units are tagged is a
property of each ReceivingArea and must be specified during **ReceivingArea
design**. The default frequency is 1 unit in 10 -- when tagging is active,
every tenth unit released from the ReceivingArea is tagged.

Tagging of individual units has two purposes.   The most obvious is that the
<u>progress</u> <u>of</u> <u>individual</u> <u>tagged</u> <u>units</u> <u>is</u> <u>shown</u> while tracing or charting the
running of the model. Each ReceivingArea is assigned a distinctive color
and a block representing the tagged unit bears the color of the
ReceivingArea where it originated.

The second purpose of tagging an individual unit is to be able to keep track
of the total time it spends in the factory. Based on these data, the
average "flowtime", "total process-time", and "total waiting-time" can be
computed. The flowtime of a unit is the time from its release from its
Receiving Area until its arrival at a Shipping Area. The total process-time
is the sum of the processing-times at Workcenters that the unit encounters
en route from ReceivingArea to ShippingArea.   The total waiting-time is the
difference between flowtime and process-time. These statistics are reported
(for each ShippingArea) in "flowtime results" (see Section E.4).

Note that the identity of a tagged unit is lost if the unit enters an
unordered Buffer. Hence if you want to follow the progress of a tagged unit
all the way from ReceivingArea to ShippingArea, and have flowtime,
process-time, and wait-time statistics, you must use FIFO or LIFO Buffers
along its route.

B.5 ShippingArea Design _____

A ShippingArea is a location from which material produced by the factory is
discharged to the outside world. Units are accepted at a ShippingArea from
the output-links from Processes (which must be established from the Process
end) or from dropoff-links from ControlPoints (which must be established
from the ControlPoint end). There is no limit to the number of Processes
and/or ControlPoints that can supply material to a particular ShippingArea.

A ShippingArea cannot be directly linked to a Buffer or to a ReceivingArea.
If you need to model such a linkage, you can do so by interposing a dummy
WorkCenter -- one with a Process having zero processing-time. The display

of the dummy WorkCenter can be suppressed so it appears that the links go
directly from the ReceivingArea or Buffer to the ShippingArea.

Your principal option in the design of a ShippingArea concerns the manner
in which shipments are made from that Area to the outside world.   The
choices are:

1. Shipment can be continuous. That is, the ShippingArea
   immediately ships each individual unit to the outside world as
   soon as it is accepted at the ShippingArea. No
   stock is held at the ShippingArea. This is the default shipment
   mechanism, assumed for each ShippingArea unless you specify
   otherwise. A continuous-shipment ShippingArea can always accept
   another unit arriving from a Process. During **run**, a continuous-
   shipment ShippingArea always appears to be "empty" -- the bar
   graph at the right side of the symbol for the ShippingArea is
   always empty.

   A continuous-shipment ShippingArea can represent its obvious
   counterpart where there is immediate shipment, but it also can
   represent any shipping mechanism or schedule that never presents
   a problem to the factory that supplies material to the Area. For
   example, a ShippingArea that always accumulates a pallet-lot of
   10 units before making a shipment would nevertheless be modeled
   as a continuous-shipment ShippingArea if it has adequate storage-
   capacity (so that it never has to refuse to accept an arriving
   unit from the factory), and if it ships whenever a pallet was
   full, rather than against some fixed schedule.

2. Shipments can be made from the ShippingArea in regular batches.
   A batch consists of one or more units shipped from the Shipping
   Area at the same instant in time. "Regular" implies that the
   interval of time between batches is more or less regular, and is
   generated automatically by an internal probability mechanism.
   Note, however, that this batch mechanism is independent of the
   time pattern with which units actually arrive at the ShippingArea
   from the factory. It is a means of modeling the demand placed
   upon the ShippingArea by the outside world, and not for modeling
   the supply provided to the ShippingArea by the factory. It
   should not, for example, be used to model the pallet-shipment
   situation described in (1) above.

   The intervals between shipments are drawn at random from a
   uniform probability distribution. You specify the minimum
   (shortest interval) and maximum (longest interval) of that
   distribution: every interval length between that minimum and
   maximum is equally likely to occur. If you specify a distribution
   for which the minimum value is the same as the maximum value, that
   of course means that every interval has exactly the same length.
   The default distribution for inter-shipment intervals has both
   minimum and maximum values of 10 timeunits.

   The size of the batch-shipment that is requested is also drawn at
   random from a uniform distribution -- but a different distribution
   from the one that supplies the inter-shipment intervals. Again,
   you specify the minimum (smallest batch) and maximum (largest
   batch) of that distribution. If the minimum and maximum are
   equal, every batch is of exactly the same size. The default
   distribution for batch-size has both minimum and maximum values
   of 5 units.

3. The schedule of desired shipments can be manually specified. That
   is, you will specify both the batch-size and the time of the next
   shipment, for each batch individually, at the time that that batch
   is to be shipped. Each time a batch is to be shipped, the
   simulation pauses and you are asked to specify the size of this

particular batch and the time of the next shipment. You can, of
course, use this mechanism to impose an actual shipment schedule
on your factory model. (However, that does not mean that the
model will automatically adjust itself to satisfy that schedule.)

4. The schedule of desired shipments can be drawn from a <u>file</u>. This is
   logically equivalent to manual-batch shipments, except that each
   specification of batch size and time-of-next-shipment is drawn
   from a stored file rather than requested "live" from the keyboard.
   See Section F.5.1.

The manner in which shipments are made at each ShippingArea is indicated
graphically by the <u>position of the link stub</u> -- the point where Process
output-links and ControlPoint dropoff-links are attached to the symbol for
the ShippingArea.   For   example, in Figure B-4,   ShippingArea S1   is
continuous-shipment, S2 is regular-batch, S3 is manual-batch, and S4 is
file-batch.

When shipments from a particular ShippingArea are made in batches, that
ShippingArea also has a <u>limited storage-capacity</u> -- that is, it can only
accommodate a fixed number of units.   The default capacity depends upon the
particular   shipment mechanism   specified, but   you can   assign   any
storage-capacity you choose. (In particular, you can assign a large
capacity, so that the ShippingArea is never unable to accept another unit
from the factory.)

When shipments from a particular ShippingArea are made in batches, units
accumulate in the ShippingArea until a shipment is made. (During **run**, this
accumulation appears as a bar graph at the right side of the symbol for the
ShippingArea.) When a request for a shipment occurs, there may or may not be
sufficient units available in the ShippingArea to satisfy the requested

_____ **Figure B-4** _____

Graphical representation of ShippingAreas with different shipment mechanisms

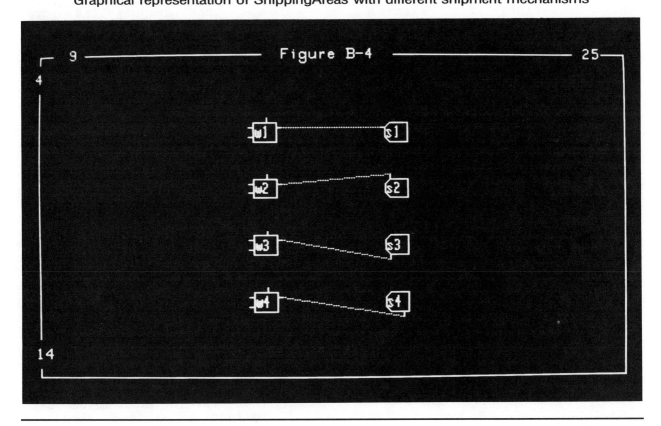

batch amount.   If sufficient units are available, the requested amount is shipped, and deducted from the stock-on-hand in the ShippingArea.   If sufficient units are not available, all of the available units are shipped, and the difference is reported as a "shortage". This shortage is treated as lost demand -- it is not backlogged for later shipment when material becomes available.

When shipments are made from a particular ShippingArea in batches, the stock on hand at that ShippingArea can be used as a "trigger" to invoke Processes at WorkCenters.   See Section B.2.1.6.   The stock at a particular ShippingArea can trigger any number of different Processes, each of which has its own trigger level and direction.   Triggers based on ShippingArea stocks are, of course, the starting point for modeling "pull" or "just-in-time" production systems.

An option for a continuous-shipment ShippingArea is to "log" (into a data file) the times when individual units arrive at the ShippingArea from the factory. This log represents the "natural delivery pattern" for the model, and can be subjected to analysis outside of the XCELL+ package. See Section F.5.2.

A ShippingArea can be supplied by the reject-output link from a Process when the "scrap option" is specified for that Process. (In fact, with the scrap option, the reject-output link must go to a ShippingArea.) In this role, the ShippingArea serves primarily to record the number of units rejected from that Process.

Each ShippingArea can be dedicated to a particular Part, but a ShippingArea can also be "universal" and accept any type of Part that is delivered to it. If the ShippingArea is committed to a particular Part, only units of that Part will be accepted.   The Part associated with a specific ShippingArea can be specified at any time in ShippingArea Design, and can subsequently be changed.

If a particular ShippingArea is committed to one type of Part this affects the output-links from Processes as well as the dropoff-links from ControlPoints.   An output-link from a Process to a ShippingArea cannot be established unless there is compatibility between the output-name of the Process and the Part accepted by the ShippingArea.   In the case of dropoff-links from ControlPoints, the link can be established, but Carriers can only make a dropoff when the Part comprising their current load is the Part accepted by the ShippingArea.

A universal ShippingArea, not committed to a particular Part, can have normal-ouput and reject-output links from any Process, and Carriers can dropoff loads of any Part from a ControlPoint connected to that ShippingArea.

B.6 Buffer Design _____

The Buffers in an XCELL+ model represent work-in-process inventory, and as such are important and interesting elements. "WIP" is not in good favor these days, and some "experts" are campaigning for its complete elimination. At the same time, manufacturing technology is moving in the direction of systems that desperately need some buffering between elements in order to operate effectively.   For example, monolithic "transfer lines" are being replaced with "flexible manufacturing systems", and synchronous materials handling systems are being supplanted by asynchronous systems such as "power and free" conveyors.

There is no question that American manufacturing practice has, in the past, tolerated higher levels of WIP than were really productive, and that there is major benefit to be obtained in reducing these levels. But at the same time, it is clear that carefully placed buffers of modest size are

tremendously valuable in increasing system thruput. In fact, perhaps the
single most important use of simulation in manufacturing systems design
today is the determination of how much WIP should be allowed, and where it
should be positioned. Examples of how XCELL+ can be used for this purpose
are given in Sections H.2 and H.3. Buffers are obviously the key elements
in these models.

Buffers are the simplest type of XCELL+ building block, in terms of the
variety of options you can exercise. Apart from the usual ability to assign
a meaningful name, your choices are:

    -- the capacity: the maximum number of units it can hold

    -- the order in which units are withdrawn.

The default storage-capacity is 10 units; the default discipline is
unordered withdrawal.

The inputs to a Buffer are the output-links from Processes. These must be
specified from **Process design**, rather than **Buffer design**, and the Buffer
must already be in place before a link can be directed to it. There is no
limit to the number of Processes that can deliver their output to a
particular Buffer. Moreover, it is not necessary that all of these
Processes be producing the same Part -- a single Buffer can accommodate
stocks of any number of different Parts.

The outputs from a Buffer are the input-links to Processes. These must also
be specified from **Process design**, rather than **Buffer design**, and again the
Buffer must already be in place before such a link can be established.
There is no limit to the number of Processes that can draw their input from
a particular Buffer.

When, during **Process design**, you specify that a Process input-link comes
from a Buffer, XCELL+ asks <u>which</u> <u>Part</u> in that Buffer is to provide the
input. The point is that while a Buffer can store many different kinds of
Parts, they are not considered interchangable, and each Process input-link
draws upon the stock of only one type of Part.

Each Buffer is considered to hold a number of "stocks" of different Parts.
Each link to a Buffer from a Process has a particular Part associated with
it. Consequently, each Buffer has stocks corresponding to the Parts of each
of its links. (This happens more or less automatically, and you don't have
to worry about it.) When you establish a link to a Buffer, a stock for the
Part associated with that link is automatically established in the Buffer --
unless such a stock already exists there.

The overall capacity limit of a Buffer limits the <u>total</u> <u>stock</u> of all the
different types of Parts in the Buffer. It may turn out (and often seems
to) that in running the model the contents of a Buffer are dominated by the
stock of only one of the several different types of Parts it can store, and
little or no space is left for Parts of other kinds. Models that include
Buffers that are shared by different kinds of Parts can exhibit very
surprising behavior, and you should treat them with great caution.

Note that the input to a Buffer cannot come directly from another Buffer or
from a ReceivingArea, and the output from a Buffer cannot go directly to
another Buffer or to a ShippingArea. If you want to model such a situation
you will have to interpose a dummy WorkCenter with a Process having zero
processing-time.

A special use of a Buffer is as the starting point of a "rework line". That
is, reject-output from a Process can be directed to a Buffer which in turn
supplies a WorkCenter where a rework or recovery Process is performed. See
Section B.2.1.2.1.

The stock-level of a particular Part in a Buffer can be used as a "trigger" to invoke a Process at some WorkCenter. See Section B.2.1.5.2. Each stock can trigger any number of different Processes, each of which can have its own trigger level and direction. Triggers that invoke a Process that is "upstream" of the Buffer, when the stock-level falls to a particular value, can be used to model "pull" or "just-in-time" (JIT) production systems.

The <u>total</u> <u>contents</u> of a Buffer, rather than the stock of a particular Part, can also be used as the basis of triggers.

The stock of a particular Part, and the total contents of a Buffer can be plotted over time as the model is run. See Section E.2.1.2.

B.6.1 Unordered Buffers

Unless you specify overwise, Buffers are "unordered" -- units of Parts of different types can be <u>withdrawn</u> <u>in</u> <u>any</u> <u>order</u>, without regard for the order in which the individual units entered the Buffer. For example, if a Buffer contains stocks of Parts A and B, if a unit of A is present it can be withdrawn, without regard for whether or not any units of B are present, and without regard for the relative arrival order of the A's and B's. The situation becomes very different when the optional ordering is specified, as described in the next section.

B.6.2 Ordered Buffers

The contents of a Buffer can optionally be <u>ordered</u>, so the withdrawal of units is either first-in-first-out (FIFO), or last-in- first-out (LIFO). The order-of-withdrawal at each Buffer is indicated graphically by the <u>position</u> <u>of</u> <u>the</u> <u>link</u> <u>stubs</u> -- the points at which Process links are attached

--- **Figure B-5** ---

Graphical representation of Buffers with different withdrawal orders

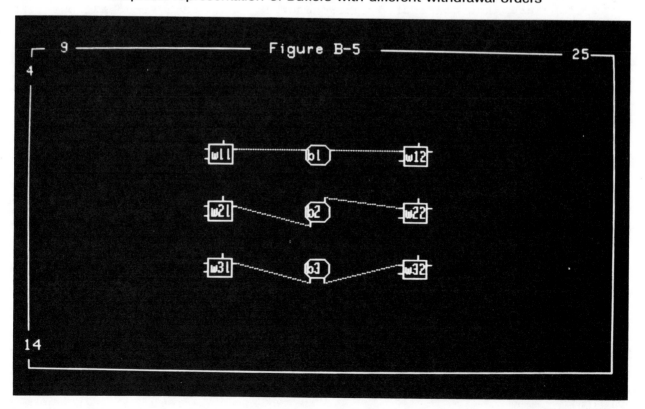

to the symbol for the Buffer. For example, in Figure B-5, Buffer B1 has
unordered withdrawal, B2 is FIFO, and B3 is LIFO.

For some situations, an ordered-withdrawal Buffer is extremely useful. For
example, a FIFO Buffer is a natural element with which to model a gravity
conveyor. However, an ordered-withdrawal Buffer containing different kinds
of Parts is a very restrictive device. For example, when a FIFO Buffer
contains a unit of Part B as its oldest content, requests for all other
types of Part from that Buffer must wait at least until that B is withdrawn.
The effect on system thruput can be devastating. Of course, a real FIFO
Buffer with different Parts would behave the same way, so the model might
faithfully predict a real disaster. In **Buffer design** it is easy to press the
<FIFO> key even if the real buffer is not strictly ordered, without
understanding the effect this can have on the performance of the model. Be
wary of ordered Buffers that serve several types of Parts -- in real systems
as well as simulated models.

Optionally, in a FIFO Buffer, you can specify the minimum holding time (MHT)
to be experienced by each unit. The default MHT is 0. This is particularly
useful in modeling conveyors -- see Section C.3.1. You can designate a
FIFO/MHT Buffer as a CONVEYOR, which distinguishes the Buffer with a
different graphical symbol, but is not different in operation from a
FIFO/MHT Buffer.

Ordered Buffers are important to the "tagging" feature of XCELL+ (see
Section B.4.1). When a tagged unit enters an unordered Buffer, its identity
is lost and it emerges untagged. This not only means that the color-coded
tag disappears from the trace screen; it also means that the flow-time,
process time, and wait time through the factory cannot be computed. Hence,
if you intend to invoke the tagging feature, it is essential that every
Buffer on the path of the tagged units be ordered.

B.6.3 Zero-Capacity Buffers

The minimum capacity for a Buffer is zero. While real storage devices that
would not hold any units would not be of much use, nevertheless
zero-capacity Buffers are very useful devices in modeling. They can be used
to overcome the restrictions on various types of elements. For example,
since there is no limit to either the number of links supplying material to
a Buffer or the number of links drawing material from the Buffer, a Buffer
can be appended to either the upstream or downstream side of a Process to
overcome the severe limitations on input to and output from a Process.

For example, Figure B-6 shows a WorkCenter W1 that has a single Process.
This "fast" Process is capable of supplying input to all three of the "slow"
Processes at W2, W3 and W4 -- but the Process at W1 is entitled to only a
single normal-output link, so it cannot be directly linked to all three
downstream Processes. The solution is to link the outut from the Process at
W1 to the Buffer B1 and to connect the input links for the W2, W3 and W4
Processes to B1, as shown in Figure B-6. However, if there is even one unit
of storage-capacity in B1, this significantly alters the way the system
operates. In general, providing storage-capacity at B1 will increase the
thruput of the system, but the point is that if you needed to model a system
without such storage, it would be very difficult without the ability to have
a zero-capacity Buffer at B1.

Similarly, the fast Process at W5 in Figure B-6 is supplied by four slow
Processes at W6, W7, W8 and W9 through Buffer B2. While it is very helpful
to have storage-capacity at B2, it is difficult to measure just how helpful
the storage at B2 is unless you can compare performance to a model with
zero-capacity at B2.

When zero-capacity Buffers are used as "distributors" and "concentrators",
as in this example, you will probably want to place the Buffer in the cell

Figure B-6

Use of zero-capacity Buffers

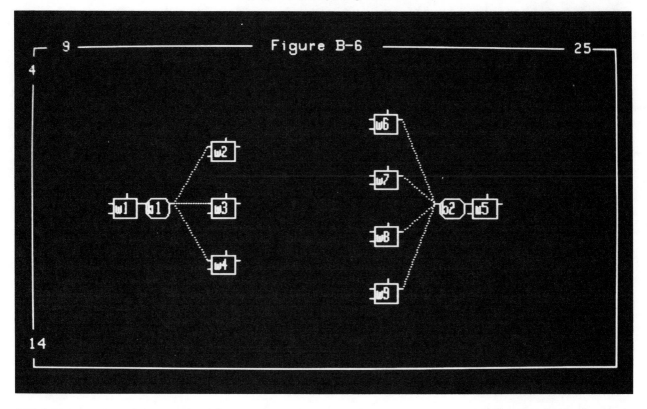

adjacent to the Workcenter, and then suppress the display of the Buffer.
When this is done, it will (almost) appear as if the multiple links are
directly connected to the Process. For example, Figure B-7 shows the same
elements as those of Figure B-6 presented in this way.

B.6.4 Request for Units

An option in **Buffer design** is the specification of a "request".   In many
respects, this is the Carrier counterpart to the trigger mechanism for
Processes in allowing dynamic control of activity.

Each stock -- that is, each different type of Part -- in the Buffer can have
its own request specified. There are four components to the specification:

> <u>level</u>: the stock-level below which a request will be issued each time
> that a unit is withdrawn from this stock. (The default level
> is 1 unit.)

> Part <u>requested</u>: the particular type of Part to be requested -- usually,
> but not necessarily, the same Part as the stock associated
> with the specification. (The default Part requested is the
> same as the Part of the stock for which the specification is
> made.)

> <u>source</u> ControlPoint: the ControlPoint where the <u>pickup</u> of the requested
> Part is to be made

> <u>destination</u> ControlPoint: the ControlPoint where the <u>dropoff</u> of the
> requested Part is to take place -- usually, but not
> necessarily, a ControlPoint with a dropoff-link to the
> requesting Buffer

Figure B-7

Alternative presentation of the elements in Figure B-6

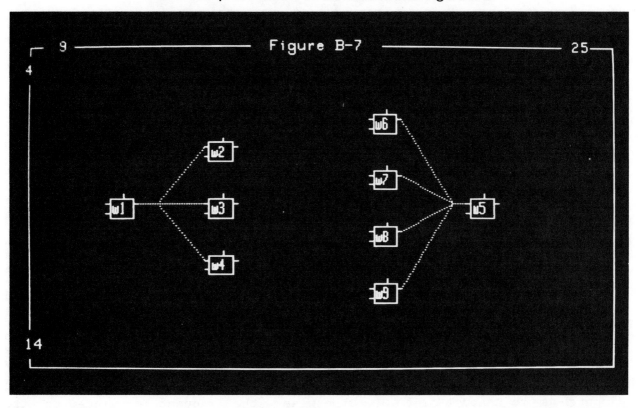

When a particular ControlPoint has been designated as the source ControlPoint in <u>any</u> <u>request</u> <u>specification</u>, that ControlPoint is automatically put into "request-only" mode. That means that pickups at that ControlPoint can only be made in response to specific requests. Note that request-only mode is a characteristic of the <u>specification</u> of requests (during **design**), and not the actual issuance of requests (during **run**).

The request mechanism makes it possible to represent "pull" systems for materials handling. In the absence of requests, materials handling is essentially a "push" system -- if units are available at a ControlPoint when a Carrier arrives, a pickup takes place and the units are advanced through the system. On the other hand, the request mechanism makes it possible to limit the pickup of units in response to the needs of the downstream elements of the model, as reflected by withdrawals from stock at a Buffer.

A chronologically-ordered list of requests is maintained at each request-only ControlPoint. As new requests are received they are added to the end of this list; as requests are satisfied, they are removed from the list. The request-only ControlPoint <u>attempts</u> to satisfy requests in the order in which they are received (first-come, first-served), but is not necessarily successful in maintaining this order. Satisfaction of requests depends upon the availability of different types of Parts for pickup at that ControlPoint. When the pickup link to a request-only ControlPoint is connected to a ReceivingArea, only one type of part is ever available for pickup at that ControlPoint -- requests for any other type of Part will remain unsatisfied on the request list. However, ControlPoints with pickup-links to Buffers or WorkCenters can pickup a variety of different types of Parts, so the requests on the list can reasonably be for different Parts.

Each time an empty Carrier becomes available at a request-only ControlPoint, the requests pending at that ControlPoint are examined to find the oldest request that can be satisfied.

Request-only ControlPoints can depend on "cruising" empty Carriers. However, it is also possible to "pre-position" empty Carriers at certain ControlPoints designated to be HoldingPoints.   The "Holding" option is specified in the **traffic control** menu. HoldingPoints serve as "staging" (or "parking") areas, and release empty Carriers to satisfy requests.   A HoldingPoint holds an (unrouted) empty Carrier until a request-release is received. The incoming Paths to a HoldingPoint represent a parking area, since Carriers are blocked on these Paths by the empty Carrier held at the HoldingPoint. (For this reason it is desirable to position the HoldingPoint and parking area on a "sidetrack" so that the movement of loaded Carriers is not blocked.)

If one or more HoldingPoints have been established, then XCELL+ automatically assigns to each request-only ControlPoint the closest HoldingPoint (closest in the sense of minimum transit-time).   Each request-only ControlPoint then signals its assigned HoldingPoint for release of empty Carriers to satisfy requests.

The following example may help explain how this all works. Suppose the stock of Part P at Buffer B has a request specification of level 2 for a unit of Part P to be picked up at source ControlPoint 4 and carried to destination ControlPoint 8. Suppose that HoldingPoint 6 has been determined to be the minimum transit-time pre-positioning point for ControlPoint 4. When the model is being **run**, each time a unit of P is withdrawn from Buffer B when the level of P at B is less than 2, then a request is sent to ControlPoint 4 for a unit of P to be sent to ControlPoint 8. If there are no other requests pending at ControlPoint 4, and an empty Carrier is already waiting at ControlPoint 4, and a unit of P is available for pickup at ControlPoint 4, then the pickup is made and the Carrier bearing P is dispatched to ControlPoint 8. Otherwise, the request is placed on the chronological request list at ControlPoint 4. If no empty Carrier is waiting at ControlPoint 4, an empty Carrier is released from the pre-positioning point at HoldingPoint 6 and dispatched to ControlPoint 4. If no empty Carrier is waiting at HoldingPoint 6, the release-request is placed on a chronologically-ordered list at HoldingPoint 6. Release-requests are satisfied, in first-come, first-served order, as empty Carriers arrive at HoldingPoint 6.

Note that, although empty Carrier release-requests are issued in response to particular Part-requests, the empty Carrier is not commited to a particular Part-request. The empty Carrier is routed to the source ControlPoint of the Part-request, and cannot be claimed by another ControlPoint en route, but once it arrives it can be used to satisfy any request at that ControlPoint. The originating Part-request may already have been satisfied (by prior arrival of another empty Carrier), or the requested Part may not be available. The point is that the empty Carrier release mechanism is intended to provide an appropriate quantity of empty Carriers at the source ControlPoint -- but not to commit particular Carriers to particular Part-requests.

These facilities make it possible to have both push and pull systems, with both cruising and dispatched Carriers in the same materials handling network. The design and tuning of such a network is a complicated process -- both in modeling and in the real world -- which is, of course, the reason that modeling is especially useful for such systems.

B.6.5 Delivery of Units

A "delivery" is almost identical to a "request", as described in Section B.6.4. The only difference is that delivery from a stock is triggered by arrival of a unit when the stock-level is greater than a specified value. (In effect, requests correspond to a "low-trigger" and bring units to the

Buffer. Deliveries correspond to a "high-trigger", and release units <u>from</u> <u>the Buffer</u>.) Each stock at a Buffer can have both a delivery specification and a request specification.

Like a request, there are four components to delivery specification:

   <u>level</u>: the stock-level above which a delivery will be issued each time
         that a unit is added to this stock. (The default level is
         0 units.)

   <u>Part</u> <u>to</u> <u>be</u> <u>delivered</u>: the particular type of Part to be delivered --
         usually, but not necessarily the same Part as the stock
         associated with the delivery specification. (The default
         Part to be delivered is the same as the Part of the stock
         for which the specification is made.)

   <u>source</u> <u>ControlPoint</u>: the ControlPoint where the <u>pickup</u> of the delivery
         Part is to be made -- usually, but not necessarily, a
         ControlPoint with a pickup-link to this Buffer)

   <u>destination</u> <u>ControlPoint</u>: the ControlPoint where the <u>dropoff</u> of the
         delivered Part is to take place

During **run**, once a delivery is triggered, a request is sent to the source ControlPoint. That is, the term "delivery" is just an alternative (high trigger) specification -- the resulting action is another request. The source ControlPoint does not know whether an arriving request is the result of a "request specification" or of a "delivery specification". It is treated exactly as described in Section B.6.4.

B.7 Design Costs _____

Each element of the factory model has <u>two</u> <u>cost</u> <u>coefficients</u> associated with it:

   1. a <u>capital</u> <u>cost</u>, representing the fixed, or investment, cost of
      including this element in the model

   2. an <u>operating</u> <u>cost</u>, representing the variable cost, per unit of
      thruput, of running this element of the model.

These costs are measured in "costunits", which you can, of course, interpret in any way that is appropriate to your particular problem.

The default values assigned to the different types of elements are the following:

	capital cost	operating cost
WorkCenter	100	5
Buffer	10	1
ReceivingArea	25	2
ShippingArea	25	2
MaintenanceCenter	25	10 (see note below)
AuxiliaryResource	25	10 (see note below)
ControlPoint	20	1
PathSegment	1	-- (same for all Segments)
Carrier	10	-- (same for all Carriers)

The cost coefficients for individual elements can be changed in the options menu. There is an <options> key in each of the design sub-menus -- **WorkCenter design, Buffer design**, etc. The costs for Pathsegments and Carriers are changed from **change Path** and **change Carrier**. All PathSegments have the same fixed cost, and all Carriers have the same fixed cost -- specify the cost for one and you have specified the cost for each one.

The total of the capital costs, and the operating costs are presented in **results** menu, accessible from **run** (see Section E.4). The capital costs and operating costs are not combined, so it is not necessary for you to be consistent in the interpretation of a capital costunit and an operating costunit. For example, each capital costunit could represent $10,000, while each operating costunit could represent only $100. (There is, of course, no reason why you cannot assign the actual dollar values to these coefficients, rather than scale them in this way.)

Note: "Operating cost" for a MaintenanceCenter has a different meaning. This is the <u>cost per service-team</u> -- a design cost in addition to the fixed cost of the Center itself. For example, the total default cost of a MaintenanceCenter with two service-teams is 45 costunits (25 + 2 x 10). This is a fixed cost that does not change with operation of the Center.

The operating cost for an AuxiliaryResource is interpreted similarly.

B.8 AuxiliaryResource Design

An AuxiliaryResource is something besides a WorkCenter needed by a Process; the AuxiliaryResource element is essentially just a home site where one or more resources of a particular type reside when not in use. In other words, creating an AuxiliaryResource site is actually creating a <u>new</u> <u>type</u> of AuxiliaryResource for Processes.

You can specify three attributes for an AuxiliaryResource site:

1. The location -- essentially immaterial, since resource travel between the site and the Processes where used is instantaneous. Just position the site "out of the way", but close enough to the active Processes so its changes during tracing will be visible.

2. The name -- the default names begin with "A".

3. The number of Resources of this type -- the default is 1.

The important specification is <u>which Processes require each type</u> of AuxiliaryResource, but this is done from **Process Design** rather than from **AuxiliaryResource Design**. See Section B.2.1.6.

Perhaps the most obvious use of an AuxiliaryResource is to represent the <u>operator</u> required to perform a Process. That is, for a particular Process to be performed, in addition to the availability of the host WorkCenter (representing a "machine"), and the material specified by the input-links to the Process, there must be an operator of the proper skill classification available. The corresponding AuxiliaryResource site is just the way to specify how many operators of that skill classification are present in the factory.

Since a Process can optionally require two different AuxiliaryResources, these could represent an operator and tooling, or two different kinds of operators, etc.

What AuxiliaryResources really represent is a very general and powerful mechanism for <u>limiting the number of WorkCenters that can be simultaneously active</u>. For example, suppose you have three Processes A, B and C and want

to allow any two, but not all three of these Processes to be active at the
same time.   Specify   that each of the three Processes requires an
AuxiliaryResource named R1, and then provide (at the R1 site) only two
Resources of this type.

Note that in operation, no queue of Processes waiting for a particular
AuxiliaryResource is maintained.   When a Resource is released by a
completing Process, a check is made to see if any idle WorkCenter can now be
put into service -- but the order of examination depends on the order in
which the Resource specification was made in **Process Design**, and not the
order in which the WorkCenters fell idle.

B.9 ControlPoint Design

ControlPoints have four distinct roles in a model:

   -- They are the junctions in Paths -- every Path orginates at a
         ControlPoint and terminates in a ControlPoint.

   -- They are the "connection" between the materials handling facilities
         and other elements -- that is, between ControlPoints, Paths
         and Carriers, and ReceivingAreas, ShippingAreas, Buffers
         and WorkCenters. ControlPoints are the only points where
         Carriers can pickup and dropoff loads.

   -- They provide "traffic-control" that determines the route and
         action of Carriers.

   -- They can serve as "ChargingPoints" to recharge Carrier batteries.

The design of ControlPoints can be quite complicated -- if you are trying to
model a modern computer-controlled materials handling system.   There is a
good deal of flexibility in the XCELL+ modeling tools, but you have to
understand a variety of different control mechanisms and understand how they
work together.

ControlPoint design is like the design of other elements in most respects.
You create a ControlPoint by pressing <add CtrlPt> when the cell-cursor is
on an empty cell.   You can change the characteristics of a ControlPoint by
pressing <change cell> when the cell-cursor is positioned on an existing
ControlPoint. There is also a Tabular Editor for ControlPoints.   The
differences between ControlPoints and other types of elements are the
following:

   -- ControlPoints have numbers rather than names. The numbers are
         assigned automatically in the order you create ControlPoints; you
         cannot change them. You can jump the cell-cursor to a Control
         ControlPoint by entering the ControlPoint number in the same way
         that you can jump to another type of element by entering its name.

   -- ControlPoints cannot be automatically copied (by the <copy cell>
         command.

   -- A ControlPoint can only be moved if it does not have any Paths
         attached to it.

   -- When you are specifying a Path from one ControlPoint and reach
         another ControlPoint where the Path terminates, **ControlPoint
         design** automatically jumps from the origin ControlPoint to the
         termination ControlPoint. (This is the only instance in XCELL+
         where the locus of **design** changes automatically).

B.9.1 Pickup and Dropoff Connections

ControlPoints are the only points in the materials handling system where Carriers can pickup and dropoff loads. If Carriers are to pickup loads at a particular ControlPoint you must specify a pickup-link from that ControlPoint to a ReceivingArea, a Buffer or a WorkCenter. If Carriers are to dropoff loads at a particular ControlPoint you must specify a dropoff-link from that ControlPoint to a Buffer, a WorkCenter or a ShippingArea. Neither a pickup-link nor a dropoff-link can go directly from one ControlPoint to another ControlPoint. (They also cannot go to either a MaintenanceCenter or an AuxiliaryResource.)

An individual ControlPoint can have both a pickup-link and a dropoff-link. However, a ControlPoint that is serving as either a HoldingPoint of a ChargingPoint (see Section B.9.6) cannot have either a pickup-link or a dropoff-link.

There is a **pickup/dropoff** menu, accessible from **ControlPoint design**, in which you can establish the pickup-link and the dropoff-link, and also can specify the times that will be required to perform a pickup and a dropoff. The default value for pickup is 1 timeunit and for dropoff is also 1 timeunit; any non-negative time can be given. Both pickup and dropoff times are constants -- there is no provision for variable pickup and dropoff times.

Pickup-links and dropoff-links are normal links -- just like the input-links and output-links of a Process. Links have no storage capacity, and they transfer units instantaneously, so they can be considered idealized conveyors. This means that the location of a ControlPoint, relative to the element at the end of its pickup-link or dropoff-link, is immaterial -- since the length of a pickup-link or dropoff-link is immaterial. However, the location of a ControlPoint relative to other ControlPoints is highly significant, since this affects the Paths between ControlPoints. See Section B.9.2.

Although each ControlPoint can have only a single pickup-link, there is no limit to the number of different ControlPoints that can be linked for pickup to a particular ReceivingArea or Buffer. Similarly, although each ControlPoint can have only a single dropoff-link, there is no limit to the number of different ControlPoints that can be linked for dropoff to a particular Buffer or ShippingArea.

However, the situation with regard to pickup-links and dropoff-links to WorkCenters is quite different. If a dropoff-link from a ControlPoint goes to a Workcenter, it becomes the X-input link for every Process at that WorkCenter. This applies not only to Processes that exist at the time that the link is established, but also to Processes that are subsequently added to that WorkCenter. This necessarily means that there is a one-to-one association between dropoff ControlPoints and WorkCenters. If a ControlPoint has a dropoff-link to a particular WorkCenter no other ControlPoint can also have a dropoff link to that same WorkCenter.

Similarly, if a pickup-link to a ControlPoint comes from a WorkCenter, it becomes the normal-output link for every Process at that WorkCenter, so there is a one-to-one association between pickup ControlPoints and WorkCenters.

When there is a dropoff-link to a WorkCenter, serving as the X-input to each of the Processes at the WorkCenter, any of those Processes can optionally also have a Y-input link. It is not necessary that all Processes at the WorkCenter have the same Y-input link just because they have their X-input link in common. When a Y-input link is specified for such Processes, it must be an ordinary XCELL+ link from a ReceivingArea, a Buffer or another Process -- it cannot be a dropoff-link from a ControlPoint.

For a Carrier to dropoff a Part to a WorkCenter, it must be a Part whose name corresponds to the name of a Process at that WorkCenter. That is,

where a Process can ordinarily use any type of Part as its X-input (when
that input comes from a ReceivingArea, Buffer or another Process), when the
source is a ControlPoint the Part serving as X-input must have the same name
as the Process itself.

If a ControlPoint has both a dropoff-link and a pickup-link, a loaded
Carrier arriving at that ControlPoint is allowed to make a pickup after
dropping off its load. However, the reverse order of actions is prohibited
-- a Carrier is not allowed to make a dropoff if it just made a pickup at
the same ControlPoint. (If you need to model such a sequence, use adjacent
ControlPoints, making the pickup at the first and the dropoff at the
second.)

B.9.1.1 Engagement During Processing

When the dropoff-link from a ControlPoint goes directly to a WorkCenter, you
can optionally specify that a Carrier performing a dropoff to that
WorkCenter be "engaged" during the processing that takes place there. The
Carrier remains at the ControlPoint for the sum of the dropoff time, the
processing time and the pickup time, rather than be held there only for the
dropoff time. When processing is complete, the finished unit from the
Process is returned to the Carrier, which then proceeds as a loaded Carrier.

When the engagement option is specified, the dropoff-link serves as both the
X-input link and the normal-output link for every Process at the WorkCenter.
Hence this is the only ControlPoint that can be connected to this particular
WorkCenter.

Note that although the Carrier entering the engaging ControlPoint is loaded,
and the Carrier leaving the engaging ControlPoint is also loaded, the
leaving Part is not necessarily the same type of Part as the entering Part
-- since the engaged Process can optionally produce output with a different
name than the Process itself.

B.9.2 Paths

A Path is a route by which a Carrier can travel from one ControlPoint to
another. A Path can connect two adjacent ControlPoints, or a Path can
consist of a connected sequence of Segments from one ControlPoint to
another.

A particular ControlPoint can have as many as four Paths -- called, in the
obvious way, top, right, bottom and left. Each Path has one of three
possible direction senses with respect to the ControlPoint:

        -- outgoing; if the Path originates in this ControlPoint

        -- incoming; if the Path terminates in this ControlPoint

        -- reversing; if the Path can change from incoming to outgoing,
                      during run, depending on traffic requirements

There is a visible distinction between these different types of Paths. For
a non-reversing Path, the incoming end is "open" as it enters the
ControlPoint. That is, the square that represents the ControlPoint has an
open side to receive an incoming Path. A reversing Path is closed at both
ends, with no visible indication of the current direction.

Although it is legal, and sometimes useful, to have a "storage loop" Path
originate and terminate in the same ControlPoint, it is more common for a
particular Path to have its ends associated with different ControlPoints.
Unless a particular ControlPoint has at least one Path capable of being
incoming, and one Path capable of being outgoing, it is not likely to serve
a useful purpose in the model.

When a Path connects non-adjacent ControlPoints, it consists of a connected sequence of Segments. Segment cells are like other elements only in that they occupy a cell. For example, if a particular ControlPoint is to have a right Path, you cannot position the ControlPoint immediately to the left of, say, a Buffer -- there would be no cell in which to place the first Segment of the Path.

Segments are unlike other elements in that they are not autonomous -- they exist only as a component of a Path between ControlPoints. Segments are not created from **design** like other elements. They are created in **Paths** menu, which is accessible only from **ControlPoint design.**

Paths are constructed by tracing their Segments with a special "Path cursor" from one ControlPoint to another. The directional sense of the Path is specified after its Segments have been specified, and does not depend upon the order in which the Segments were specified (although the default sense is non-reversing, in the order drawn). The directional sense can be changed in **change Path.**

Segments do not have names or numbers -- there is no reason to refer to them individually. There is a fixed cost associated with each Segment, but it is not an individual cost, as for other types of elements. All Segments cost the same amount.

Similarly, the drawing of individual Segments cannot be suppressed; the entire Path is either suppressed or displayed.

A Path has a <u>length</u> and a <u>transit-time</u>. The length of the Path is simply the number of Segments it contains. The length is significant because it determines the storage capacity of the Path -- each Segment can be occupied by a single Carrier, and each Carrier can bear a single unit of load. Hence, you must position your ControlPoints so there is a clear space between them, in which to add a Path, and so that the number of Segments in the Path provides a suitable amount of Carrier accumulation capacity. You do not have to be particularly concerned with the position of ControlPoints relative to the elements to which their pickup-links and dropoff-links connect -- since these links do not consume floor space (they can cross other elements), and transport over these links is instantaneous regardless of length. Only the clarity of the graphical presentation suggests the placement of ControlPoints close to the elements they serve for pickup and dropoff.

B.9.2.1 Reversible Paths

Optionally, a Path can be <u>bi-directional</u> or <u>reversible</u> -- that is, its directional sense can change dynamically during the run of the model according to traffic requirements. This capability is generally not necessary to model current forms of AGV systems, but it permits modeling various mono-rail systems with reversing Carriers. Since any Path can be reversible, you can construct very complicated networks of Paths -- but BE WARNED, it is deceptively easy to construct such networks, and very difficult to make them behave reasonably.

The reversible option is specified in **change Path** menu. You are automatically in **change Path** when you complete the initial specification of the cells that the Path covers. You can return to **change Path** by placing the **design** cursor on any Segment of the Path and pressing <change cell>.

Don't confuse the reversible option with the key that <changes direction> of a Path. The latter is a permanent change. You can later change it (by repeating the same key) but the Path does not dynamically change its own direction during **run.**

A reversible Path works in the following way. Regarding the Path from the point-of-view of the ControlPoint at one end of the Path, at any instant the reversible Path is in one of the three following states:

reversible-empty -- no Carrier is currently on the Path

reversible-incoming -- one or more Carriers are currently on the
                       Path headed for this ControlPoint

reversible-outgoing -- one or more Carriers are currently on the
                       Path headed away from this ControlPoint

A Carrier at this ControlPoint, seeking an outgoing Path, can enter a reversible-outgoing Path or a reversible-empty Path (thereby converting that to a reversible-outgoing Path). It can, of course, also enter an ordinary outgoing Path. It cannot enter a reversible-incoming Path (or an ordinary incoming Path). You can think of it as following the normal "one-way bridge algorithm":

1. A vehicle approaching an empty bridge from either direction can enter immediately.

2. A vehicle approaching a bridge where the traffic is currently moving in the favorable direction can enter immediately.

3. A vehicle approaching a bridge where the traffic is currently moving in the unfavorable direction must wait until the bridge is empty before entering.

The difficulty in modeling reversible Paths is that there is no waiting area in which a Carrier can wait until a reversible-incoming Path becomes reversible-empty. If a Carrier wanting to enter a reversible Path simply waits at the exiting ControlPoint, the incoming traffic is blocked and cannot (ever) exit the Path. The Path will never become reversible-empty, and at least this particular ControlPoint is deadlocked.

Reversible Paths are a new, and little-tried, feature of XCELL+. We are currently experimenting with several deadlock-avoidance algorithms, and it will probably be possible to make XCELL+ smarter in future releases, in terms of finding alternative Paths to avoid deadlock -- but at the moment, that is primarily your responsibility. Note that networks with a single Carrier are safe -- the deadlock described above cannot occur -- but the addition of a second Carrier immediately makes things enormously more complicated.

B.9.2.2 Transit-Times

Carrier speed is specified indirectly in terms of the "transit-times" of the ControlPoints and PathSegments. To speed up the Carriers, you reduce the transit-times of the cells they must traverse.

Each ControlPoint and each PathSegment has a separate transit-time. The total traverse time for a Path is simply the sum of the transit-times of the Segments that constitute the Path.

The default transit-time for a ControlPoint is one timeunit; this can be changed to any non-negative value.

The default traverse time for a Path is one timeunit for each Segment of the Path. You can specify a different traverse time for a Path immediately after its creation, or later in **change Path**. In either case, the traverse time you specify for the Path is divided equally among the Segments of the Path to determine the transit-times of the individual Segments.

B.9.3 Carriers

Carriers are elements with two unique properties, in comparison with all other types of elements:

    -- Carriers are mobile, where all other types of elements have a
        fixed position on the factory floor.

    -- Carriers do not have a cell of their own, but are superimposed on
        some ControlPoint or PathSegment.

Every ControlPoint and every PathSegment can accommodate exactly one Carrier. The total number of Carriers in the model is, of course, dependent on the number of times you specify <add Carrier> in **ControlPoint design** and **change PathSegment**. For example, to have five Carriers in the system, you must <add Carrier> at five different ControlPoints and/or PathSegments during design.

Although each Carrier has an identifying number, shown in **detailed display**, **results** and on the optional Gantt Chart (but not in the trace or plot display), all Carriers are functionally equivalent. They have the same capability, cost the same amount, and travel at the same speed(s).

During the **run** of a model, each Carrier has the following properties (which change as the run progresses):

    -- <u>physical</u> <u>location</u>: superimposed on some ControlPoint or PathSegment

    -- <u>loaded</u> or <u>empty</u>: if loaded, the Carrier contains one unit of a
        particular type of Part

    -- <u>routed</u> or <u>unrouted</u>: if routed, it bears the ControlPoint number of
        its destination (which appears within the Carrier symbol
        in the normal-scale trace display)

    -- <u>state</u> <u>of</u> <u>battery</u> <u>charge</u>: expressed as a fraction of the full-charge
        run-time that remains

    -- <u>status</u>: any of the following:
                - in transit
                - performing dropoff
                - waiting for dropoff
                - performing pickup
                - waiting for pickup
                - engaged during processing
                - held for release-request
                - blocked by traffic
                - manually frozen in place
                - having batteries charged

B.9.3.1 Carrier Speed

Carrier speed is specified indirectly -- by specifying the transit-time for each cell the Carrier must cross. See Section B.9.2.2.

All Carriers have the same speed characteristics. By default, empty Carriers travel at the same speed as loaded Carriers, but you can change that by giving an "empty Carrier speed adjustment" (faster or slower), in **change Carrier**, accessible from **change Path** for a Segment where a Carrier is present.

You can also effectively change the speed of all Carriers by changing the transit-times of all ControlPoints and Paths. There is a convenient, automatic way of doing this in **change Carrier**.

B.9.4 Traffic-Control Rules

The most complex aspect of **ControlPoint design** is the specification of Carrier traffic-control rules -- the specification of what a Carrier does as it enters a ControlPoint, and which outgoing Path it takes as it leaves the ControlPoint.

The first thing to understand is the control of routed Carriers. A routed Carrier has a definite destination -- the ControlPoint number of the destination is shown within the Carrier symbol on the trace display as the model is run.   The control of a routed Carrier is the same, regardless of whether the Carrier is loaded or empty:

-- When a routed Carrier headed for ControlPoint D enters ControlPoint
     E en route to D, the Carrier is unaffected by traffic-control
     rules in force at E. It is also not affected by pickup or dropoff
     opportunities at E. After experiencing the transit-time for E,
     the Carrier leaves E along whichever outgoing Path provides
     the fastest route from E to D. "Fastest" is determined as if this
     were the only Carrier in the model -- that is, without concern for
     traffic congestion. (The fastest route is determined using
     reversing Paths in the most favorable direction.)

-- When a routed Carrier headed for ControlPoint D enters ControlPoint
     D it immediately becomes unrouted. It is then treated in
     exactly the same way as it would be if it had arrived as an
     unrouted Carrier. The rules governing treatment of unrouted
     Carriers are given in the following sections.

Note that a Carrier cannot become routed unless there is some feasible path from its current location to its destination ControlPoint. Destinations are not assigned to Carriers if they are not accessible from the Carrier's present location.

Carriers without a specific ControlPoint as a destination are said to be "cruising" -- whether loaded or empty. Routed Carriers move single-mindedly towards their destination ControlPoint, waiting as necessary for traffic congestion, but ignoring all pickup and dropoff opportunities on the way, and all local traffic-control rules at the intermediate ControlPoints. On the   other hand,   cruising Carriers move according to the   local traffic-control rules of each ControlPoint they enter, and if empty, make the first offered pickup, and if loaded, make the first appropriate dropoff. These two modes of Carrier control are entirely compatible -- cruising and routed Carriers can be used in the same model, and indeed, in the same ControlPoints and Paths.

Traffic-control at a particular ControlPoint is either manual or automatic. Manual means that each time an unrouted Carrier is ready to leave the ControlPoint, the run pauses and you are asked to select the outgoing Path for the Carrier.   Automatic means that the traffic-control rules specified for that particular ControlPoint are applied.   Different rules are applicable to the control of loaded and empty Carriers, as described in Sections B.9.4.1 and B.9.4.2, respectively.

The default traffic-control rule for determining the departure Path from a ControlPoint is used unless you have specified other rules for the particular ControlPoint. The default is the same, regardless of whether the (unrouted) exiting Carrier is loaded or empty:

          Choose among the outgoing Paths from the ControlPoint in
               clockwise rotation.

For example, if a particular ControlPoint has top, bottom, and left outgoing Paths, the default exit selection sequence from that ControlPoint would be:

          top, bottom, left, top, bottom, left, top, ... etc.

B.9.4.1 Automatic Traffic-Control of Loaded Carriers

As an unrouted Carrier loaded with a unit of Part P enters a ControlPoint D, the following rules are applied:

1. If there is a dropoff-link from ControlPoint D, and if the element at the end of that link can <u>immediately</u> accept a unit of P, begin the dropoff Process. (The unit is instantaneously available at the end of the dropoff-link, but the Carrier is "tied up" for the "dropoff-time" specified at ControlPoint D.)

2. If the dropoff element cannot immediately accept a unit of P, but the loaded-WAIT option has been specified for ControlPoint D, wait until the dropoff element can accept a unit of P.

3. If no dropoff takes place, the Carrier remains loaded with a unit of Part P, and experiences the "transit-time" for ControlPoint D.

If a dropoff takes place, at the end of the dropoff-time, the Carrier proceeds as an empty Carrier. It experiences the transit-time for ControlPoint D, and then exits from D according to the rules for an empty Carrier, as described in Section B.9.4.2 below.

If no dropoff takes place, when the Carrier loaded with a unit of Part P has completed its transit of ControlPoint D and is ready to leave D, the following rules apply. Note that at this point it does not matter whether the Carrier entered ControlPoint D loaded with P and failed to dropoff the load, or whether the Carrier entered D empty and picked up the load P at D:

1. If a "Part-destination" list has been specified for ControlPoint D, check to see if Part P is on that list. If so, assign the corresponding destination for P to the Carrier, making it a routed Carrier.

2. If no Part-destination list has been specified for ControlPoint D, or if Part P is not on that list, and if a "destination sequence" for loaded Carriers has been specified for ControlPoint D, determine the destination from that list and make the Carrier a routed Carrier.

3. Otherwise, determine the exit direction for the Carrier by the default clockwise rotation.

The destination-sequence for loaded Carriers provides a cyclic sequence of ControlPoint numbers that are assigned to successive exiting loaded Carriers, in order, starting again from the beginning when the sequence is exhausted. For example, if the destination-sequence 2,4,5,5 has been specified for ControlPoint D, the first loaded Carrier exiting from D will be routed to ControlPoint 2; the second to ControlPoint 4, the third and fourth to ControlPoint 5; the fifth to ControlPoint 2; etc. The destination sequence can be used to arbitrarily distribute the outgoing traffic from a ControlPoint and, by repeating certain ControlPoint numbers on the list, to distribute the traffic with arbitrary assymmetry. Note that a destination-sequence consisting of a single ControlPoint number will direct all unrouted loaded Carriers exiting from D to a particular ControlPoint.

A variation on the use of the destination-sequence is applied if the "balance load" option is specified for ControlPoint D. If load-balancing is specified, and the destination-sequence 2,4,5,5 is specified, then <u>each time</u> a destination assignment is sought for a loaded Carrier, it is assigned to whichever of ControlPoints 2, 4 and 5 has the fewest loaded Carriers currently en route to it. Note that the repetition of ControlPoint 5 on the list is immaterial when the balance load option is in effect.

Note that, with or without load-balancing, the destination-sequence is independent of the type of Part on the Carrier. Each loaded Carrier is treated the same way, regardless of the type of Part it contains.

B.9.4.2 Automatic Traffic-Control of Empty Carriers

As an unrouted empty Carrier enters a ControlPoint D, the following rules are applied:

1. If the "empty skip" option is in effect for ControlPoint D, and a sufficient number of empty Carriers have not been passed through D since the last pickup, pass this Carrier through without attempting a pickup.

2. If there is a pickup-link to ControlPoint D, and if a unit of any type of Part is immediately available from the element at the end of the pickup-link, the Carrier begins the pickup Process. (The unit is instantaneously withdrawn from the element at the end of the pickup-link, but the Carrier is "tied up" for the pickup-time specified at ControlPoint D.)

3. If there is no unit available from the element at the end of the pickup-link, but the empty-WAIT option has been specified for ControlPoint D, the Carrier waits at D until a a unit is available for pickup.

4. If no pickup takes place, the Carrier remains empty, and experiences the "transit-time" for ControlPoint D.

If a pickup takes place, at the end of the pickup-time the Carrier proceeds as a loaded Carrier. It experiences the transit-time at ControlPoint D, and then exits from D according to the rules for loaded Carriers, as described in Section B.9.4.1 above.

If no pickup occurs, when the empty Carrier has completed its transit of ControlPoint D and is ready to leave D, the following rules apply. Note that at this point it does not matter whether the Carrier entered ControlPoint D empty and failed to make a pickup, or whether the Carrier entered ControlPoint D loaded and succeeded in making a dropoff at D:

1. If a "destination sequence" for empty Carriers has been specified for ControlPoint D, determine the destination from that list and make the Carrier a routed Carrier. Otherwise, determine the exit direction for the Carrier by the default clockwise rotation.

The destination-sequence for empty Carriers provides a cyclic sequence of ControlPoint numbers that are assigned to successive exiting empty Carriers, in order, starting again from the beginning when the sequence is exhausted. For example, if the destination-sequence 7,7,4 has been specified for ControlPoint D, the first empty Carrier exiting from D will be routed to ControlPoint 7; the second to ControlPoint 7; the third to ControlPoint 4; the fourth to ControlPoint 7; etc. The destination sequence can be used to arbitrarily distribute the outgoing traffic of empty Carriers from a ControlPoint and, by repeating certain ControlPoint numbers on the list, to distribute the traffic with arbitrary assymetry. Note that a destination-sequence consisting of a single ControlPoint number will direct all unrouted empty Carriers exiting from D to that particular ControlPoint.

B.9.4.3 Request-Only ControlPoints

If the specification of a "request" or a "delivery" (see Sections B.6.4 and B.6.5) at any Buffer in the model specifies ControlPoint S as the "source" of the unit to be moved, then ControlPoint S becomes a "request-only" ControlPoint and the rules governing pickup of loads at S are quite different.

Pickups are allowed at a request-only ControlPoint only in satisfaction of specific requests or delivery orders issued by actions at a Buffer. A chronologically ordered list of requests and delivery orders is maintained for ControlPoint S. Each time an empty Carrier arrives at S, this list is searched, looking for the oldest request that can currently be satisfied. Each request or delivery order on the list includes destination information, so that when a request or delivery order is satisfied, the loaded Carrier is routed to the appropriate destination.

You can also make provision to dispatch an appropriate number of empty

Carriers to ControlPoint S to satisfy requests and delivery orders at S. Empty Carriers can be pre-positioned in the system by specifying the empty-HOLD option at one or more ControlPoints. These ControlPoints then become "HoldingPoints" -- staging or parking areas for empty Carriers. When there are one or more such HoldingPoints, XCELL+ automatically figures out which HoldingPoint is the best source of empty Carriers for every other ControlPoint. Then, each time a request or delivery-order is received at ControlPoint S, an empty Carrier is released from the HoldingPoint closest to S, and that Carrier is routed to S. The mechanism is entirely automatic -- except for your specification of certain ControlPoints as HoldingPoints.

B.9.5 Zone Control

Each ControlPoint belongs to some "zone" (the default is zone number 1). Each zone has a limit on the maximum number of Carriers it can contain. This limit is enforced only during run of the model. In design, you can exceed the limit by specifying <add Carrier> at cells in the zone more times than the zone limit, but when the model is run no Carriers will be allowed to enter the zone unless the current number is below the limit (hence any excess introduced in design will eventually be dissipated).

Zone membership is specified in the options menu of ControlPoint design. In this same menu you can change the zone Carrier limit (from any ControlPoint within the particular zone). (The default zone limit is large enough so that an incoming Carrier is never zone-blocked.)

A zone consists of a certain set of ControlPoints and all Paths that are incoming to those ControlPoints. This means that zone entry for a Carrier always takes place as that Carrier seeks to leave a ControlPoint in a different zone. If the zone to be entered already contains the maximum number of Carriers permitted, the Carrier seeking entry is blocked until some other Carrier leaves the new zone.

B.9.6 Charging of Carrier Batteries

In some situations the necessicity of charging the batteries that supply driving power for the Carriers is an important consideration. The time during which Carriers are out of service can be significant, affecting both the requisite number of Carriers and the overall performance of the system. Moreover, the interaction between charging requirements and other aspects of system management makes modeling especially important.

The XCELL+ facilities for this purpose are the following:

   -- One or more ControlPoints can be designated as "ChargingPoints". This is done in the **options** menu. A ChargingPoint is used only for the purpose of charging Carrier batteries -- that is, it cannot also have a pickup or dropoff-link, nor can it serve as a HoldingPoint. It cannot have an "empty-skip" option, nor a "empty-WAIT" or "full-WAIT" option.

   -- The "running time for a fully-charged battery" can be specified. This value applies to all Carriers. Each Carrier has a "time-meter" that records the time remaining until the battery is exhausted. This time is depleted only by running-time -- that is, by the transit-time of each cell the Carrier traverses. Time spent blocked, or in pickup or dropoff, is not counted.

   -- The "reserved-time" can be specified. This value applies to all Carriers. It represents the level of time-remaining at which the Carrier is in need of recharging and must seek out a ChargingPoint.

-- The "charging-time" can be specified. This value applies to all
   ChargingPoints and all Carriers. It is the time during which a
   Carrier will be held at a ChargingPoint to be recharged. Note
   that XCELL+ ChargingPoints only accommodate a single Carrier at a
   time, so to model "double-outlet charging stations" the XCELL+
   charging-time must be adjusted appropriately.

Each ControlPoint is continually on the lookout for passing Carriers that
are in need of recharging. Each time an unrouted, empty Carrier enters a
ControlPoint, it is checked to see if its remaining-time is less than the
reserved-time. If so, the Carrier is routed to the nearest ChargingPoint.

If no ChargingPoints are designated in the model, the entire charging
mechanism is inoperative -- the Carriers' remaining-time is not reduced and
they run indefinitely without recharge.

Since we were unable to figure out any reasonable way of dealing with
Carriers whose battery becomes completely discharged before they can reach a
ChargingPoint, and we were unwilling to just leave them dead on the Path,
XCELL+ simply records the fact that a Carrier "became disabled" due to a
discharged battery -- but in fact, allows the Carrier to continue to run.

C

Design Strategies and Techniques

C.1 The Order of Designing Components _____

In the design of a factory model it is not necessary to specify all the characteristics of an element when you first create it, since you can later come back to design and change the element -- even during a pause in running the model. This means that there is <u>no required order</u> of creating elements. However, there are some orders of creation that are more convenient than others, in the sense of requiring less jumping back and forth between elements.

For example, since a MaintenanceCenter must exist before you can specify it as the provider of maintenance service to a particular WorkCenter, it is more convenient to create the MaintenanceCenter first, before creating the WorkCenter. The penalty for not doing things in this order is not serious, since all you have to do is temporarily leave WorkCenter design, create the required MaintenanceCenter, and then return to WorkCenter design to specify the maintenance characteristics of the WorkCenter.

Similarly, the source of an input-link to a Process must exist before you can specify the link in Process design, and the destination of an output-link must exist before you can specify that link. Hence, it is more convenient to create the source and destination elements before entering Process design. But again, the penalty for not doing things in the most convenient order is just having to leave Process design temporarily, and return later.

In general, this suggests that it is convenient to build a factory model from the <u>outside in</u>. That is, first create all the ReceivingAreas and ShippingAreas that you can anticipate needing. (If you miss some, you can always add them; extra ones can be removed; they can be moved from one location to another; you can return to change their characteristics.) Second, specify the Buffers, AuxiliaryResources and MaintenanceCenters as best you can. Finally, create the WorkCenters and Processes.

C.1.1 The Required Sequence of Creating Elements

The following is a summary of the sequence dependencies in constructing a factory model:

1. The source element of an input-link must be in place before the link can be specified in Process design.

2. The destination element of an output-link must be in place before the link can be specified in Process design.

3. A ShippingArea must be in place before the <scrap> disposition of reject-output can be chosen in Process design.

4. A Buffer must be in place before the <rework> disposition of reject-output can be chosen in Process design.

5. A MaintenanceCenter must be in place before <assign MtnCtr> can be specified in WorkCenter maintenance.

6. A Buffer, batch-mode ReceivingArea or batch-mode ShippingArea must be in place before a trigger for a Process can be specified in switching rules.

Default elements will be automatically created if you place the link-cursor on an empty cell and press <select>. The default element types are the following:

1. For an X-input or Y-input link, the default is a ReceivingArea.

2. For a normal-output link, the default is a ShippingArea.

3. For the scrap disposition of reject-output, the default is a ShippingArea.

4. For the rework disposition of reject-output, the default is a Buffer.

5. For the <assign MtnCtr> action, the default is a MaintenanceCenter.

While the automatic creation of these default elements will sometimes be convenient, it is probably still a good idea to create elements of the proper type, in the right cell, from design, rather than rely on these defaults. (A warning message is issued whenever a default element is created.)

C.1.2 The Order of Creating Processes at a WorkCenter

If a WorkCenter has more than one Process, the order in which competing Processes are performed depends in part on the order in which the various Processes were added to the WorkCenter in WorkCenter design. A complete description of Process selection rules is given in Section B.2.1.5. Here, we describe the implications for certain applications.

When competing Processes on the same WorkCenter have identical priorities, the order in which those Processes are chosen depends on the order in which they were created:

> When there is an unresolved tie at a WorkCenter as to which Process should be started next, the Processes are chosen in an order that is the OPPOSITE from that in which they were created.

If a systematic rotation among Processes is desired, and the sequence being followed is not the one you want, you can change it by deleting and re-creating Processes. However, this is a tedious task, so it is advisable to give some thought to this issue before creating multiple Processes with the same priority.

An example of where this feature is useful is a factory operated on a cyclic schedule, in which items are produced in a fixed, repeating sequence with batch-sizes that depend on the item. For example, if there are 5 parts (A through E) and the desired sequence is A, B, C, D, E, then you should create the Processes in order E, D, C, B, A at each WorkCenter. Each process can be given the appropriate batch-size.

As a final note, it is important to recognize the role that the batch-size plays in breaking ties. For example, consider the situation when no triggers are in use and priorities are all equal. If no batch-size is specified for a Process, it will run as long as there is material available, regardless of other Processes. Only when the supply for the incumbent Process is interrupted does any other Process have a chance to seize the WorkCenter. Therefore, in most applications with more than one Process at a WorkCenter, a fixed batch-size is necessary to ensure change among the Processes. Specifying a batch-size of 1 is often appropriate. It may seem equivalent to no-batch-size, but in fact, ensures rotation among Processes for which material is available.

C.2 Dummy and Composite Elements: Methods to Extend XCELL+'s Capability _____

Composite elements are combinations of WorkCenters, Buffers, and other basic elements that serve to represent a single functional element of a real system. The WorkCenters and Processes in XCELL+ are compromises between generality and convenience. For example, each Process is limited to at most two inputs (X and Y) and two outputs (normal and reject). This is adequate to model a wide variety of real processes, and is simple to understand and use. However, when the real process has more than two inputs or outputs, then some extra effort is required. This and other modeling problems may be solved by using composite elements.

Composite WorkCenters often involve "dummy Processes". A dummy Process is defined as a "Process with zero processing-time and zero setup-time". It has no counterpart in the real factory being modeled. A dummy WorkCenter is one that has only dummy Processes.

This section is intended to suggest some ways such artificial Processes can be employed, but it cannot begin to exhaust the possibilities.

The overall appearance of a factory model that involves composite elements can be significantly improved by selectively suppressing the display of the various supporting elements, and displaying only the primary element in each composite. (Recall that display suppression is an option in display detail.)

C.2.1 Multiple Delivery Schedules in Receiving

Consider a receiving operation that handles a variety of different products, each having its own delivery schedule. There is a storage area for receiving, and it is shared among all the products.

No single XCELL+ element can model such an operation directly. A Buffer can accommodate multiple parts, but has no schedule of input. A ReceivingArea has at most a single delivery schedule. Hence, what you need is an element that has some of the characteristics of a Buffer and some of the characteristics of a ReceivingArea.

The solution is a composite element consisting of multiple ReceivingAreas feeding a single Buffer. Each ReceivingArea accepts a particular type of part, with its own delivery schedule. However, since ReceivingAreas cannot directly supply material to a Buffer, you must interpose a dummy WorkCenter, with an input-link from the ReceivingArea and an output-link to the Buffer. Each dummy WorkCenter has a single purpose: to move one type of material from its ReceivingArea to the Buffer. Since the processing-times and setup-times of the dummy Processes are all zero, there is no delay in delivery of material to the Buffer. Arriving units are transferred immediately and instantaneously, up to the capacity limit of the Buffer.

An example with three parts is shown below. ReceivingArea RA and dummy WorkCenter WA generate the schedule for part A and deliver it to the Buffer. Parts B and C are treated similarly. ("PT" in the diagrams denotes "processing-time".)

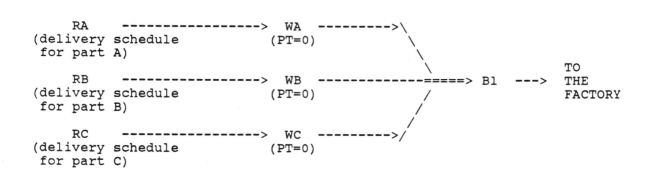

Note that the total storage capacity of this composite element includes the capacity at RA, RB and RC, as well as that at B1. As long as B1 is not full, arriving material is moved immediately to B1 and the storage capacity at the separate ReceivingAreas is not used. However, as soon as B1 becomes full, the dummy WorkCenters are blocked and material "backs up" in the ReceivingAreas.

An alternative solution to this problem would be to use a single dummy WorkCenter with three dummy Processes having equal priorities, instead of the three dummy WorkCenters shown above. This behaves in exactly the same way as the version shown.

C.2.2 The Failure and Repair of Automatic Storage Devices

Consider an automatic storage device whose less-than-perfect reliability is a significant factor in the problem being modeled. A Buffer is the obvious basic component to use, except that Buffers are perfectly reliable. A solution, shown in the diagram below, is to "attach" a WorkCenter W1 to the Buffer B1 to take advantage of the maintenance mechanism associated with WorkCenters. This WorkCenter, attached upstream of B1, can be considered to simulate a loading mechanism for the Buffer. Hence, in this case the processing-time should be small, but not zero.

```
    --------> W1  --------> B1 --------->

            (maintenance
              at M1)                                   M1
```

Note that if the storage device is to fail randomly, it is important to have a non-zero loading time at W1, since random failures in XCELL+ are based on <u>operating time</u> rather than clock time, so a WorkCenter with zero processing-time will never fail.

Normally, material would flow quickly through W1 into B1. But when W1 breaks down, or has scheduled maintenance, it effectively shuts off the flow of material into B1 and can represent a breakdown or maintenance of B1. As noted earlier, this really represents breakdown of the device that <u>loads</u> the storage area, since only the input to B1 is blocked by the suspension of processing at W1; withdrawals from B1 can still occur. Placing W1 downstream of B1 would suspend withdrawals, but not input, thereby representing failure of an <u>unloader</u> of the storage area. Presumably, when a real storage device fails, both input and withdrawals are suspended. (There is no easy way to use two WorkCenters, above and below B1, and perfectly synchronize the maintenance activity of these WorkCenters.)

A more complex representation is needed if failure of the storage area halts both input and withdrawals. The key is to use the WorkCenter as a mechanism that both loads and unloads the Buffer, as with many "carousel" storage devices. In this case, one WorkCenter, W2, represents the transfer device, and it has two processes: LOAD to transfer units into B1, and UNLOAD to remove units from B1. Maintenance of W2 shuts down both the LOAD and UNLOAD Processes. This is shown in the diagram below, where W2 and B1 together are the composite element representing the automatic storage device.

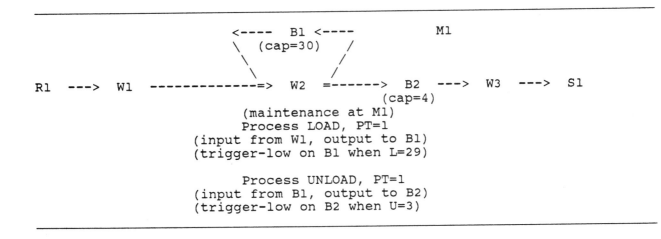

In this example, the capacity of the automatic storage unit, B1, is 30. An automatic machine, W3, has an input magazine, represented by B2, that holds 4 units.

LOAD is (must be) triggered to shut off when the Buffer is full. If this is not done, the loader/unloader can become deadlocked. (With a full Buffer, if there is a unit in LOAD, UNLOAD cannot operate.) UNLOAD is triggered on the downstream Buffer B2 so that material is not removed from B1 until it is needed.

Multi-product storage is even more complex. If the Buffer B1 provides storage for different Parts, W2 needs a separate load and unload Process for each Part that it places in B1. Furthermore, to avoid a deadlock, the loading Processes must be <u>triggered</u> <u>on</u> <u>the</u> <u>total</u> <u>contents</u> of B1, rather than the stock of a particular Part. That is, if all slots are full (regardless of which Parts occupy them) all loading should stop.

C.2.3 Generalized Assembly by Composite WorkCenters

Consider an assembly process in which three components are assembled. This must be modelled by a composite element, because a single Process allows at most two input components. This is illustrated by W1/W2 in the diagram below. The ReceivingAreas R1 and R2 supply the X-input and Y-input to a "dummy" Process on W1. The output of this Process is the X-input of the "real" WorkCenter W2, and material from R3 is its Y-input. The real Process at W2 has the characteristics of the process being modeled -- processing-times, setup-time, yield, etc.

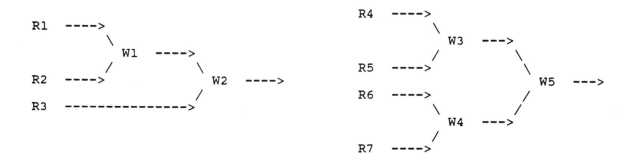

The appearance of the model is identical to a two-stage assembly process. The only difference is that the dummy Process on W1 has zero processing-time and perfect yield. Collectively, W1/W2 behave like a 3-input Process.

Similarly, W3/W4/W5 represent a 4-input Process. In this way, WorkCenters and Processes can be cascaded to whatever depth is necessary to accommodate the required number of inputs.

If the display of W1 is suppressed, W2 will appear to be a 3-input Process. Similarly, suppressing the display of W3 and W4 will make W5 look like a 4-input Process.

C.2.4 Dis-assembly Processes

To model a dis-assembly process, a "multiplier" can be specified for a Process, so that each unit produced becomes N identical units of output (see Section B.2.1.2.3). For example, a slitting operation on roll stock can produce 3 units of 12 inch width stock from 1 unit of 36 inch input stock.

If disassembly produces non-identical items, as in cutting lumber, dummy Processes may be used to rename the output. To illustrate, suppose that each unit of Part P is dis-assembled into 5 units of Part P1 and 3 units of Part P2, so that a total of 8 units are derived from each unit of Part P. In the diagram below, WorkCenter W1 has a Process that multiplies P into 8 units. The processing time corresponds to the real dis-assembly time. WorkCenter W2 has two dummy Processes, P1 with batch size 5 and P2 with batch size 3. Both draw inputs of P from Buffer B1 and transform them (in zero time) to P1 and P2. That is, they simply rename them.

```
--------> W1 --------> B1 ----------> W2 ----------->

         Process P       (cap=0)        Process P1
         (multiplier 8)                 (batch-size 5)

                                        Process P2
                                        (batch-size 3)
```

Note that the Buffer B1 is necessary to allow more than one destination for the output of WorkCenter W1. However, setting its capacity to zero assures that there is no possibility of real storage taking place inside the composite element represented in the diagram.

Another way to accomplish the same result is illustrated below. When Part P is finished at WorkCenter W1, it is delivered to a dummy Buffer B1. An instant later, dummy WorkCenter W4 withdraws the unit from B1 and delivers it to the dummy ShippingArea S1. Its momentary stay in B1 triggers the two dummy WorkCenters W2 and W3 to produce the required units of P1 and P2, using the unlimited supply of material from dummy ReceivingArea R1. Buffers B2 and B3 provide space to receive the parts as they come out of the composite WorkCenter.

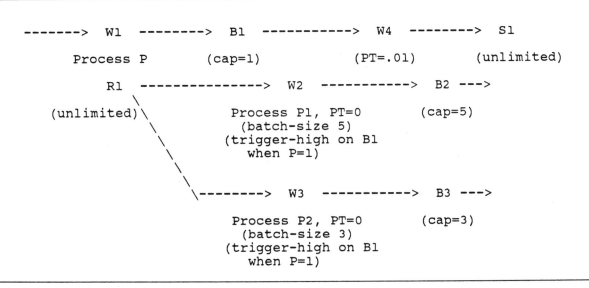

Using this trick, Part P disappears from the system rather than being transformed to P1 and P2. Although this is not what happens in the factory, the results are the same.

However, one weakness of this method is that it does not model blocking of W1. That is, if there is insufficient space to store P1 and P2, WorkCenters W2 and W3 are blocked, but W1 continues to operate. Hence, this model should be used only if there is adequate storage space for all situations downstream of the dis-assembly process.

C.3 Materials Handling Elements

The standard input-links and output-links of a Process represent a sort of idealized materials handling device. They have <u>infinite</u> <u>speed</u> and <u>no</u> <u>storage</u> <u>capacity</u> (regardless of the length of the line representing the link). In many situations, where materials handling times are negligible compared to processing times, and storage during materials handling is negligible compared to the storage capacity of Buffers, ReceivingAreas, and ShippingAreas, standard links are adequate modeling elements. However, where materials handling considerations are significant aspects of the problem, standard links alone may not be sufficient.

You can construct composite elements of varying degrees of complexity with which to realistically model materials handling devices, but it is easy to get carried away in this regard, and provide a degree of detail that is not really necessary. Perhaps the most effective strategy is to start with a very simple model, and selectively and gradually enhance the materials handling elements where there is demonstrable and significant lack of verisimilitude.

C.3.1 Conveyors

When a standard link, with zero transit-time and zero storage capacity, is not an adequate representation of a real conveyor, there are a variety of

ways in which you can use a "composite link" to improve the realism of the
representation. The simplest is just to use a Process at a WorkCenter to
represent the conveyor, with the processing-time representing the transit-
time:

```
                    (_____conveyor_____)
from
a real              ---------------->  W1  ---------------->            to
WorkCenter                                                              next real
                                                                        WorkCenter
```

The limitation is that this "conveyor", although having realistic transit-
time, has a storage capacity of only one unit.

An obvious but dubious improvement is to use a composite link consisting of
a Buffer and a WorkCenter, as shown in the diagram below. The Buffer
represents the storage capacity of the conveyor, and the processing-time of
the Process at the WorkCenter represents the transit-time.

```
                    (_____conveyor_____)
from
a real              ----------> B1  ---------> W1 ---------->            to
WorkCenter                                                               next real
                                                                         WorkCenter
```

The problem that makes this representation of limited use is the fact that
the effective transit-time depends on the number of units on the conveyor
(that is, in B1). For example, if the processing-time at W1 is T, then the
transit-time when B1 is empty is T; when B1 contains one unit the transit-
time is 2T; etc. You could set T so that T multiplied by the average
contents of B1 is equal to the intended average transit-time, but there are
probably not many situations for which this is a useful approximation.

A very general, but costly, "solution" is to represent an asynchronous
conveyor by a sequence of WorkCenters, as shown below. The processing-time
of the Process at each WorkCenter represents the time to transit one
"sector" of the conveyor, where a sector is defined as an area that can be
occupied by at most one item. The transit-time of the conveyor is the sum
of the individual processing-times; the storage capacity is the number of
WorkCenters that constitute the conveyor.

```
                    (_____conveyor_____)
from
a real              ----->  W1  --> W2  --> W3  --> W4  --> W5  ----->            to
WorkCenter                                                                        next real
                                                                                 WorkCenter
```

Using the <copy> command in **design**, the construction of such a conveyor is
less burdensome than it might seem. Unfortunately, the limitation on the
total number of WorkCenters in a model prevents widespread use of this
technique, but it can be used sparingly to model critical conveyors. Note
that just because you use this technique for one conveyor in a model, you
are not obligated to use it for all conveyors.

By suppressing the display of the basic elements in any of these representations of a conveyor, the composite link will look like a standard link, but behave very differently.

C.3.1.1 Modeling Conveyors with FIFO Buffers

Buffers can optionally preserve the identity of individual units and permit first-in-first-out (FIFO) ordering. Since this is the way a real conveyor behaves, it may seem obvious that a FIFO Buffer should be used in any representation of a conveyor. However, it is not always necessary, and since a FIFO Buffer is more "expensive" than an unordered Buffer, you should only specify FIFO ordering when this improves the representation. ("Expensive" means that FIFO Buffers run more slowly than unordered Buffers, and also consume a limited resource in the model called a "unit" -- see Appendix 1.)

When a conveyor handles <u>more than one type of Part,</u> FIFO ordering is crucial, since the units are not interchangeable and the order in which different types of Part enter the conveyor must be preserved for the order of discharge. But when there is only one type of Part, the units are logically indistinguishable, so that specifying FIFO ordering increases the cost but not the realism of the model.

However, FIFO ordering in a Buffer also allows the option of specifying the <u>minimum holding time</u> (MHT) for units in the Buffer. This feature permits a major improvement in the representation of conveyors. In many situations, a FIFO/MHT Buffer alone is a reasonable representation of a conveyor (making the techniques of the previous section generally unncessary).

There is a Buffer ordering option called "CONVEYOR" -- but this is functionally identical to FIFO ordering with a minimum holding time. The only difference is the use of a different symbol in the display to signify the use of this Buffer as a conveyor.

Note, however, that a FIFO/MHT Buffer represents a conveyor where there is no minimum spacing between units. This has two effects. First, if a batch of units arrives simultaneously, they may all go into the FIFO/MHT Buffer simultaneously. Second, if the output end is blocked, it is possible for several units to complete their minimum holding times, and therefore be available for essentially simultaneous discharge. There would be no delay as the next unit "moves forward to discharge", as would be experienced on a real conveyor. In many cases, these considerations would be negligible and a FIFO/MHT Buffer alone is an adequate representation of a conveyor. However, when it is not adequate alone, a composite using a FIFO/MHT Buffer feeding a WorkCenter to represent the unloading/indexing time could be used. When necessary, you could also include an upstream Workcenter to represent a loader.

But let us repeat our warning. Just because XCELL+ allows you to model conveyors to any required level of detail, does not mean that you are obligated to model conveyors in great detail when they are not critical to the model's overall performance. As a general rule, try not to drive tacks with a sledgehammer.

C.3.1.2 Modeling Conveyors with Paths and Carriers

The most detailed, and presumably most realistic model of a conveyor in XCELL+ is constructed using a loop of Paths, and a large number of Carriers. To construct such a conveyor from point A to point B:

1. Create a ControlPoint J at point A. Link J to whatever element will place material on the conveyor. Note that since a ControlPoint has only a single pickup-link, if there is more than one element providing material, it will be necessary to use a Buffer to aggregate the flow. Connect the pickup-link from J to the Buffer.

In **traffic-control** rules at J, have empty Carriers WAIT for pickup.

Set the pickup-time at J appropriately.

2. Create a ControlPoint K at point B. Connect the dropoff-link from
   K to whatever element will remove material from the conveyor.
   Since K can have only a single dropoff-link it may be necessary
   to interpose a Buffer at this point also.

   In **traffic-control** rules at K, have loaded Carriers WAIT for
   dropoff.

   Set the dropoff-time at K appropriately.

3. Run a Path from J to K, and a return Path from K to J. The length
   of the forward Path from J to K determines the storage capacity of
   the conveyor -- each PathSegment will potentially store one unit
   of material.

   Suppress the display of the return Path from K to J.

   Set the transit-time of the return Path from K to J to a very
   small time (0, for example).

   Set the transit-time of the forward Path from J to K to an
   appropriate value -- divided equally over the Path Segments.

   Set the transit-times at J and K appropriately -- perhaps 0.

4. Add Carriers to J and K, and to all the Segments on the forward
   Path from J to K.

The "conveyor" described above operates as a constant-speed power-and-free
conveyor. An example of a conveyor modeled in this way is shown in Figure
C-1.

Many variations are possible, including continuous loop, synchronous powered
conveyors.   But note that there must be <u>at least</u> <u>one cell</u> in the loop
without a Carrier -- or none of the Carriers can move.

─────────────────────────────── **Figure C-1** ───────────────────────────────

Example of a conveyor modeled with Paths and Carriers

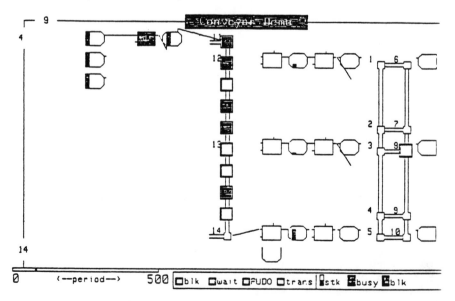

Note, however, that just because conveyors can be modeled in this level of detail, you are not obliged to use such detail unless conveyors constitute a critical element in your model. For many models ordinary links, or the mechanisms of the preceeding Section provide an adequate representation of a conveyor.

C.3.2 Movement of Units in Batches

Material is often moved in batches, with the batch size determined by the capacity of a container or a pallet.   This can be modeled by a composite element consisting of Buffers and triggered Processes. The simplest version of this uses only a single dummy WorkCenter.

Consider the scheme in the diagram below. Part P is to be moved in pallets that hold 2 units each. Buffer B1 represents five pallets, since it has a storage-capacity of 10 units. All Processes have batch-size of 2, equal to the capacity of one pallet. The real Process at WorkCenter W1 is triggered to begin when there are 2 or more empty spaces in the Buffer. Hence, when W1 begins a pallet load, there is certainly at least one empty pallet available.

The dummy Process at WorkCenter W2 is triggered to begin when there are 2 or more units in B1, which would indicate that there is at least one full pallet available for use. This provides the supply for WorkCenter W3, the next real element. In turn, W3 is triggered when an empty pallet is available in the next downstream Buffer, B2.

```
------->  W1  ------->  B1  -------->  W2  ------->  W3  ------->  B2  --->

     trigger-low   (cap=10)   trigger-high   trigger-low   (cap=10)
       on B1 when              on B1 when     on B2 when
         P=8                      P=2           P=8
       batch=2                  batch=2       batch=2
                                PT=0
```

If several Parts are made on the line, the triggers may be needed to simulate some other aspect of scheduling.   In this case, two dummy WorkCenters would be needed for each Buffer, one on the input side and the other on the output side of the Buffer. The scheme would be the same as in the previous example except that a new dummy WorkCenter would be inserted between W1 and B1. Its design would be exactly as described for W1 (above) except that it would have zero setup and processing-times. This would serve to block W1 whenever there is not an empty pallet, and leave W1's trigger mechanism free for other duties.

C.3.3 A Palletizer

A more detailed model of a process in which pallets are used can represent the time required to load and move the pallet. For example, an automatic palletizer may have three different characteristic times. The first, t1, is the time to add one unit to a layer on the pallet. The second, t2, is the time to move the loader up to the next level once a layer is finished. The third, t3, is the time to remove the full pallet and replace it with an empty one.

The diagram below represents a 4-layer palletizer. Each layer consists of 9 units. Process P has zero setup time and processing-time t1 to represent loading within a layer. The batch-size is 9 so that this process, once begun, will continue until a layer is full.

```
    R1   ---------->         <--- B1 <---    ---------------------->  S1
 (unlimited)              \  \  (cap=9)  /  /                    (unlimited)
                          \   \         /  /
    input of  -------->>=======>   W1  ===========---->  B3  ----->  output of
    Parts P               /   \         \                           full pallets
                         /     <--- B2 <---
                              (cap=4)
```

****************** Processes at WorkCenter W1 ********************

Process P   Process Layer, produces L   Process F
batch=9   trigger-high on B1 when P=9   trigger-high on
output to B1   batch=1   B2 when L=4
PT=t1, setup-time=0   input from r1, output to b2   batch=1
                             PT=t2, setup-time=0   input from R1
                                                            output to B3
Process P1   Process L1   PT=t3
trigger-high on B1 when P=9 trigger-high on B2 when L=4   setup-time=0.
batch=9   batch=4
input P from B1, output to S1 input L from B2, output to S1
PT=0, setup-time=0   PT=0, setup-time=0

The second Process, Layer, is triggered to produce 1 unit (of L) when there
is a full layer (P=9) in B1. L is stored in B2. Each unit of L in B2
represents an entire layer on the pallet. Processing-time is t2 to simulate
moving to the next layer.

Then, dummy process P1 removes all of the units of P from B1 in zero time.
These are discarded from the model by sending them to ShippingArea S1.
Thus, each time a layer is completed, it is skimmed off and replaced by one
unit of L.

Finally, when there are 4 Layers in B2, the third Process, F for Full, is
engaged. It produces one unit of F and places it in B3. Dummy Process L1
then removes the layers and throws them away in S1.

The individual units of P have been destroyed in this model. In their place
is one F (full pallet) for each 36 units of P. If the pallet is to be
disassembled in the same factory model, some sort of disassembly process
must be simulated. Two examples were given in an earlier section. A third
method is to essentially reverse the above model.

This model will not work unless one is careful with the order in which the
processes are created. The order should be P, P1, Layer, L1 and then F.
This assures, for example, that Process F is carried out before L1. If L1
went first, then there would no longer be 4 units of L in the Buffer to
trigger F. The Processes must all have the same priority.

Finally, the three Buffers in the diagram may be replaced by one Buffer of
capacity at least 9+4+1. Parts P, L and F would all share this buffer. They
were separated here to make the explanation easier.

C.3.4 Overflow of Materials Handling Systems: Queues with Balking

Normally, when a Buffer is full, any WorkCenter that feeds into the Buffer
will be blocked when it finishes a unit. The WorkCenter waits until a unit
is withdrawn from the Buffer, so that it can deliver its finished unit.
However, in some situations, when a storage area becomes full, <u>additional
arriving material is lost</u> to the system. For example, on a bottling line, a

jamup may cause bottles to fall on the floor and break. In queuing theory, such an event is referred to as <u>balking</u>, because the "customer" leaves upon encountering a queue that is too large.

This may be modeled by using a dummy WorkCenter with two Processes per part, with all Processes triggered on the contents of a Buffer. For example, in the diagram below, the storage area represented by Buffer B1 has capacity for 10 units and experiences overflows. The dummy WorkCenter W1 has Process A1 that is triggered to be active when there is space in the Buffer, and Process A2 that becomes active when the Buffer is full. When active, A2 disposes of arriving units by sending them (in zero time) to the dummy ShippingArea S1.

```
                         ----->  S1
                        /     (unlimited)
input                  /
to the       ------>  W1  -------->  B1  -------->    output
storage                                              from the
area          Process A1                             storage area
              PT=0, setup-time=0
              output to b1
              trigger-low on B1 when contents = 9

              Process A2
              PT=0, setup-time=0
              output to S1
              trigger-high on B1 when contents = 10

           (similar Process pairs for each Part type)
```

Each Part type that uses the storage area must pass through W1, and therefore must have two corresponding Processes there -- one for storage and one for overflow.

C.4 Ovens and Other Batch Processes

There are many processes that operate simultaneously on more than one unit. Heat treating is a common example in which a batch of parts is loaded into an oven for a period of time that is (nearly) independent of the size of the batch. The parts in a real process may or may not be identical to each other.

Since a WorkCenter may only process one unit at a time, a composite element must be used to represent an oven (or similar batch processor). A Buffer may be used to represent the inside of an oven, with a WorkCenter to load and unload. The oven's baking time can be represented by the setup-time of the unloading Process.

For a single type of Part, one method is illustrated in the diagram below. Buffer B2 is the oven, and WorkCenter W1 is the loader/unloader. The Processes on W1 are LOAD and UNLOAD. LOAD is triggered when a full batch (in this case 5 units) is in the upstream Buffer B1. A setup-time of 1 represents the time required to move a batch into the oven. UNLOAD is triggered when the oven is full (5 units). However, UNLOAD does not take place until after a setup-time of 31, which represents the baking time of 30 timeunits, plus 1 timeunit to move the batch out of the oven.

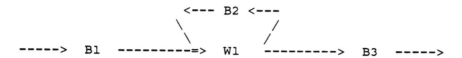

```
                            <--- B2 <---
                           \         /
                            \       /
     ----->  B1  ---------=>  W1  --------->  B3  ----->

        Process LOAD at W1          Process UNLOAD at W1
        trigger-high on B1 when P=5 trigger-high on B2 when L=5
        batch=5                     batch=5
        input from B1, output to B2 input from B2, output to B3
        PT=0, setup-time=1          PT=0, setup-time=31
```

There is nothing in this model to prevent the oven from becoming blocked, unable to discharge its output when finished. Since that could have rather disastrous consequences for the batch (or partial batch) that is stuck inside, one should be particularly careful in designing the system.

If more than one type of Part uses the same oven, but only one type may be baked at a time, then the extension of the above example is straightforward. There must be two Processes at W1 for each part (one to load and the second to unload), and each of these may be triggered in a manner analogous to the single-Part case, shown above. If no priorities are set, the use of the oven will tend to rotate among the various Parts, depending primarily on which is first to attain a complete batch in the input buffer. However, if the load Processes are given different priorities, then lower priority items will remain in the input buffer longer, being passed by the Parts with higher priority.

C.4.1 Continuous Flow Devices

There are certain manufacturing processes in which pieces move continuously through "treatment" on a steadily-moving conveyor. For example, heat-trating, curing, chilling, air-drying, and electronic burn-in are often done in this manner. For modelling purposes, there is no difference between such a continuous flow process, and a conveyor. The model in Section C.3.1.1, using a FIFO/MHT Buffer, is particularly appropriate for this situation.

However, it is once again extremely important to allow sufficient flow capacity to handle the discharge from the process. If the discharge from the FIFO/MHT Buffer is blocked, units may be "overcooked" by staying too long in treatment. (This may, of course, be a problem in the real system as well.)

C.5 Miscellaneous Alternative Modeling Schemes _____

C.5.1 Semi-Automatic Machines

MaintenanceCenters are basically just a means for making WorkCenters unavailable for processing for varying amounts of time. Although the nominal purpose is to model machine breakdowns and scheduled maintenance there are many other uses of this mechanism.

For example, the "service-team" at a MaintenanceCenter could represent the operator of a group of semi-automatic machines. The time between "failures" could represent time the machines could run attended; the "repair" time could represent the time the operator required to put the machine back into service. A MaintenanceCenter with more than one service-team would represent a group of operators sharing responsibility for a common set of machines.

C.5.2 Multiple Shifts

A second example is the use of scheduled maintenance mechanism to vary the number of shifts that different WorkCenters are available. For example, suppose some WorkCenters are scheduled for three-shift operation, and others only for two-shift operation. You could schedule eight hours of "maintenance" every sixteen hours, by a MaintenanceCenter with enough service-teams so that no WorkCenter would ever have to queue for "service".

C.5.3 Combination of Scheduled Maintenance and Random Failure

XCELL+ WorkCenters can have either scheduled maintenance or random failures, but a single WorkCenter cannot have both.   If both are required for a particular WorkCenter, you can approximate this by appending a dummy WorkCenter.   Scheduled maintenance can then be assigned to the dummy, and its occurrence will shut down the real WorkCenter by blocking the flow of material.   Note that in such a composite, the random failure must be assigned to the real WorkCenter; random failure depends on busy-time, and dummy Processes have no busy-time.

Note that this dual WorkCenter is only an approximation of a real machine that experiences both scheduled maintenance and random failures.   For example, in this approximation the primary WorkCenter could still be finishing its unit while the appended WorkCenter is shut down for scheduled maintenance.   (The primary WorkCenter would be blocked as soon as it finished the incumbent unit, since it cannot dispose of it to start another unit.) Hence, it would be a good approximation only if the processing-time is significantly less than the repair time.   It is also possible that the dual WorkCenter could experience both scheduled maintenance and random failure simultaneously, so the approximation would be good only if both scheduled maintenance and random failure are relatively infrequent events so that the chances of simultaneous occurrence are negligible.

C.5.4 Alternative Routings

A situation in which a part has an alternative WorkCenter, perhaps employed only in emergencies, can sometimes be adequately modelled using the trigger mechanism.   Failure, or overload, of the primary WorkCenter for a task will presumably cause some stock level to build up. This can be employed as a "high-trigger" for a Process on an alternative WorkCenter.

In the diagram below, Part P is normally withdrawn from B1 and processed at WorkCenter W1. However, when the stock level at B1 reaches 10, WorkCenter W2 is triggered to carry out an identical Process. This would bypass W1, for example, during maintenance. The alternative WorkCenter W2 may have other Processes not related to Part P.   If so, one should carefully consider triggering, batch-sizes and priorities. For example, should P get priority over other parts that W2 normally produces?

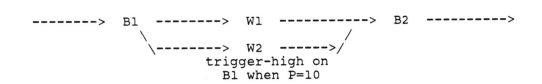

C.5.5 Dynamic Line-Balancing

In a serial production facility (a production line), tasks are assigned to workstations with an attempt to maintain a balance. If all workstations have

equal average processing-time, the line is said to be balanced. However, it
may be impossible to divide the operations in a manner that achieves perfect
balance. Moreover, if there is any randomness in processing-time, the line
will have temporary imbalances, although on the average, the work at the
various different workstations is balanced.

Buffers may be inserted between workstations to alleviate blockage due to
variability in processing-times, but if the average processing-times are
unequal, there is no way that buffers can eliminate idle-time at the faster
workstations.

In practice, workers can cooperate to balance the line "on the fly" or
dynamically. For example, if inventory builds up between two workstations,
the first workstation takes on a larger portion of the overall task,
effectively slowing down. This temporarily reduces the workload at the
second workstation, since it has less to do on each unit, presumably
allowing it to catch up. When the inventory between the workstations has
been reduced to a "normal level", both workstations return to their normal
portion of the overall task. In a similar manner, the second workstation
can assume a larger portion of the task if the first workstation momentarily
falls behind. This, of course, assumes that each worker is trained and
equipped to perform different fractions of the task, and that both attitude
and working rules permit such flexibility. It might be useful to study a
simulation of this process, to determine just how effective it might be in
increasing line throughput, before attempting to encourage such a practice
in the actual factory.

To model this for two WorkCenters, W1 and W2, each must have two Processes.
Let Process A represent the normal share-of-work for both WorkCenters. Let
Process B represent the adjusted share in which W1 has increased processing
times, and W2 has reduced processing-times. At W1, Process B can be thought
of as Process A, followed by one extra task. At W2, Process B is Process A,
minus the first task of the operation. We shall refer to the task that is
passed back and forth as the "flexible task".

The following diagram shows an example in which the flexible task takes 4
timeunits.

```
-------->  W1  ----------->  B1  --------------  W2  ----------->
           Process A                             Process A
           PT=8                                  PT=13
           trigger-low on B1
              when A=1
           batch-size=1

           Process B                             Process B
           PT=12                                 PT=9
           trigger-high on B1                    rename Part to A
              when A=2
           batch-size=2
```

Because Process A is 3 units faster at W1 than at W2, the second WorkCenter
falls behind. However, when inventory in B1 reaches 2 units, W1 switches
over to Process B and maintains that Process for 2 units. Meanwhile, W2
still has some units of A to finish, and since this is still slower than W1,
inventory continues to increase. However, as soon as the A units are
cleared out, W2 switches to B and can catch up.

Note that Process B on W2 renames the part before sending it on. This is
important because once the unit has finished both WorkCenters, there is no

distinction as to whether it was processed by A or B. The same tasks have
been done in the same order.

> (A study of such dynamic line-balancing, using XCELL+, showed that
> substantial increases in production are possible. In a production line
> of five stages, with random variation in processing-times, improvements
> of as much as 25% were achieved simply by having the "workers" shift
> parts of the task so as to try to keep the buffers between workstations
> "half-full". See Ostolaza, McClain and Thomas: "Use of Dynamic State-
> Dependent Assembly-line Balancing to Improve Throughput" in <u>The</u> <u>Journal</u>
> <u>of</u> <u>Manufacturing</u> <u>and</u> <u>Operations</u> <u>Management</u> (1990).)

C.6 Alternative Models of Supply and Demand _____

Normally, <u>neither</u> <u>supply</u> <u>nor</u> <u>demand</u> <u>will</u> <u>wait</u> in XCELL+. That is, if
material arrives when the ReceivingArea is full, it is lost to the system
("rejected").   Similarly, demand that occurs in excess of the material
available in a ShippingArea is also lost ("shortage"). In this section,
some tricks are suggested to build models that represent other assumptions
on supply and demand.

C.6.1 Standing-Order Systems

A standing-order system has three components:

1. A fixed order quantity Q, arriving at fixed intervals T.

2. An emergency order policy, used in case stock falls below r1.

3. A cancellation policy, used in case stock exceeds r2.

The simplest version of this policy cancels one order for quantity Q if r2
is exceeded, and places an extra order for Q if stock falls to r1. In that
case, the policy has the four parameters Q, T, r1 and r2. This policy may be
implemented using two dummy WorkCenters W1 and W2, one Buffer B1, and two
ReceivingAreas R1 and R2 to form a composite ReceivingArea.

For example, consider a company that has a standing-order policy, where
arriving shipments are kept in a storage area of capacity r2 until needed in
the factory. The model is shown in the diagram below.

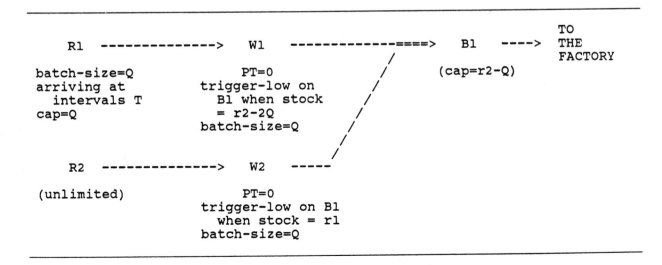

Storage in this model occurs in two elements -- the ReceivingArea R1 and the
Buffer B1.   Since the   former has capacity   equal to one   batch Q,   and the
latter has   capacity r2   - Q, the   total storage   capacity of   the composite
ReceivingArea is Q + r2 - Q or r2, as intended.

The dummy WorkCenter W1 moves Q units from R1 to B1 at regular intervals of
time T. However, if B1 is too near capacity to accept a full batch, W1 is
disabled. If batches arrive while W1 is disabled, the first is stored in R1
and the rest are lost to the system, simulating cancelled orders.   On the
other hand, if stock at B1 falls to r1, the other dummy WorkCenter W2 is
enabled and delivers an emergency order of size Q immediately. For this to
work properly, r1 <= r2 - Q.

Several variations are possible. For example, rather than turning away
entire orders, partial orders can be accepted up to the available storage
capacity by disabling the trigger and batch-size of W1. However, in this
case W1 can, in effect, store one unit from each batch and hence the
capacity of B1 should be reduced by 1 unit to accurately reflect the storage
capacity of the system.

A fixed or random delay for emergency orders can be included by adding a
dummy Buffer B2 and WorkCenter W3 as shown below. Setting the expected
processing-time for each unit in the emergency order (at W2) equal to L/Q
delays completion of the order for an average of L periods. The order
accumulates in the dummy Buffer B2 until the batch is complete.   Then the
dummy WorkCenter W3 is triggered and passes the emergency order on to the
factory.

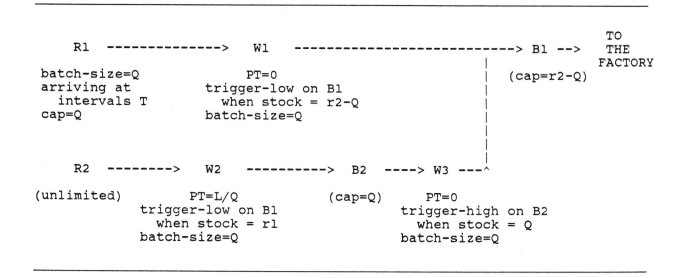

C.6.2 Backlogging Demand

When a ShippingArea is used to define a demand process, the   assumption is
that demand is lost if there is no waiting item. To model a situation in
which demands will wait, we can create a queue of orders.   In the diagram
below, the factory has three elements R1 (raw material ReceivingArea), W1
(the entire factory, represented as a single WorkCenter) and B1 (a Buffer
that represents the shipping dock. (WorkCenter W1 could, of course, be
replaced by a complete model of the factory.)

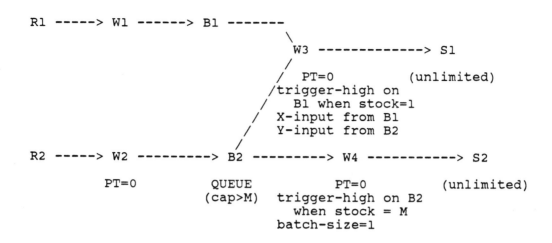

```
    R1 ------> W1 ------> B1 -------
                                    \
                                     W3 -------------> S1
                                    /
                                   /  PT=0          (unlimited)
                                  /trigger-high on
                                 /    B1 when stock=1
                                /   X-input from B1
                               /    Y-input from B2
    R2 -----> W2 ---------> B2 ---------> W4 -----------> S2
              PT=0          QUEUE         PT=0         (unlimited)
                           (cap>M)   trigger-high on B2
                                        when stock = M
                                        batch-size=1
```

Seven elements are used to simulate demand. A ReceivingArea R2 simulates the arrival of orders, which are immediately funneled to a Buffer B2 (the queue) by the dummy WorkCenter W2. There they are stored until one of two things happens:

> When a unit of product is finished by the factory and arrives at the shipping Buffer B1, the dummy WorkCenter W3 withdraws one order and one finished item and assembles them to form a unit of sales, which is sent to the ShippingArea S1.

> When the backlog of waiting orders reaches a prespecified level M, the dummy WorkCenter W4 is triggered to remove one order from the queue and send it to lost sales, portrayed by the dummy ShippingArea S2. This puts a limit on the length of the queue of unfilled orders, and simulates a cancelled order due to too large a backlog.

To ensure that units are not withdrawn from the shipping Buffer B1 prematurely, the assembly Process W3 is not triggered unless there are orders in the queue, B2.

C.7 Inventory Control Policies _____

Triggers allow production decisions to be based on the level of a particular local inventory -- the stock in a specified Buffer, batch-mode Receiving-Area, or batch-mode ShippingArea. However, this can result in myopic (nearsighted) decision making, and in many situations decisions as to which parts to produce should be based on the total amount of stock anywhere in the model.

For example, consider a ten-stage production line with the first Process triggered to begin when finished goods inventory falls below a given level. Of course, the finished goods inventory remains below the trigger level until the order makes its way through the factory and into inventory. Hence, there can be ten partially finished units in the system before the first unit reaches finished goods. After inventory has reached the desired level, the trigger is disabled, but the ten units still in the pipeline continue to be processed. Hence, an overstock occurs. Triggering on total stock throughout the model solves this problem.

This section explains how to create a mechanism to keep a running count of the total stock of a part, starting at any point in the system.

C.7.1 Echelon Inventory

"Echelon stock" is defined as the total number of a units of a part that have been manufactured but have not yet left the system. For example, if we make a special stainless steel nut that is used in several end products, the echelon stock of these nuts is the stock on hand plus the unit or units currently being manufactured, plus all of the nuts that have been installed on end products that have not yet been shipped.

Hence the echelon stock of a particular part is incremented when a Process begins a unit of that part, and decremented when a unit of that part exits the system, or when a unit of another part that includes a unit of the particular part exits the system. The example discussed below assumes a serial factory, or production line. (All items follow the same routing, with no alternative processes.)

A simple factory is shown below. It makes one product, P. Raw material arrives at R1 in unlimited amounts. There are two WorkCenters, W1 and W2, separated by a Buffer, B2. Finished goods are stored at S1 until a demand occurs.

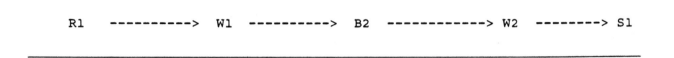

This factory's form is not particularly important for the discussion except for the following characteristic:

> The ShippingArea has storage capacity for only one unit, and demand occurs as requests for single units at some finite rate.

If this is not the case, modifications would have to be made. The unit capacity and the unit demands are used as a counter.

In the diagram below, the "real" factory consists of W1, B2 and W2. The other elements are dummies:

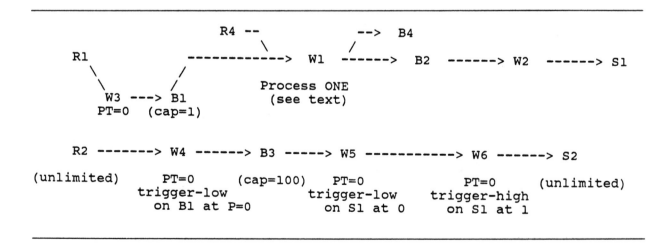

The dummy production line that begins at R2 generates "records" rather than real products. These are stored in Buffer B3 until a demand occurs, and then they are removed. The quantity in B3 corresponds to the level of echelon stock. The trick is to time the "arrivals" into B3 to coincide with the start of a new unit of product P, and "departures" from B3 to coincide with shipment.

Coordinating "production start" and "arrival of records" is accomplished as follows. All raw material must pass through Buffer B1. Whenever stock is required by the factory, inventory drops to zero in B1 for an instant. That event triggers dummy WorkCenter W4 to place one "record" into B3.

WorkCenters W5 and W6 serve to remove a record whenever a real unit leaves the system. W5 is triggered when ShippingArea S1 is emptied. Thus, when a real demand is satisfied, W5 pulls a record out of B3. The record remains at W5 until W6 is activated. When another part is finished in the factory and arrives at ShippingArea S1, W6 is activated and W5 is switched off. The records stored in B3 are unaffected, but the record that was still in W5 is withdrawn, clearing it for the next transaction.

Finally, some special initialization is required. When the factory is empty, the dummy Processes at W4 and W5 are both "on". It is important for one record to be processed so that W5 will be filled and blocked. (Remember that the unit in W5 does not count as echelon stock, since it has been removed from B3.) This happens automatically when the factory simulation is initialized. However, a unit of P also gets delivered to the factory in that interval, and it does not get counted.

To get around this problem, a dummy Process (called ONE) is created at the entrance to the factory, W1. This activity is given top priority, a batch-size of one, and is triggered when the stock level at dummy Buffer B4 is zero. The processing time for ONE is set to 0.01 so that the factory is blocked by this Process for a very short interval. When ONE has produced one unit, it goes into the Buffer at B4 and stays there forever, which permanently turns off the dummy Process. The factory is then free to operate normally, and all inputs of raw materials are properly counted thereafter.

Finally, it should be noted that this method does have an effect on the system. In particular, the addition of the dummy WorkCenter W3 and Buffer B1 places two more units of storage in the system. In the example given here, it does not matter because the supply at R1 is infinite. However, if there is a finite supply and limited capacity at the ReceivingArea, the dummy elements W3 and B1 effectively expand the capacity, and one should allow for that effect in the design.

The same would be true if the ShippingArea were different from our factory. For example, if the capacity of the ShippingArea exceeds 1, we would need a dummy WorkCenter and Buffer to count the departures.

C.7.2 Echelon Inventory Position with Backorders

When demand is backlogged, ordering policies often use <u>inventory position</u>, which is defined as "units on hand + units on order - <u>units backlogged</u>". This measure can be negative, indicating that the backlog of orders exceeds the amount in process plus on hand. For a company that produces only "to order", the inventory position is always negative (unless orders are cancelled after production has begun).

The method of measuring inventory position combines two other tricks. First, we need a method to store demands. This is covered in section C.4.2, Backlogging Demand. Second, we need to be able to measure the quantity in process, which was covered in the previous section.

The diagram below shows a model in which these elements are combined. The factory consists of the ReceivingArea R1, WorkCenters W1 and W2, and Buffers B2 and B3. It manufactures a single product, P. In this design, B3 represents storage for the ShippingArea. The rest of the model consists of dummy elements for keeping score.

Demand is simulated by arrivals of orders at the ReceivingArea R3. The arrival interval is chosen to best represent the demand process. These orders are immediately stored in B7 by the dummy Process at W7. Demand is satisfied at the dummy WorkCenter W8 where one order from B7 is assembled with one item from B3 to produce one sale.

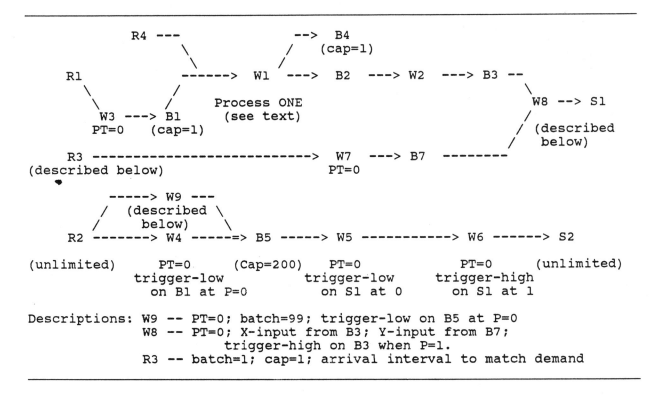

```
          R4 ---                    --> B4
                \               /     (cap=1)
                 \             /
    R1            ------->  W1  --->  B2  ---> W2  ---> B3 --
      \          /                                          \
       \        /            Process ONE                     W8 --> S1
        W3 ---> B1           (see text)                     /
        PT=0   (cap=1)                                     / (described
                                                         /    below)
          R3 -------------------------------> W7  ---> B7 --------
          (described below)                  PT=0
```

```
          -----> W9 ---
         /  (described \
        /     below)    \
    R2 -------> W4 -----=> B5 -----> W5 -----------> W6 ------> S2

  (unlimited)     PT=0      (Cap=200)  PT=0            PT=0        (unlimited)
                trigger-low          trigger-low     trigger-high
                on B1 at P=0         on S1 at 0      on S1 at 1
```

```
Descriptions: W9 -- PT=0; batch=99; trigger-low on B5 at P=0
              W8 -- PT=0; X-input from B3; Y-input from B7;
                    trigger-high on B3 when P=1.
              R3 -- batch=1; cap=1; arrival interval to match demand
```

The inventory position is measured by the contents of the Buffer B5. It is initialized with 99 units of dummy stock by the WorkCenter W9. One more unit enters B5 during initialization. Therefore, the nominal level in B5 is 100 units, indicating an inventory position of zero.

The inventory position (stock at B5) is increased by the dummy Process at W4 whenever the contents of B1 drops to zero, indicating that the real factory has just withdrawn raw materials and started one unit. The dummy WorkCenter W5 reduces the position by one unit whenever an order arrives at R3.

As in the case of echelon stocks, there is a dummy Process added to W1 to block the factory from starting until all of the dummy WorkCenters and Buffers have been initialized. The name of the process is ONE, and it draws raw material from R4, produces one ONE in time 0.01, sends it to B4 and is thereby turned off.

The average contents of Buffer B7 equals the average number of outstanding backorders. The average contents of Buffer B5 (less 100) is the average inventory position. Since position equals echelon stock - backorders, the average WIP inventory (including finished goods) can be computed from the average contents of B5, minus 100, plus the average contents of B7.

C.8 Flexible Manufacturing Systems as Closed Systems __

Many research studies have modeled a Flexible Manufacturing System (FMS) as a closed queuing system -- that is, a queuing system with a fixed number of units and no input and no output. The justification for this approach is that some real FMSs are maintained at a constant level of work-in-process. Whenever a unit is removed from the system, it is replaced immediately with

another unit. In a closed system, any work-in-process that is in the system
when it is established remains there permanently, circulating through the
WorkCenters. Hence, the real system is similar to a closed one.

A closed system can be modeled in XCELL+ using the following technique. The
key is to design an "injector", which loads a fixed number of units into the
system at the beginning of the run and then "turns off". The rest of the
system is designed as a loop, with no input other than the injector, and no
output. For example, in the diagram below, WorkCenter W1 and Buffer B1
represent the injector. There are two types of Parts, A and B.   At W1,
dummy Process A withdraws units from ReceivingArea RA and sends them (in
zero time) to Buffer B1, where they enter the loop. ReceivingArea RA is in
manual-batch-mode (see Section B.4). When the run of the model begins, you
are prompted to specify the size of the first arriving batch; the
appropriate response is the <u>total</u> <u>number</u> <u>of</u> <u>Parts</u> <u>of</u> <u>type</u> A to be injected
into the system. You then specify that the next batch will arrive at some
very distant time in the future, so that, in effect, there is no further
input. Similarly, Part B is injected from RB.

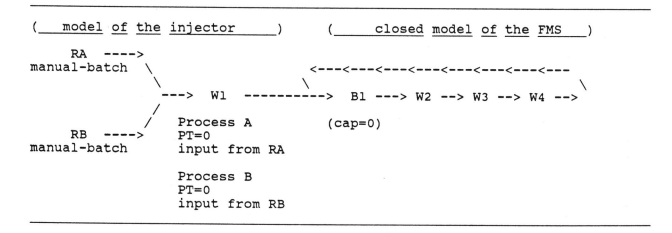

In general, an FMS includes materials handling as well as manufacturing
elements, and one of the critical design factors is the number of units that
may be in the system at once; call this N. N includes units that are being
worked on, units in transit, and units that are in storage (if that is part
of the FMS). In the model, the capacity of Buffer B1 is zero so that it
does not represent storage that has no counterpart in the real system. If
there are storage areas in the real FMS, then they would of course appear as
non-zero-capacity Buffers in the right side of the diagram. If there are
such real storage areas, they could serve as injection points, and the dummy
Buffer B1 would be unnecessary.

In using such a model, it is important that the total number of units loaded
into the system be less than than the total capacity N for work-in-process.
If this is not done, the model will deadlock.

D

Analysis of a Factory Model

D.1 The Analysis Menu _____

The analysis menu is accessible from main -- in parallel to design and run. Analysis has two purposes:

1. To <u>check</u> the model to see if there are obvious omissions or inconsistencies in the design.

2. To <u>estimate</u> the theoretical flow capacity of the model, ignoring variability, and making several simplifying assumptions.

The checking phase of analysis corresponds roughly to the overall check of a computer program that is performed by a compiler before attempting the execution of the program. This final check can detect many kinds of "global" errors that are not apparent in the examination of the individual statements in the program as they are written. In the same way, in building a factory model you can construct elements that are locally valid, but that do not make sense in the context of the overall model. XCELL+ analysis can detect some of these anomalies, and your use of analysis after design, or repeatedly during design, will save you time in the long run.

You should regard checking as part of your <u>design task</u>, and use it repeatedly during the course of construction of a model. However, as for a computer program, automatic checking can detect only certain simple classes of errors, and the burden of testing and validation of the model is still essentially yours.

The estimation phase of analysis calculates the flows and bottlenecks in the factory model <u>ignoring all sources of variability</u>. It is not, in general, a substitute for actually running the model in order to measure its performance, but it does provide a convenient and useful "base case" against which to compare the results of running the model. It is a useful preliminary step to running the model, and may to some extent reduce the necessity of making "calibration" runs. It is a valuable feature, and one not often provided in simulation systems.

Unfortunately, XCELL+ analysis cannot yet cope with the flexibility introduced by use of the asynchronous materials handling facilities -- ControlPoints, Paths and Carriers.

D.2 Structural Checking _____

For the most part, XCELL+ can prevent you from making local errors in constructing an individual element. But you retain your inalienable right to construct a model that doesn't make any sense. For example, elements can be linked together in such a way that there is no continuous path for material to move through the factory. To a modest extent, the checking phase of analysis can detect such problems. It examines the overall model for a variety of suspicious constructions. These are legal constructions, but sufficiently unusual to be worth calling to your attention.

It is best to use analysis repeatedly during design, perhaps after each major section of the model is finished and while it is still fresh in your mind. Analysis will then probably report some problems arising from the fact that the model is as yet unfinished, but you should be able to recognize these conditions and distinguish between them and real mistakes. As your models become more complicated, with multiple Processes at each WorkCenter, and different stocks in each Buffer, you will find the analysis functions of XCELL+ increasingly useful (at least up to the point where you start to use the materials handling facilities).

A simple example of a possible problem that is detectable by analysis is a Process for which no input has been specified. For a very simple model, the omission would be obvious in the graphical display of the model, and you would not need analysis to call it to your attention. However, as models become more complicated, the graphical display is no longer always adequate to clearly present all of the relationships. In particular, since Processes share a WorkCenter and the links of all Processes are superimposed on each other in the display, it is easy to omit a link without the omission being apparent in the display. It is, of course, legal and sometimes useful to have a null-input Process, but it is much more often the case that this is an oversight -- hence analysis calls it to your attention.

Similarly, as the density of elements in the display increases, it is sometimes necessary to put elements in adjacent cells. The fact that the graphical symbols for the elements are touching each other does not mean that the elements are linked -- but you cannot tell that from the display. The checking phase of analysis provides effortless detection of such omissions.

The conditions checked are the following:

  1. a WorkCenter without any Processes

  2. a Process without any input-links

  3. a Process without normal-output link

  4. a Process with normal- and reject-output links to the same cell

  5. a Buffer that contains no stocks

  6. a stock in a Buffer without any input-links

  7. a stock in a Buffer without any output-links

  8. a ReceivingArea without any output-links

  9. a ShippingArea without any input-links

  10. a Process whose normal-output has no possible path to a
      ShippingArea

  11. a Process without some input path back to a ReceivingArea

  12. a MaintenanceCenter that does not service any WorkCenters

  13. an AuxiliaryResource that does not service any Processes

  14. a ControlPoint with no incoming Path

15. a ControlPoint with no outgoing Path

16. a request or delivery specification without a source or destination

17. a request or delivery specification for which there is no Path from the source to the destination

18. a request or delivery specification with no pickup-link at the source or no dropoff-link at the destination

19. a request or delivery specification with no feasible way to acquire the required Part at the source, or to discharge the Part at the destination.

The anomalies found in the checking phase are classified as either a "warning" or a "serious" problem. The latter will presumably cause some segment of the model to be inoperative if it is run. Even for problems analysis considers warnings, you should make sure you understand why the situation is being reported, since the warning may in fact be a symptom of a more serious structural error.

Although this checking is generally helpful, it is certainly not an absolute guarantee of the correctness of a factory model, nor is it always necessary for a model to completely satisfy the checking routine in order to be useful. For example, a partially designed model, with many apparently serious anomalies, may still be capable of running and producing useful results. Conversely, a model in which checking discovers no problems may nonetheless be rife with logical flaws and produce nonsensical results.

D.3 Flow Analysis

Flow Analysis involves the calculation of <u>flows</u>, <u>utilizations</u>, <u>cycle-times</u>, and <u>minimum</u> <u>process</u> <u>batch-sizes</u>. These are discussed in the following sections.

The flow of material through a factory model is measured in material units (just called "units") per timeunit. Each unit can, in fact, represent a single piece, or it can represent a pallet, totebox, carton, barrel, or whatever the physical entities are that are moved through the factory. The timeunits are also general, undimensioned units, so you can let one timeunit represent whatever amount of real time is appropriate.

Units originate at a ReceivingArea, and presumably finish their travels at a ShippingArea. In between, they travel along links, passing through WorkCenters and Buffers. (There is no flow of units through MaintenanceCenters or AuxiliaryResources.)

D3.1 Flow through a Process at a WorkCenter

The concept of a "Part" is used in XCELL+ to denote a particular type of unit. A unit becomes a unit of Part "P" either by being the output of a Process named P, or by being the output of a Process where the output is explicitly renamed P (see Section B.2.1.2). The unit retains its identity as P until it is transformed to some other Part by another Process. In particular, it retains its identity as P when it enters a Buffer. The supply of Part P in a Buffer is called the "stock" of P in that Buffer.

When a unit of Part P is supplied as input to a Process, it is transformed to the Part associated with the output of that Process. It <u>may</u> continue to be P, if the output of the Process is P, but the output can just as well be specified to be some other Part, say Q.

This sounds confusing, but it is actually very flexible and powerful. For example, you can retain the identity of a particular Part P through a sequence of Processes on different WorkCenters just by specifying the output of each of these Processes as P.   However, you have the alternative, at any point, of declaring that the input components have now become a composite with a different name -- just by assigning that new name to the output of the (assembly) Process.

Reviewing the relevant characteristics of a Process, each Process has

1. A name, normally associated with the output of the Process. Optionally, the normal-output of a Process can be assigned a name different from that of the Process itself.

2. Two input links, called X-input and Y-input; either one, or both, can be used. Units arriving along either link consist of some specific Part.

3. Two output links, called N-output for "normal" and R-output for "reject".

The flow of units through a particular Process is the number of units which undergo <u>initial</u> <u>processing</u> by that Process. That means that if processing must be repeated (because a rejected unit is recycled) this is not counted as a second unit of flow.

The flow diagram for a Process is different depending upon whether rejected units are

1. recycled at that Process (R-output link circles back to input of the Process)

2. reworked elsewhere (R-output link goes to a Buffer, from which units move to a Process for rework)

3. scrapped (R-output link goes to a ShippingArea)

In the flow diagrams below, we show the flow on the various links, even though these flows are not reported. "r" denotes the fraction of work rejected (fraction of R-output).

─────────────────────────── **Figure D-1** ───────────────────────────

Flow through a Process at a WorkCenter

(1) When R-output is recycled at this Process:

```
                                <-------- R-output; flow = fr/(1-r)
                              \        /
  X-input; flow = f  --->      \      /
                           \     \   /
                            \     \ /
                             ---> --> W --------> N-output; flow = f
                            /
  Y-input; flow = f  --->
```

(2) and (3) When R-output is reworked elsewhere or scrapped:

```
                                        R-output; flow = fr/(1-r)

                                      -------------------->
   X-input;              --->        /
   flow = f/(1-r)           \       /
                             -------> W --------> N-output; flow = f
                            /
   Y-input;               --->
   flow = f/(1-r)
```

D3.2 Flow through a Stock at a Buffer

A stock at a Buffer is the supply of a certain part in that Buffer. A stock can receive input over one or more input links, and release output over one or more output links. (There is no limit to the number of input links or output links associated with a particular stock.) The input links come from either the N-output or R-output of a Process at a WorkCenter.   Note that the output name of the supplying Process has the same name as the stock -- both are handling units of the same Part.

The output links from a stock can go to either the X-input or Y-input of a Process at a WorkCenter. In this case, the Process may or may not have the same name as the stock, since the Process may be viewed either as continuing work on the same Part, or as incorporating a unit of the input Part into an output Part with a different name.

The flow through a stock at a Buffer is the sum of the flows on all its input links. This is, of course, equal to the sum of the flows on all its output links, since in steady-state a factory model is conservative -- units are neither created nor destroyed.

─────────────────────────── **Figure D-2** ───────────────────────────

Flow through a stock in a Buffer

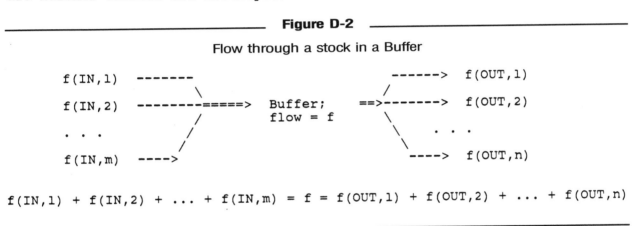

$$f(IN,1) + f(IN,2) + \ldots + f(IN,m) = f = f(OUT,1) + f(OUT,2) + \ldots + f(OUT,n)$$

D3.3 Flow through a ReceivingArea

The units at a ReceivingArea are designated as units of a particular Part. Units from a ReceivingArea can go to the X-input or Y-input of any Process. One ReceivingArea can supply input to any number of Processes, whether those are Processes for one Part or Processes for many different Parts (since a Process named "A" does not necessarily have to have Part "A" as input).

The flow from a ReceivingArea is simply the sum of the flows over all of the links from that ReceivingArea.

D3.4 Flow into a ShippingArea

Unlike ReceivingAreas, ShippingAreas do not have to be dedicated to a particular Part -- although optionally that can be done.

Units arrive at a ShippingArea from either the N-output or R-output of any Process. One ShippingArea can accept units from any number of Processes, and if the ShippingArea is not dedicated to a particular Part those Processes can deliver a variety of different Parts. However, if the ShippingArea is dedicated to one Part -- say "P" -- then only Processes that produce P can deliver to that ShippingArea. (Recall that a Process can produce P either because the Process itself is named P, or because it has renamed its output as P.)

Although not required, it is a useful practice in a multi-Part model, to have a separate ShippingArea for each different Part that is a final product. (You can choose names for each ShippingArea to reflect the type of material accepted there.) This will cause the flow for each type of unit to be reported separately.

The flow to a ShippingArea is simply the sum of the flows over all of the links to that ShippingArea.

D3.5 Conservation of Units

The flows in a factory model obey a set of linear equations that enforce the conservation of units in the model. In general, the solution of this set of equations is quite complicated, due to the possibility of recirculating flows along rework paths. However, when the rework paths are sufficiently restricted, the equations can be solved with relative ease. This is the task of Flow Analysis.

Hence, if the "rework elsewhere" option has been used for any Process at any WorkCenter, Flow Analysis gives up on solving these equations (and warns you that it cannot proceed).

The idea is essentially to calculate the flows elsewhere in the model that are necessary to yield certain desired flows to the ShippingAreas. That is, it is a "pull-oriented" computation. There are three situations with regard to flow to a ShippingArea:

1. If a ShippingArea receives scrap units (R-output from a Process) it is assumed that there is no desired flow, and the flow is only an unfortunate by-product of other desired flows.

2. If a ShippingArea is not operating in regular-batch mode -- that is, if it is either unlimited, or in manual-batch mode -- you must specify the desired flow by means of an interactive dialog Your specification must be in terms of the

   (number of units of material) per (timeunit).

3. If a ShippingArea is in "regular-batch" mode, the flow is computed as

   (average batch size) / (average time between batches)

   This gives the average number of units per timeunit.

Flow Analysis starts with these desired output flows from the ShippingAreas and works backward through the links of the model. Given the desired flow at each ShippingArea, Flow Analysis must "allocate", or partition, that flow over the set of incoming links to that ShippingArea. It does the same thing for the incoming links to each stock in a Buffer. From these allocated flows it is able to compute the necessary flow through each Process at a WorkCenter, and eventually from each ReceivingArea.

D3.6 Allocation of Flows over Multiple Incoming Links

When a ShippingArea or stock in a Buffer has only a single incoming link, there is no question of how to distribute the required flow over a set of links. In this case, the calculation is straightforward. However, if any ShippingArea or stock in a Buffer has multiple input links, then Flow Analysis must somehow allocate the total flow over the several links -- and as a result, the calculation may be only an approximation to the true flow.

The flow allocation strategy is simply to divide the required flow over (most of) the incoming links equally:

  If a ShippingArea, or a stock in a Buffer, has a required flow of f units per timeunit, and has n input links (excluding links from the

R-output of Processes) then the flow is distributed equally over these
links. That is, for each non-R-output link, the flow is f/n units per
timeunit.

This strategy essentially assumes that the model involves similar facilities
operating in parallel. That is, if there is more than one incoming link, it
is assumed that the mechanism of supply at the origin of all of those links
is similar. In a particular model, the validity of the results produced by
Flow Analysis must be judged as heavily dependent upon the validity of this
assumption of supply symmetry.

D3.7 Utilization of WorkCenters

A WorkCenter in a factory model can be in any one of several states:

IP	in processing; performing useful work
ID	idle; no input available
IR	in repair; undergoing maintenance
IS	in setup; preparing to process a different Part
BL	blocked; unable to dispose of finished output
QR	queued for repair

If each of these symbols represents the fraction of available time a
Workcenter spends in that state then:

$$IP + ID + IR + IS + BL + QR = 1$$

We define the utilization of a particular WorkCenter as IP -- the fraction
of time the WorkCenter spends in useful work.

One of the principal reasons for constructing and running a simulation model
is to get some idea of how the time of each WorkCenter is broken down among
these states. Essentially, the productive capacity of a model is a function
of the utilization of its WorkCenters.

In some idealized sense, a perfectly balanced factory of perfect
WorkCenters, running at capacity, could achieve 100% utilization of every
WorkCenter -- they would always be in state IP. But the imperfect
WorkCenters that must be used in real factories may exhibit variability in
processing-times, less than perfect yield, and require some maintenance
attention. It is also the case that WorkCenter capacity is "lumpy" -- a
group of identical WorkCenters work in parallel, and the capacity of the
group is typically not smoothly and continuously variable. Hence, perfect
balance is difficult, if not impossible, to achieve.

Another complication is that the processing (IP) state is the useful state
-- the WorkCenter is performing useful work. Only when the WorkCenter is in
the IP state can material flow through the WorkCenter. On the other hand,
unless the WorkCenter is totally saturated, there will necessarily be some
fraction of the available time when it is not in processing. Utilization is
essentially the fraction of available time spent in state IP.

Although, in general, high utilization is a good thing, you cannot
reasonably set out to achieve 100% utilization of each WorkCenter. A
perfectly balanced factory model is often useful in theoretical studies, but
it is rarely a realistic representation of an actual factory. Ordinarily,
there are some "bottleneck" WorkCenters that "saturate" first, and thereby
limit the level of utilization of other WorkCenters. It is also often
useful to run a model at less than maximum capacity to study its behavior
under those conditions.

In general, the IP state is "good", and the ID, IR, IS, BL and QR states are
"bad". But it is instructive to examine the source of each of these other
states more carefully:

IR (repair) is characteristic of the particular WorkCenter. It is desirable to have IR small, but it is generally a parameter given to the model, rather than a result produced by the model.

QR (queued) is a result of the model -- a factor that you seek to minimize. But of course the value of a reduction in QR must be balanced against the cost of the maintenance facilities that are necessary to achieve the reduction.

BL (blocked) is the purest kind of bad -- there is no offsetting economy or virtue. It is a major goal of the simulation model to identify and measure blockage so that the design can be altered to reduce it.

IS (setup) is, to some extent, determined by the characteristic of the WorkCenter and the Processes that it performs. That is, the length of time taken to perform a particular setup is presumably given. However, the fraction of time spent in state IS depends upon the <u>frequency</u> of setup, as well as the length of each setup, and this depends to a significant extent on the structure of the model and the rules used to schedule the Processes. The length of a single setup may also depend on what Process preceded the incoming Process, which is represented by the "major" and "minor" setup times of XCELL+.

ID (idle) is an ambiguous and interesting state. When you are modeling a "push" facility, ID is bad -- you are presumably trying to arrange things to achieve as great a throughput capacity as possible. However, when you are modeling a "pull" facility, the total amount of ID is essentially determined by the specification of demand. You can rearrange it, and trade it for IS, BL and QR, but it is not inherently reducible.

Two general principles of utilization are relevant:

1. The <u>principle</u> <u>of</u> <u>maximum</u> <u>realizable</u> <u>utilization</u>

Assuming that the fraction of time in state IR is given, and not something determined by the model, the available time is actually $(1 - IR)$, and utilization should be measured against this, rather than against 1. Hence the <u>maximum</u> <u>realizable</u> <u>utilization</u> M is

$$M = (1 - IR) \times 100$$

This holds whether IR represents scheduled maintenance, or random breakdowns.

2. The <u>principle</u> <u>of</u> <u>process</u> <u>work</u> <u>utilization</u>

Let P represents the set of k different Processes performed at a particular WorkCenter, and pi be one of those Processes. Further, let

   fi   be the flow rate of Process pi

   ti   be the mean time to perform Process pi on a single unit
         (excluding setup time, if any)

   ri   be the fraction of units rejected after Process pi

   ui   be the utilization of the Workcenter by Process pi

   U   be the total Process utilization of the WorkCenter,
         expressed as a percentage

Then U = 100 * ui   for all k of the Processes pi in P, and

ui = fi x ti   if ri=0

= fi x ti   if ri>0 and rejected units are reworked
                   elsewhere or scrapped

= (fi x ti)/(1-ri)   if ri>0 and rejected units are recycled

The maximum realizable utilization of the WorkCenter is M, and its required utilization is U. If U >= M then the WorkCenter is said to be <u>saturated</u> (or oversaturated). That is, there is no time left after repair and processing to devote to the states ID, IS, BL or QR.

If U < M, then IP will not take up all the available time, and the balance will be (somehow) divided among ID, IS, BL and QR.

D3.8 Minimum Cycle Times

If a WorkCenter is not saturated, then M - U percent of the time will be spent in the ID, IS, BL or QR states. Consider the situation where none of this "excess" time is "wasted" in the idle (ID), undesirable blocked (BL), or queued (QR) states. Then all the excess time is available to be devoted to setup, the IS state. Since each setup requires a fixed amount of time, this available time (M-U) effectively establishes a limit on the <u>frequency of setup</u> -- that is, if the WorkCenter is setup more often than this limit, there is insufficient time to perform both the necessary setup and the required production. As a result the time available for production (IP) is necessarily reduced.

Let si represent the setup time required to prepare the WorkCenter to perform Process pi. Let S be the sum of the si, for all k Processes in the set P.   Consider a "complete cycle" on this WorkCenter to be a period of time during which the Workcenter performs each of the k Processes once and only once.   Assume that the k Processes are numbered (or renumbered, if necessary) in the order in which they appear in the cycle. The length C of the cycle is the length of time from the setup of the first Process in the cycle pl to the completion of the processing of the last Process pk in the cycle (after which the WorkCenter begins the setup of pl to start the next cycle). Assume that the major-setup time is the same as the minor-setup time for each Process, so S is a constant amount of time, independent of the order of Processes within the cycle. Then

C = s1 + n1 x t1 + s2 + n2 x t2 + ... + sk + nk x tk

C = S + n1 x t1 + n2 x t2 + ... + nk x tk

where ni is the number of units produced by Process pi in the cycle.

Now consider some (long) period of time T, during which this cycle is repeated many times. Assume an ideal situation in which the WorkCenter is never idle, blocked or queued for repair. Then

1 = IP + IR + IS

Recognizing that IP and IR are given, by the required flow and the WorkCenter breakdown characteristics, this means that the fraction of time in setup is

IS = 1 - IP - IR

The amount of time during T in setup is

T x IS = T x (1-IP-IR)

The number of cycles during T is T/C, and each cycle requires S total time to make the k setups. Hence

$$T \times (1-IP-IR) = (T \times S)/C$$

$$C = S/(1-IP-IR)$$

$$1 - IR - IP = (M - U)/100$$

Thus C is the minimum cycle-time. For any cycle length less than C, there would be too frequent setup, and the increased fraction of time in IS would necessarily cut into IP -- the required flowrate could not be met. Conversely, for any cycle length greater than C, the available time (after IP and IR) would not be totally consumed by setup, so there would be some time in states ID, BL or QR.

D3.9 Minimum Process Batch-Size

You do not have explicit control over the cycle-time in the model. However, you have explicit control over the minimum batch-size for each Process, which indirectly determines the cycle-time. (See Section B.2.1.5.) The fixed batch-size is the minimum number of consecutive units of a particular Process that must be completed before another Process can interrupt and take over the WorkCenter.

The number of units that will be produced by Process pi during the minimum length cycle is

$$f_i \times C$$

If you specify a batch-size that is less than this value, the cycle-length will be less than C, setup will be too frequent, and the required flowrates will not be achievable.

Consequently, the choice of batch-size is directly related to saturation, since it determines the amount of time that must be spent in setup. Flow Analysis calculates and reports these minimum batch-sizes. But note that this calculation depends upon the calculated flowrates, hence also depends upon the symmetry assumption used in calculating flows.

The greater the utilization of a WorkCenter, the greater the minimum batch-size must be for the Processes at that WorkCenter -- since there is little time to spare for setup. If a WorkCenter is saturated, it has no time to spare for setup, so theoretically the minimum batch-size must be infinite. A batch-size of 999999 is reported in this case, which you should interpret as a sign of saturation. That is, 999999 means there is no reasonable batch-size that will allow this WorkCenter to do all the work that is required of it.

D3.10 An Example of Flow Analysis

Consider the following example, for the simple factory model shown in Figure D-3.

The detailed characteristics of this model are:

ReceivingAreas

R1   unlimited supply

R2   regular-batch arrivals; batch-size (25,25); time between
          arrivals (45,55); storage-capacity 50

Figure D-3

Factory model for Flow Analysis

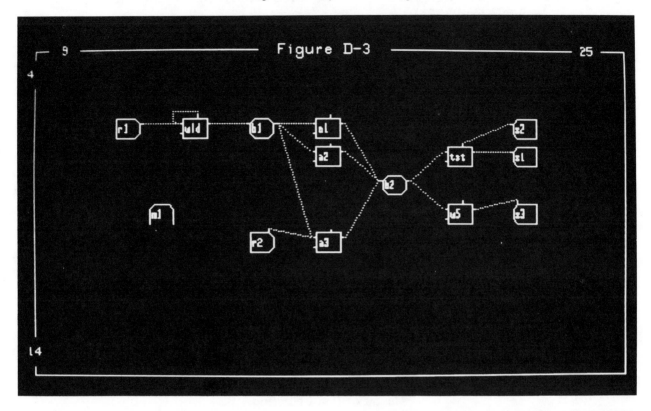

ShippingAreas

S1   continuous shipment

S2   continuous shipment

S3   regular-batch shipments; batch-size (3,7); time between
      shipments (8,12); storage-capacity 50

Buffers

B1   capacity 10; stock P1

B2   capacity 10; stocks P1, P2

WorkCenters/Processes

WLD/P1   setup 10,10; proc-tm CONS (1);   rej 10%, recycled

A1/P1   setup 5,5;   proc-tm UNIF (1,3); rej 0%

A2/P1   setup 5,5;   proc-tm UNIF (1,3); rej 0%

A3/P1   setup 10,10; proc-tm UNIF (3,5); rej 0%; batch size 10

A3/P2   setup 20,20; proc-tm CONS (.4);   rej 0%; batch size 25

TST/P1   setup 12,12; proc-tm UNIF (.6,1.2); rej 20%, scrap to s2

W5/P2   setup 4,4;   proc-tm CONS (.8);   rej 0%

Maintenance Characteristics

One MaintenanceCenter, with one service-team, servicing the
following WorkCenters:

    A1   random brkdn; expn time betw brk, mean 45; expn repr, mn 5

    TST   random brkdn; expn time betw brk, mean 95; expn repr, mn 5

    W5   random brkdn; expn time betw brk, mean 45; cons repr, 5

    A2   random brkdn; expn time betw brk, mean 20; expn repr, mn 5

    A3   scheduled; interval 45; expn service, mean 5

Figures D-4 and D-5 are the results displayed when Flow Analysis is used
with a desired flow of 0.8 unit per timeunit specified for ShippingArea s1.
The resulting expected flow to S2 is (3+7)/(8+12) = 0.5 units per timeunit.
Figure D-4 is the result of the <list utilization> action in Analysis;
Figure D-5 is the result of <list flows>.

These results are obtained as follows:

   1. With a desired flow of 0.8 to S1, and a reject rate of 20% for
      Process P1 at WorkCenter TST, the flow rate from P2 at TST must be
      1.0.

————————————————————————————— **Figure D-4** —————————————————————————————

Result of ‹list utilization›

Wkctr	Util'zn	Max ut'zn	Saturated?	Min cycle time
wld	111.111	100.000	YES	999999.00
a1	66.667	90.000	NO	21.43
tst	90.000	95.000	NO	240.00
w5	40.000	90.000	NO	8.00
a2	66.667	80.000	NO	37.50
a3	153.333	90.000	YES	999999.00

2. The input flow to stock P1 at Buffer B2 is assumed to be drawn
   equally from the three supplying Processes, hence 0.333 for
   Process P1 at each of the WorkCenters A1, A2 and A3.

3. The flow rate of P1 through Buffer B1 is 1.0.

4. The flow rate of P1 from WorkCenter WLD is 1.0. Since Process P1
   at WLD has 10% of its output recycled, and has a processing-
   time of 1, its utilization is $1.0 \times 1/(1-0.1) \times 100 = 111.111$,
   which is, of course, impossible.

5. The utilization of WorkCenter A3 is $(0.333 \times 4 + 0.5 \times 0.4) \times 100 =$
   153.333, where the utilization of both A1 and A2 is
   $(0.333 \times 0.2) \times 100 = 66.667$.

6. Since there is extra time available at A1 and A2 to do more
   processing of P1, WorkCenter A3 is not required to work on
   P1 at all. (Note that A1 and A2, working at their maximum
   attainable utilizations of 0.9 and 0.8 respectively, can
   achieve a flow of 0.85 units of P1.)

The table below summarizes the results obtained by actually running the
model for 10,000 timeunits. (This was preceded by a "run-in period" of 500
timeunits, after which result collection was re-started.) It is instructive
to compare these actual results to the estimates produced by Analysis.

_____ **Figure D-5** _____

Result of ‹list flows›

CELL			FLOW(units/timeunit)	
Rcg Area	r1		.587	
Rcg Area	r2		.293 with rec'g flow of	.500
Wkctr	wld	Proc P1	.587 min batch size: 17	
Wkctr	a1	Proc P1	.196 min batch size: 2	
Wkctr	tst	Proc P1	.587 min batch size: 17	
Wkctr	w5	Proc P2	.293 min batch size: 2	
Wkctr	a2	Proc P1	.196 min batch size: 2	
Wkctr	a3	Proc P2	.293 min batch size:999999	
Wkctr	a3	Proc P1	.196 min batch size:999999	
Buffer	b1	Stock P1	.587	
Buffer	b2	Stock P2	.293	
Buffer	b2	Stock P1	.587	
Shp Area	s1		.470	
Shp Area	s2		.117	
Shp Area	s3		.293 with shp'g flow of	.500

element				flow (units/timeunit)	
RecArea	R1			.738	
RecArea	R2			.233	(.267 rejected)
WkCtr	WLD	Proc	P1	.738	
WkCtr	A1	Proc	P1	.345	
WkCtr	TST	Proc	P1	.738	
WkCtr	W5	Proc	P2	.232	
WkCtr	A2	Proc	P1	.301	
WkCtr	A3	Proc	P2	.233	
WkCtr	A3	Proc	P1	.092	
Buffer	B1	stock	P1	.738	
Buffer	B2	stock	P2	.233	
Buffer	B2	stock	P1	.738	
ShipArea	S1			.593	
ShipArea	S2			.146	
ShipArea	S3			.232	(.269 shortage)

WkCtr	Utilization: processing	setup	maintenance
WLD	82.09	0.00	0.00
A1	68.89	0.00	16.16
TST	66.43	0.00	10.06
W5	18.53	0.00	9.43
A2	59.94	0.00	22.25
A3	46.07	27.82	12.58

D.4 Bottleneck Analysis

Bottleneck Analysis starts with values of desired flow at each Shipping-Area, and works backwards (upstream in the model) from there to determine whether or not the model can deliver these flows. Bottleneck Analysis starts by asking you to specify the desired flow for each ShippingArea that receives the normal-output from some Process.

The WorkCenter utilizations are analyzed (by repeated use of Flow Analysis), and the resulting flows are scaled so that

  1. no WorkCenter exceeds its capacity

  2. one or more WorkCenters have utilization exactly equal to capacity.

The WorkCenters with utilization equal to their capacity are, of course, the bottlenecks in the model, and Bottleneck Analysis reports the flow that is delivered with these bottleneck WorkCenters working exactly at capacity.

For the example given above, Flow Analysis with desired shipping flows of 0.8 for S1 and 0.5 for S3 lead to an overload at both WorkCenters WLD and A3. Desired flows of 0.72 and 0.45 (scaling both flows downward by a factor of 0.9) determines that A3 is still overloaded. Finally, after the initial flow has been scaled downwards by a factor of 0.5875, WorkCenter A3 has utilization exactly equal to a maximum realizable utilization -- its capacity. In effect, Bottleneck Analysis automatically searches for this limiting scaling factor. In doing so, it retains the relative balance between flows that you specified initially.

Figures D-6 and D-7 show the displays that result when Bottleneck Analysis is used with desired relative flows of 0.8 at S1 and 0.5 at S2. Figure D-6 is produced by the <list utilization> key, and D-7 is produced by <list flows>.

Figure D-6

Result of ‹list utilization›

Wkctr	Util'zn	Max ut'zn	Saturated?	Min cycle time
wld	65.217	100.000	NO	28.75
a1	39.130	90.000	NO	9.83
tst	52.826	95.000	NO	28.45
w5	23.478	90.000	NO	6.01
a2	39.130	80.000	NO	12.23
a3	90.000	90.000	YES	999999.00

Figure D-7

Result of ‹list flows›

CELL			FLOW(units/timeunit)	
Rcg Area	r1		1.000	
Rcg Area	r2		.500 with rec'g flow of	.500
Wkctr	wld	Proc P1	1.000 min batch size:999999	
Wkctr	a1	Proc P1	.333 min batch size: 7	
Wkctr	tst	Proc P1	1.000 min batch size: 240	
Wkctr	w5	Proc P2	.500 min batch size: 4	
Wkctr	a2	Proc P1	.333 min batch size: 12	
Wkctr	a3	Proc P2	.500 min batch size:999999	
Wkctr	a3	Proc P1	.333 min batch size:999999	
Buffer	b1	Stock P1	1.000	
Buffer	b2	Stock P2	.500	
Buffer	b2	Stock P1	1.000	
Shp Area	s1		.800	
Shp Area	s2		.200	
Shp Area	s3		.500 with shp'g flow of	.500

E

Running a Factory Model

The purpose of building a factory model is to be able to run it. Although the exercise of constructing the model may in itself sharpen your understanding of the factory just by forcing you to study carefully the characteristics of individual elements, and the relationships between elements, the primary benefit of modeling lies in the performance measurements you can obtain from running the model.

Your objective in running the model is to obtain <u>insight</u>, and not just data. You need to discover <u>how</u> the model works, and not just that it does work. In general, you need <u>comparative</u> <u>results</u> -- to learn how the performance of the model changes in response to changes in structural characteristics. There is as much art to running a model effectively as there is in constructing it. Some of the general issues involved in the use of a model are discussed in Section H. Section E is concerned with the tools XCELL+ provides for you to use while you run the model.

E.1 The Run Menu

The **run** menu is only accessible from **main**. To go back and forth between **design** and **run**, you must pass through **main**. Run mode and **design** mode present different kinds of information, so as you move back and forth between them, the display screen changes. For example, Figure E-1 shows a typical "trace" display in **run**.

As you enter **run** menu, the model does not immediately start running. The model is "paused" and you are really in **pause** menu. The initial **pause** menu appears as follows:

tagging	display detail	controls	modify state			begin run	back to main

Later, after the model has been run and the model-clock is no longer at 0, the **pause** menu includes the key, and the key is replaced by <resume run>. <modify state> is no longer shown, since that can only by done at time 0:

tagging	display detail	controls			results	resume run	back to main

Figure E-1

An Example of the trace display during run

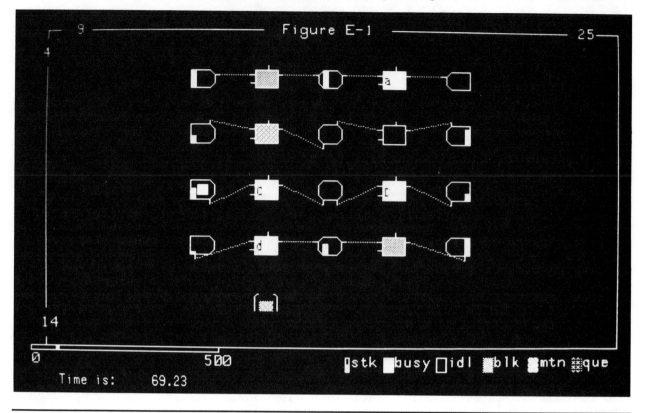

The **pause** menus offer the following choices:

<start/stop tagging>   Invoke/disable unit-tagging feature to track the
                    progress of units as released to the factory from
                    ReceivingAreas. See Sections B.4.1 and B.6.2.

<display detail>   Examine the complete characteristics of a single
                    cell. (There is a "selection screen", with a
                    cell-cursor, as in **design**, with which you select
                    the particular cell to display.)

<controls>   Specify a variety of "run control" and display options.
             See Sections E.2.

<modify state>   Before starting the run, manually change the state of
                 Buffers and ReceivingAreas. See Section E.5.

<results>   Display (or print) the results of the run, up to this
                 point, in tabular form. See Section E.4.

<begin run> or <resume run>   Leave **pause**, and begin (or resume)
                            running the model.

<back to main>   Leave **pause** and return to **main**.

Once you press the <begin run>, or <resume run>, key you have left **pause** and
are "running" -- but in fact, the <u>model</u> <u>still</u> <u>does</u> <u>not</u> <u>start</u> to run and you
are still in manual control. This is admittedly rather confusing, but once
you figure it out, it gives you a very useful degree of control.

Perhaps the easiest way to understand the situation is to compare it to control of an automobile. **Pause** corresponds to "neutral"; **running** means you have put the vehicle "in gear", so that forward motion is enabled, but the vehicle does not actually begin to move until you depress the accelerator. Similarly, as you enter **run** from **pause**, you have enabled motion, but you are still in control of speed. Think of your model at this point as running at zero speed. If, at this point, you press the <automatic run> key, you have, in effect, pressed the accelerator to the floor, and the model will "take off" and run at full speed. Alternatively, if you press <one step>, the model will lurch ahead "one step", and then stop and wait for further instructions. (Alas, XCELL+ does not yet have a "reverse gear" that will allow you to run time backwards -- which would sometimes be very useful.)

The **run** menu is as follows:

suspend draw			one step	slower	faster	auto run	pause

The keys of this **run** menu give you the following choices:

<suspend/resume draw> This simply suspends the drawing of changes on the display screen. The model is still running, but the only way you can tell this is by watching the clock advance. When you are running with drawing suspended, this key becomes <resume draw>, so you can resume the active display.

The purpose of <suspend/resume draw> is optionally to relieve the computer of the task of changing the display screen. Relieved of this burden, the model runs approximately five times as fast.

<one step> Advance the model by taking all the actions that occur simultaneously at this point in time. The clock will advance to the next time when an action occurs.

<slower> Insert one artificial delay (approximately 0.25 seconds) between re-draws of the display screen. Each time you press <slower> an additional 0.25 delay is inserted. The purpose is to slow the changes in the display screen to the point where you can follow them visually. There is a "speedometer" to show how much delay you have inserted.

<faster> Remove one delay between re-draws of the screen. The <faster> key only appears when some amount of artificial delay is present.

<automatic run> Run the model automatically, at whatever speed you have specified with the <suspend draw>, <slower> and <faster> keys.

<pause> Leave **run** and return to **pause** menu.

In addition to the <pause> key, there are several other ways that the model can automatically return from **run** to **pause**:

    -- The clock reaches the "end of a period". (The "time thermometer"
            is filled to the right limit.)

    -- The "plot" overlay reaches the right limit of the screen --
            see Section E.2.1.2.

    -- The "chart" reaches the right limit of the screen --
            see Section E.2.1.3.

    -- The model becomes "deadlocked".

E.1.1 Deadlock During Run

"Deadlock" simply means that the factory has reached a point such that there
will be no further progress. That is, there will be no further movement of
material, or change of state of any element, no matter how long the run
would continue. Consequently, the run is automatically paused at the point
where deadlock is detected.

For example, suppose you try to run a model that consists of, say, a single
Buffer. Deadlock will be reported immediately, since nothing "works" in
this model.

Deadlock can, of course, be achieved in more subtle ways. For example,
suppose there is a set of Processes on a particular Workcenter that all draw
input from a common Buffer. If the Process that is currently active has a
fixed "batch-size", and is in the middle of processing a batch when the
Buffer becomes filled with some other type of part, at least this portion of
the model is deadlocked. The Process cannot release the WorkCenter until
the batch is finished, and the batch cannot finish because the proper type
of input material is not available in the Buffer. On the other hand, the
material that is in the Buffer cannot be withdrawn since the Process(es)
that need it cannot be started on the WorkCenter. As a result, no further
material can be added to the Buffer. Whether or not the effect of this
local deadlock propagates throughout the model depends on the overall
structure of the model.

Note that only complete deadlock is automatically detected -- when the
entire model can make no further progress. Your model may suffer local
deadlock situations such as the one described above, without issuing an
explicit warning. It is surprisingly easy to construct models that exhibit
deadlock -- particularly multi-product models -- and you must be alert for
the symptoms. Deadlock, of course, can occur in real factories as well as
models, so simulation is useful to discover combinations of structure and
operating disciplines that can result in deadlock.

Unfortunately, any model that has at least one batch-mode ReceivingArea or
one batch-mode ShippingArea can never be in complete deadlock. Even if
everything else is totally blocked, arrivals or shipments will continue.
Hence in this case the automatic deadlock detection is unable to assist you
by reporting that your model has ceased to make progress.

E.2 Run Controls _____

Run control is a menu accessible from pause in which you select options that
control the nature of the run and the type of information displayed. The
run control menu is the following:

audible alarms	re-start results	re-start run	new r-n seed	display options	change view	period length	no change

Run control offers the following options:

      <audible alarms> Move to a menu in which you can turn ON or OFF a
                                    variety of audible signals that sound when
                                    certain conditions arise in running the model.
                                    See Section E.2.1.4.

      <re-start results> Clears the result accumulators, and resets
                                    the model clock to zero -- but does not alter
                                    the state of the model. See Section E.6.

      <re-start run> Clears results, resets the model clock to zero, and
                               resets the state of the model to "empty and
                               idle". Prepares to start the run over again
                               from the beginning. <re-start run>
                               automatically leaves **run control** and returns
                               to **pause**

      <new random-number seed> Gives you the opportunity to specify the
                                    "seed" used as the starting point for the
                                    "random number generator". See Section E.6.1.

      <display options> Moves to a **display option** menu in which you specify
                                the form of the **run** display screen.
                                See Section E.2.1.

      <change view> Moves to a menu in which you can reposition the
                               display window, and change the scale of
                               the display. See Section A.6.

      <period length> Gives you the opportunity to change the length of
                               the "data-collection period". The run
                               automatically pauses at the end of each
                               period. See Section E.4.1.

      <no change> Leaves **run control**, and returns to **pause**.

E.2.1 Display Options

There are three distinctly different types of display available during the
run of a model:

      <trace> The instantaneous state of each element in the current window
                          is shown. This is the default form of display.

      <plot> A graph of the contents of one particular Buffer is overlaid
                       on the trace display.

      <chart> A Gantt Chart of the state of selected WorkCenters, Carriers,
                       MaintenanceCenters and AuxiliaryResources is shown

These are described in detail in the following sections. Your choice among
these displays is made in **display options**, which is accessible from **run
control**. The <no change> key in **display options** returns you to **run control**.

All the different types of run display are generated "live", in "real-time",
as events occur during the running of the model, and <u>presented</u> <u>immediately</u>.
You are able to view the action as it takes places. (Some other simulation
systems produce a "history file" as the model is run, and then repeatedly
process the data in that file to generate various displays.)

Direct and immediate viewing means that the various types of run display in
XCELL+ are <u>alternatives</u>.   You cannot, for example, trace the action of the
model for a certain interval, and then immediately view the events of the
same interval in some other form -- say in a Gantt Chart. However, you can

Figure E-2

Example of the tracing form of run display

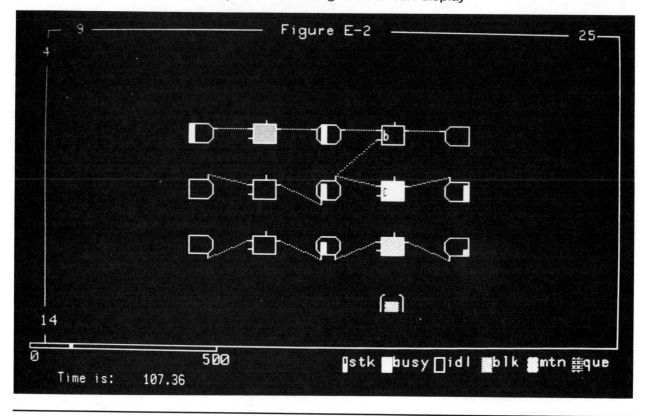

easily accomplish this, using the File Manager, if you anticipate the need to re-examine the events in the interval. You simply store the model at the beginning of the interval, and later retrieve the model, in the state that existed at the beginning of the interval, and run again from that point -- presumably using an alternate form of display.

The generation of displays in real-time, as the model is running, permits tremendous flexibility in interaction with the model. You can return to design to change the characteristics of the model, and then <resume the run> of the changed model, from the point where you <paused> before making the change. For many types of changes it is not necessary to re-start the run from the beginning.

E.2.1.1 Tracing of the Running of a Model

Tracing shows the state of each element of the model at each instant in time. The display changes as the state changes. This is the default form of run display. Figures E-1 and E-2 are examples of the tracing display.

The tracing display is changed every time the model clock advances (which is not quite the same as saying "for every event" since several events can occur at the same point in time). This coincides with the forward progress associated with the <one step> key.

The information shown in the trace, for each type of element, is the following:

WorkCenters:
      1. The WorkCenter symbol is color-coded to identify the following
         states:

      a. busy processing
      b. in setup
      c. idle, no material available
      d. idle, has received X-input, waiting for Y-input
      e. idle, has received Y-input, waiting for X-input
      f. blocked, cannot dispose of output
      g. undergoing maintenance
      h. queued, waiting for maintenance
      i. manually pulled "offline" (labelled as "OL")

2. Only the input-links and output-links of the current Process are shown.
3. The name of the current Process is shown when the WorkCenter is busy processing, or is in setup.

ReceivingAreas:
1. The stock currently available is shown as a bar-graph at the left-side of the symbol. This is scaled so that the full height of the symbol represents its storage-capacity, and the area filled on the screen represents the fraction of storage-capacity that is currently full. An unlimited-supply ReceivingArea is considered to have a capacity of 1 unit, which is always full -- hence the bar graph is always completely filled in. (Recall that you can distinguish among different arrival modes by the position where the links join the ReceivingArea symbol.)
2. Each time a unit is released from the ReceivingArea, a yellow block flashes in the right section of the ReceivingArea.

ShippingAreas:
1. The stock accepted, but not yet shipped, is shown as a bar-graph at the right-side of the symbol. This is scaled so that the full height of the symbol represents its storage-capacity, and the area filled on the screen represents the fraction of storage-capacity that is currently full. A continuous-shipment ShippingArea is always shown as empty. (Recall that you can distinguish among different shipment modes by the position where the links join the ShippingArea symbol.)
2. Each time a unit is accepted at the ShippingArea, a yellow block flashes in the left section of the ShippingArea.

Buffers:
1. The total stock in the Buffer is shown as a bar-graph, scaled to the capacity of the Buffer. When the bar reaches the top of the symbol, the Buffer is full. (Recall that you can identify the ordering discipline at a Buffer by the position where the links join the Buffer symbol -- see Section B.6.2.)

MaintenanceCenters:
1. The fraction of the available service-teams working is shown as a bar-graph. If there are no WorkCenters currently queued the bar is color-coded to match the "in maintenance" state of a WorkCenter. If one or more WorkCenters are queued, the bar is color-coded to match the "queued" state of a WorkCenter.

AuxiliaryResources
1. The fraction of the total number of Resources that is currently working is shown as a bar-graph.

Carriers
1. The color of the outer border indicates the current state, according to the color key shown on the screen.
2. The color of the interior indicates whether the Carrier is empty or loaded.

　　　3. If the Carrier is "routed" the number of the destination
　　　　　ControlPoint is shown.

When tagging is in effect (see Section E.3) the trace also shows the
presence of a tagged unit as a color-coded block superimposed on the symbols
for the different types of elements.

There is also a "period thermometer" that shows the passage of time from the
beginning to the end of the period, and a "speedometer" showing the number
of "delays" you have inserted (using the <slower> and <faster> keys).   On
the period thermometer, a mark is made each time an event occurs in the
model -- for example, the completion of a unit by a Process, or the arrival
of a batch at a ReceivingArea.   Consequently, the filled-in segments of the
thermometer represent "busy periods", when there were frequent changes of
state, and the dark areas are intervals when the model clock advanced but
there was no change of state.

E.2.1.2 Plotting Buffer Stock

The plotting option permits a more detailed observation of the contents of a
particular Buffer.   It provides a graph of the contents of the selected
Buffer, with respect to time, overlayed on the lower third of the trace
screen. (If this overlay obscures the most interesting part of the window,
you can always reposition the window in **change view**. It may also be helpful
to change to <reduced scale> when plotting.)   An example is shown in Figure
E-3.

When the Buffer selected for plotting contains stock of more than one part
there are three choices available:

──────────────────────────────── **Figure E-3** ────────────────────────────────

Example of plotting Buffer contents

Time is: 428.47

<total only> Plot only the sum of all types of parts in the Buffer.
(This is chosen automatically when there is only
one type of part in the Buffer.)

<select part> To specify one particular type of part, to overlay the
total contents as shown in Figure E-3.

<maximum part> Overlay the total contents with a graph of the stock
that happens to have the greater count at each
instant in time. (This option is less useful
than it might seem, since the plot does not
indicate which part has the greatest stock at
each point.)

When the plot reaches the right limit of the screen, there is an automatic
pause. The <resume run> key clears the plot section of the screen, and
starts plotting again from the left as the run resumes. You can also
<expand> and <reduce> the horizontal time scale of the plot from pause mode.

Plotting is particularly useful in identifying bottlenecks in the model,
since a Buffer upstream of a bottleneck will tend to gradually fill up. The
rate and character of the buildup may not be apparent in tracing, but it is
unmistakable when the Buffer contents are plotted. Similarly, a Buffer that
is very lightly used generally suggests that it is located downstream from a
bottleneck.

The solution to imbalance problems revealed by plotting the contents of a
Buffer is not, in general, just to increase the size of the Buffer --
although some would argue that this has been the traditional American remedy
for the problem. It is at least encouraging that there is increasing
awareness that a bulging buffer is only a symptom of a problem, and that the
problem should be identified and cured, rather than just masked by an
increase in buffer capacity. There may even be increasing understanding of
the different functions that a buffer performs (absorption of processing
time variation, protection against breakdown, etc.) Perhaps when the current
crusade for "zero inventory" systems has run its course, an era of rational
buffer design can emerge. (See Section G.3.)

The current version of XCELL+ does not yet have the capability of plotting
the contents of a batch-mode ReceivingArea or a batch-mode ShippingArea. If
you need to plot the contents of one of those elements you will have to
resort to a composite element, such as those described in Section C.2. For
example, to plot the contents of a batch-mode ShippingArea you can insert a
dummy Buffer just upstream from the ShippingArea with a dummy WorkCenter
between them to move units. A Process in the dummy WorkCenter can be
triggered by stock in the Buffer to periodically transfer units to the
ShippingArea. Plotting the stock in the dummy Buffer in the composite
element is approximately equivalent to plotting the contents of the simple
ShippingArea that it represents.

E.2.1.3 Gantt Charting

The classic way to summarize state information for a collection of machines
is the "Gantt Chart" (named for Henry Gantt who introduced the scheme in
1917). Essentially, it involves a bar-graph for each machine, synchronized
against a common time-scale. Powerful as the concept is, it is impractical
to do much manipulation of a Gantt Chart with pencil and paper, and even the
various mechanical implementations that have been devised over the years
have made only modest gains in practical utility. However, with modern
computer graphics the full potential of this idea can be realized.

The charting option is essentially an automatically-generated Gantt Chart.
The states of various WorkCenters, Carriers, MaintenanceCenters, and
AuxiliaryResources are plotted over time. An example is shown in Figure E-4.

The chart consists of color-coded blocks to show the length of time each element spends in each different state. The color-coding of the states is the same as for the corresponding states during tracing. The states shown are:

    <u>WorkCenters</u>:
        a. busy processing
        b. idle, no material available
        c. idle, has received X-input, waiting for Y-input
        d. idle, has received Y-input, waiting for X-input
        e. blocked, cannot dispose of output
        f. undergoing maintenance
        g. queued, waiting for maintenance

    <u>MaintenanceCenters</u>:
        a. idle, no service-team active
        b. at least one team providing service
        c. queued, at least one WorkCenter waiting for service

    <u>AuxiliaryResources</u>:
        a. idle, no Resource being used
        b. busy, at least one Resource in use

    <u>Carriers</u>:
        a. upper and lower edges of bar show Carrier state:
            in transit, pickup/dropoff, blocked, wait/hold/frozen
        b. center of bar shows whether loaded or empty.

When the tagging option is in effect (see Section E.3) the Gantt Chart also shows the processing of tagged units by a colored bar superimposed on the normal busy block. The color corresponds to the color of the blocks used to

─────────────────────────────── **Figure E-4** ───────────────────────────────

Example of Gantt Chart

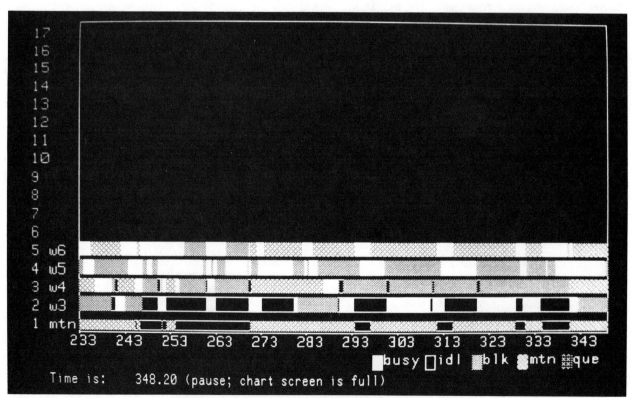

show presence of a tagged unit in the tracing display, and identifies the ReceivingArea that was the source of the unit. The progress of a tagged unit is obvious on the Gantt Chart, and the relative amounts of time spent waiting and being processed is readily apparent.

There are 25 lines on the XCELL+ Gantt Chart. The first 25 WorkCenters, Carriers, MaintenanceCenters and AuxiliaryResources that you create are automatically assigned to lines of the chart, in the order they are created. However, you have complete control over what elements are charted, and the order in which they appear on the chart. That is, you can assign line numbers, from 1 to 25, to any combination of WorkCenters, Carriers, MaintenanceCenters and AuxiliaryResources. You can also expand or reduce the (horizontal) time-scale of the chart.

The charting option is particularly useful in assessing relative balance in utilization between WorkCenters -- bottlenecks are readily apparent in the comparative density of the bars. It is also useful in showing the extent of queuing for maintenance when too few service-teams are available to provide immediate service.

E.2.2 Audible Alarms

Information can also be conveyed audibly by means of a set of alarms. You can turn ON any combination of the following alarms:

-- a WorkCenter becomes blocked (cannot dispose of its output)

-- a Buffer becomes full (blocking the entry of another unit)

-- a batch-mode ReceivingArea becomes empty (and cannot supply a request for material)

-- a batch-mode ShippingArea becomes full (and cannot accept an offered unit)

-- a WorkCenter requiring maintenance cannot get immediate service and is queued.

These alarms are controlled in audible alarms menu, which is accessible from run control.

The audible alarm can be used with any of the different display screens, or when running with "drawing suppressed". The audible alarms are most effectively used to call attention to relatively rare events that might be overlooked in the visual displays. Audible alarms are also useful to give a sense of the frequency of problems in a high-speed production run without visual displays.

Each different type of alarm has a distinctive pitch, which means the different types of problems are identifiable, and problems that propagate through the model often have recognizable sound signatures. This also means that it is probably inevitable that some users will spend time generating melodious factory models. It may, in fact, give new meaning to the process of "tuning a production line".

E.3 Unit Tagging

"Unit tagging" is an optional mode of running. When tagging is turned ON, by pressing the <tagging> key in pause menu, individual units are identified (that is, "tagged") as they are released from a ReceivingArea into the factory. The identity of the unit is preserved as it moves through the factory, until it reaches a ShippingArea or an unordered Buffer -- whichever it encounters first.

When a tagged unit reaches a ShippingArea, the total time that elapsed since its release from its ReceivingArea is recorded. This is generally called its "flowtime" through the factory. Flowtime has two components:

    -- processing-time: the sum of the processing-times of individual
                         operations performed (by Processes) as the unit moved
                         from ReceivingArea to ShippingArea

    -- waiting time: the difference between the flowtime and the
                     processing-time for the unit.

For each ShippingArea, the average value of flowtime, processing-time, and waiting time, for tagged units, is reported in <flowtime> in results menu (see Section E.4).

Although the display screens look somewhat different when tagging is in effect, tagging is a <u>run</u> <u>option</u>, and not a display option. That is, it affects the underlying running of the model, and the way data is collected, independent of what form of display is being used. When you turn tagging ON, it remains ON until you turn it OFF, regardless of what types of display you choose. You can suspend drawing, and tagging will still continue.

When tagging is in effect, and the trace or plot display option is chosen, a square block representing each tagged unit moves through the factory. The block is color-coded to identify the particular ReceivingArea from which it was released into the factory. An example is shown in Figure E-5. The colored tagged block takes the place of the yellow block indicating release from a ReceivingArea and acceptance at a ShippingArea.   The colored tagged block also appears in WorkCenters and Buffers as the tagged unit moves through the factory.

_____ **Figure E-5** _____

Identification of tagged units in the trace display

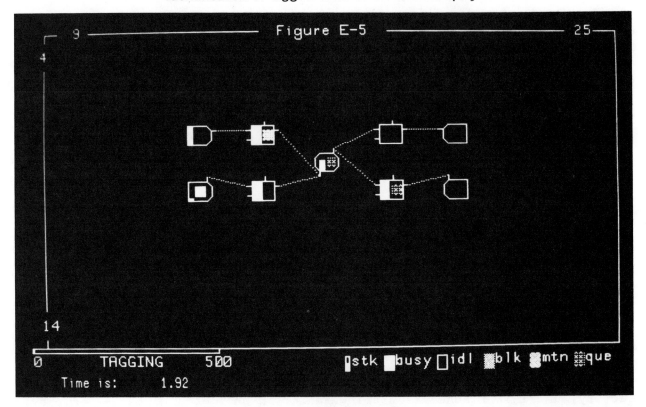

When a tagged unit enters an ordered Buffer, the colored block shows only as the unit initially enters the Buffer. The block disappears when the following (untagged) unit arrives, even though the tagged unit is still in the Buffer. (There may be more than one tagged unit in the Buffer at the same time, so the block indicates only the most recently arrived unit.)

However, the identity of the tagged unit is preserved in the Buffer, and the colored block reappears in the next element downstream on the unit's path, when the unit leaves the Buffer.

Remember that encounter with an unordered Buffer removes the tag from a unit. The unit itself is, of course, preserved, but it is no longer tagged, and on its eventual arrival at a ShippingArea, the flowtime, processing-time time, and waiting time is not recorded.

The frequency of tagging is a characteristic of the particular ReceivingArea where the tagged unit originates. The default frequency is "tag every 10th unit". You can change the frequency in ReceivingArea design. See Section B.4.1.

Tagged units also appear on the Gantt Chart, as a colored overlay on the "busy-block" for a WorkCenter while a tagged unit is being processed. The Gantt chart is particularly useful in showing the relative amounts of processing and waiting time for individual units.

E.4 Results _____

There is a separate **results** menu, accessible from **pause**. In **results** menu, you can <u>display</u>, or <u>print</u>, any of the following types of results obtained from running the model. Both period and cumulative results are given:

-- <u>cost</u> <u>summary</u>; capital and operating costs for each type of element

-- <u>thruput</u>; for each ShippingArea:
        a. units accepted
        b. batch shipments not satisfied ("shortages")

-- work-in-process <u>inventory</u>; for each Buffer, and each batch-mode
            ReceivingArea and ShippingArea:
        a. current total stock (all parts)
        b. maximum stock level (highwater mark)
        c. minimum stock level
        d. average stock level

-- <u>WorkCenter</u> <u>utilization</u>; for each WorkCenter:
        a. percent of time busy
        b. percent of time in setup
        c. percent of time in maintenance (both service and queued)
        d. percent of time blocked (cannot dispose of output)

-- <u>MaintenanceCenter</u> <u>utilization</u>; for each Center:
        a. percent of time at least one team in service
        b. percent of time at least one WorkCenter queued

-- <u>AuxiliaryResource</u> <u>utilization</u>; for each AuxiliaryResource:
        a. percent of time at least one Resource is in use
        b. average number of Resources busy

-- <u>Carrier</u> <u>utilization</u>; for each Carrier:
        a. current status
        b. current location
        c. number of loads carried
        d. percent of time loaded

```
-- flowtime; for each ShippingArea:
            a. number of tagged units received
            b. average (over all tagged units) flowtime
            c. average total processing-time
            d. average total waiting time
```

E.4.1 Period vs. Cumulative Results

A run is divided into time periods of equal length. The default period length is 500 timeunits, but you can change this length in **run controls**. The run automatically **pauses** at the end of each period. The relative position within the current period is indicated as the "period thermometer" of the tracing screen is filled in, from left to right.

Results are collected for the current period. At the end of the period, the period results are added to the cumulative (complete run) results, and the period results are cleared to start over. This does not in any way change the state of the model -- it just clears the counters that keep track of throughput for the period.

Sometimes results for a particular period may appear to be slightly inconsistent. For example, the number of units shipped plus the number in the Buffers and WorkCenters may not equal the number of units received. However, this is just a consequence of the fact that both the number shipped and the number received were cleared to 0 at the beginning of the period (and the numbers of units in WorkCenters and Buffer were unchanged).

E.4.2 Printed Output

There are three different kinds of printed output:

1. Each of the "results", described in the previous section, can be printed, rather than displayed on the screen. The <print> key in the results menu directs information to the printer rather than the screen.

2. The complete model -- structure as well as state information -- can be printed. This is done by the <print model> key in change display mode, which is accessible from main.

3. The screen-image of any of the different displays can be dumped directly to a printer. A screen-dump MSDOS utility is pre-loaded with XCELL+, so all you have to do is press the <Print Screen> key. (This is a permanently-labelled key on the PC keyboard, and not one of the XCELL+ command keys.) Function key f9 will also cause the same action.

E.4.3 Result Output to a File

By default, all XCELL+ printed output is directed to printer-port LPT1. This specification can be changed in <set specs> in change display. Specifying a file name for the PRINTPORT (for example, XLP.OUT) will direct printed output to that file (rather than to the printer). It can be be processed by some other package -- a spreadsheet, or a graphics package, for example.

E.5 Manual Change of State _____

Before the run begins (that is, at time 0) you can manually set the initial contents of Buffers and batch-mode ReceivingAreas. However, note the distinction between changing the number of units in the Buffer (state information) and changing the capacity of the Buffer (structure information). Structure must be changed by going back to **design**, via **main**, while state can be changed in **modify state** mode, reached from **pause**.

Note that by manually changing the state of the factory model you can produce results that are inconsistent. For example, by specifying an initial Buffer content greater than zero you create a situation where more units are reported as shipped than were received at ReceivingAreas.

E.6 Data Collection Practice

When you start the run of a new factory model, it is "empty and idle". That is, all the Buffers, batch-mode ReceivingAreas and batch-mode ShippingAreas are empty, all the WorkCenters are idle, and all Carrier batteries are fully-charged. This is a highly unrealistic state for a factory -- it rarely occurs in real factory operations.

Many simulation studies are concerned with measuring performance of a model under "steady-state" conditions. These are conditions under which results do not depend upon <u>when</u> the measurement is taken. That is, the expected value of capacity measured starting at time T1 should be the same as the capacity measured starting at time T2. However, steady-state in a real factory is almost as unrealistic as empty-and-idle. Real factories are subject to time-dependent demands, machine breakdowns, etc., and are always in a more-or-less transient condition.

Hence, the question of <u>how</u> and <u>when</u> you obtain measurements from your model is important in establishing the validity and significance of those results. It is often useful to measure steady-state performance as an idealized limit on factory capacity, even when you know that realistically such conditions will never exist. However, unless you are conducting a theoretical study such as the one described in Section G.3, you should also be interested in the model's transient behavior. That is, how it responds to <u>increases</u> or <u>decreases</u> in demand, or how it recovers from a period in which there happened to be numerous machine breakdowns. It is very hard to understand a model's transient behavior from printed summaries of statistics, so the dynamic displays of an interactive system such as XCELL+ are particularly valuable.

E.6.1 Initial "Run-in"

Whether you are studying steady-state or transient behavior, the results generated at the beginning of the run when it is more-or-less empty-and-idle are unrealistic, and in general, your results are improved by <u>excluding the data from some initial "run-in" or "warm-up" period</u>. It is advisable to run the factory model for a while until the "pipeline is filled", and something like steady-state is reached, and then begin your measurements. It is hard to advise exactly how long this run-in period should be, but it should certainly last until material has begun to emerge from all ShippingAreas.

The problem is simply that data produced during this unrealistic warm-up time represents circumstances that you probably do not wish to study. Even if you make very long runs, the results are tainted by inclusion of this unrealistic initial performance. You can ignore the first period, but first period data are included in the cumulative data unless you take action to exclude them.

The way to exclude data obtained during the run-in period in to press the <re-start results> key in run control. This clears counters, utilization statistics, etc., and resets the model clock to zero -- but <u>does</u> <u>not</u> <u>alter</u> <u>the</u> <u>state</u> of the model . That is, the status of WorkCenters, the contents of Buffers, etc., is unchanged, preserving the conditions that were achieved by the start-up interval. These conditions now become the initial conditions for the "real run" during which data are collected.

Although it is difficult to specify exactly how long the run-in period should be, there is the general reassurance that even a brief interval is better than none. A simple, consistent practice would be to always start data collection when the system automatically pauses after the first period. (Do this from run control during the pause.) However, the default period length of 500 timeunits may be unreasonable for this purpose, depending on how you scale the timeunits in the model, so it may be necessary to change the period length (also from run control).

E.6.2 Random Number Generation

When any of the options that involve a probability distribution are used, the results of a run depend on a sequence of pseudo-random numbers automatically generated within XCELL+. The particular values in the sequence depend upon the particular "seed" value with which it starts. Given a particular seed, the program generates a certain sequence of random-numbers. Given the same seed again, the program will regenerate precisely the same sequence of random-numbers (so they are not really random at all).

Each time you <re-start run>, in **run control**, the random-number sequence is started over -- with the same seed. Consequently, runs should be precisely reproducible. (The value of the seed is displayed in **run control**.)

To make runs that are <u>statistically independent</u>, to facilitate formal statistical analysis of results, you can supply different seeds by pressing <new random-number seed> in **run control**. To restore the default seed, simply enter 0 as the seed. (Zero is not itself a valid seed.)

Relatively long runs should have very little dependence on the particular random-number seed used to start the run. However, if you are only making short runs -- say to study short run transient behavior -- it is advisable to replicate the run (make additional independent runs with other seeds) to see how sensitive the results are to the particular sequence of random numbers used.

The random-number mechanism is different in Release 4 than in previous releases of XCELL+. In Release 4 each entity that requires a sequence of random-numbers (for example, for processing-times of a particular Process) <u>has its own sequence</u> (where previously, all entities drew from a common sequence, as numbers were needed). This means that the sequence that is experienced by a particular entity is <u>independent of the action of other entities</u>. In most cases, this should reduce the inherent variability of results, and improve the comparability of results between different runs.

F

The File Manager

F.1 The File Manager Menu

There is only one workspace in XCELL+, and this accommodates exactly one factory model, called the "current model". The current model is the only one you can change (in **design**), and the only one you can run (in **run**). However, in the course of a simulation study there will ordinarily be many different versions and copies of the model. For example:

1. During construction of the model, you should frequently store a copy as a "checkpoint" to allow you to recover from all manner of disasters.

2. When exploring various alternatives, you should store the "base" upon which the alternatives are built.

3. During the run of a model, you should store a "starting point" to avoid having to repeat the "run-in" period (see Section E.6.1). (This way, you can afford to use a longer and more effective run-in.)

4. During the run of a model, you should store the status at key points in time, so that you can return and re-start the run from such points -- to run with different options or conditions.

All but one -- the current model -- of these versions and copies will be stored as data files on disk. These are ordinary MSDOS files, and can be moved, copied, and erased by MSDOS commands when you are in the MSDOS environment, rather than the XCELL+ environment. However, XCELL+ has a built-in **file manager** that is self-contained and self-sufficient. It is not necessary for you to leave XCELL+, or to know anything about file manipulation in MSDOS in order to manage the collection of XCELL+ models on disk.

The **file manager** menu is accessible from **main**, in parallel to **design** and **run**. The **file manager** menu is the following:

set log/ batch	merge factory	assign disk	erase file	list files	retrieve factory	store factory

The actions associated with these keys are the following:

<set log/batch> -- to specify the names of the files to be used for
          file-batch arrivals at ReceivingAreas and file-batch
          shipments at ShippingAreas, and the names of the files to
          be used to log arrivals and shipments.

<merge factory> -- to copy one particular factory model from disk to
          the workspace and <u>merge</u> the incoming model with the existing
          model in the workspace

<assign disk> -- to designate which disk drive is to be considered
          the current drive -- where the files that contained stored
          factory models reside. This designation of the current
          disk remains in force until you make another assignment.

<erase file> -- to erase one particular file, on disk, containing a
          factory model.

<list files> -- to list the names of the files containing factory
          models that reside on the current disk drive.

<retrieve factory> -- to copy one particular factory model from disk to
          the workspace (and in the process, destroy the current model
          in the workspace).

<store factory> -- to copy the current factory model from the worksapce
          to a file on the current disk drive. (The contents of the
          workspace are not changed by this action.)

Note: Previous versions of XCELL+ had a <change factory name> key in the
      file manager menu. This seldom used key was moved to **set specs** in
      change display (to make room for <merge factory>). Note however that
      factory name (shown in the top line of the floor display) need not be
      the name of the file in which the model is stored. In fact, since
      most models are stored in a variety of versions and states during the
      course of an investigation, at most one of the files could have the
      same name as the factory itself.

F.2 The Use of Stored Models _____

The obvious reason for storing a model is simply to preserve it from the end
of one session to the beginning of the next. Since the contents of the
workspace are lost when you leave XCELL+ and return to MSDOS, or when you
simply turn off the computer, if you contemplate any further use of the
current model, you must store it on disk before the workspace is lost.

Experienced computer users store their work much more often than only at the
end of each session. They have heard (or experienced) too many horror
stories of failures that have destroyed the results of many hours of work.
Computers can fail, electric service can be interrupted, and there is even
the possibility that the last bug has not yet been eliminated from the
XCELL+ package. The effort required to frequently store the current status
of your work is cheap insurance against painful catastrophes.

In addition to saving these "backup" copies, there are many ways in which
the file system can be used during the course of a simulation study. When a
factory model is stored, it always includes <u>both</u> <u>the</u> <u>structure</u> <u>and</u> <u>the</u> <u>state</u>
of the model. If you store a model during a pause in running the model, you
can later retrieve that model and resume the run from precisely the state
that existed when it was paused prior to being stored. This means that the
file system provides a means with which you can <u>reverse</u> <u>the</u> <u>passage</u> <u>of</u> <u>time</u>
in the running of the model.

For example, suppose you store factory model F in file FN at time T1. That
is, model F has been run from time 0 to time T1, then the run is paused, and

the **file manager** is used to copy the current model F from the workspace to a
file named FN on the disk in the current disk drive. You can then continue
running model F (which remains unaltered in the workspace) to time T2.
Record the results of running the model from T1 to T2. Now retrieve file FN
(destroying model F at T2 in the workspace). The workspace now contains
model F, precisely as it was at time T1. You can now re-run model F, from
T1, with perhaps a different form of display (say, chart rather than trace)
than was used in the previous run from time T1. This can, of course, be
done any number of times.

Alternatively, you can retrieve the model F as it existed at time T1 and
make some change in its structure (by returning to **design**) to create some
variation called model F'. You can then run the model F' from time T1 to
T2, and compare the difference in performance between model F and model F'
when the two models are run over the same time period from T1 to T2.

Most simulation studies involve a comparison of alternative models. In many
cases there is a high degree of similarity between the models. To use your
time efficiently you should develop a base form of the model up to the point
where the alternative forms diverge. Store the base form, and retrieve it
to serve as the starting point for each of the alternative forms.

Since there is only one current model, if you retrieve a stored model you
necessarily destroy whatever had been the current model.   The **file manager**
therefore offers you a last chance to store the current model before it
would be overwritten or destroyed by retrieving another model, but does not
keep track of whether or not you have made changes since the last time you
have stored a model.

If you attempt to overwrite an existing model file with a new one, you will
be asked to confirm this action before it is performed.   That is, you must
confirm that it is, in fact, your intention to destroy an existing model
stored on disk by storing a new model on that disk using the same file name.
(You cannot have two files with exactly the same name on the same disk at
the same time.)

F.2.1 Merging Factory Models

The <merge factory> action (new in Release 4) allows a model incoming from
disk to be merged with the model already in the workspace (rather than
replace the current model, as in <retrieve>). It works as follows:

   -- the display is (temporarily) switched to reduced-scale (to show as
        much of the current model as possible)
   -- you must designate (with the cursor) the cell that will be the
        upper-left corner of the incoming model
   -- specify the name of the file for the incoming model

The incoming model is reduced to the smallest rectangle of contiguous rows
and columns that contains all the entities of the model.   The upper-left
corner of this rectangle is placed at the location you specified. The total
rectangle of the incoming model may overlap occupied cells in the existing
model, but no occupied cell in the incoming rectangle can fall on an
occupied cell of the existing model.

The two models are actually merged as follows:

   1. Default attribute values remain those of the existing model
        (regardless of those of the incoming model).
   2. Names of incoming entities are retained if they do not clash with
        names of the existing models (otherwise new default names are
        assigned).
   3. Part-names (hence Process-names and stock-names) of the incoming
        model are retained if they match Part-names in the existing model
        or if they are unique (not used in the existing model). If they

clash with entity-names of the existing model they are replaced with new default Part-names.

4. Zone-assignments of ControlPoints in the incoming model are preserved, but not the Carrier limits in those zones.

5. The state of the resulting merged model is automatically cleared to initial conditions and runtime 0 (as if <re-start run> were given).

There are many ways to use this <merge> facility:

-- to build and test major sub-models separately, and then merge sub-models for final runs and presentation
-- to easily replicate complex sections of a model
-- to build a library of "standard" factory elements to be re-used
-- to replicate entire factories into the same model (to facilitate making parallel runs with different random-number sequences to assess the inherent variability of results.

F.3 File Names _____

The files in which factory models are stored are ordinary MSDOS data files, and the rules for determining file names are those imposed by MSDOS. The file-suffix for these files is XL4.

MSDOS file names are limited to eight characters. Letters and digits can be intermixed; it is generally good practice to begin each name with a letter. A few special combinations are "reserved" by MSDOS for its own use -- for example, CON and NUL -- and MSDOS will protest if you happen to use one of these. (The reserved names are all three or four characters long.) Certain punctuation characters can also be used in a file name, but not all punctuation characters are legal. (In particular, the period is not legal.) If you do not already know the rules for which punctuation characters are allowed, it is easiest and safest to stick to letters and digits.

No distinction is made between upper and lower case letters in file names. For example:

             FACT23   fact23   Fact23

are equivalent ways of entering the same file name.

As noted above, the file name is not necessarily or automatically the same as the factory name, as shown at the top of the factory floor display window. Factory names can be longer (up to 40 characters), need not be a single word (that is, blank is a legal character), and any punctuation character can be included.

Although factory names and file names need not be the same, it is generally a good practice to choose file names to suggest the nature of the model stored in the file. The file name is often an abbreviation, or acronym, of the factory name, with a suffix identifying the version in this particular file. For example, different versions of a factory model named "Final Assembly Department", might be stored in a sequence of files named "ASM1", "ASM2", "ASM3", etc. A copy stored during a pause in a run at time 500 might be stored as "ASMT500".

Since file names are necessarily short, it is often not possible to make them completely descriptive of the characteristics of the model contained in the file. Consequently, it is often useful to maintain a careful external (paper) record of exactly what model, at what point in time, is in which file.

F.4 Incompatibility between Release 4 and Previous Xcell+ Model Files _____

The file format of a model created by Release 4 of XCELL+ is <u>not</u> the same as the file format of a model created by previous releases. Hence Release 4 cannot directly retrieve a model stored by a previous release. (Release 4 uses an XL4 file suffix to avoid confusion; previous releases used an XLP suffix.)

However, a one-way bridge between the releases is provided in the form of the "XCELL+ File Conversion Program". This is a separate program, supplied with XCELL+, that retrieves a model stored by the previous release, and re-stores it in the form required by Release 4. A model stored by the Conversion Program can then be retrieved by Release 4 and used just as if it had been created by Release 4 in the first place.

There is no comparable return path from Release 4 files to earlier releases, because Release 4 models include features that have no counterpart in earlier releases.

The Conversion Program is external to XCELL+ and is invoked from MSDOS (not from within XCELL+) by giving the command

        XLCONV   <return>

After the program is loaded, and the XCELL+ logo appears on the screen, the menus are very similar to those of the **file manager** in XCELL+. Simply retrieve a model that was stored by an earlier release, and then store that model in another file (in the Release 4 form).

F.5 Auxiliary Files _____

In addition to the disk files that are used to save factory models, there are also several kinds of files used to provide external communication to and from XCELL+.

F.5.1 Batch-Arrival and Batch-Shipment Files

XCELL+ allows batch-mode ReceivingAreas to draw the sequence of arriving batches from a file, rather than have each batch specified individually by hand (see Section B.4). Batch-mode ShippingAreas can similarly draw a shipping schedule from a file (see Section B.5).

The default file names are XLPRABAT and XLPSABAT for, respectively, the arrivals file and the shipments file. Other file names can be specified in the <set log/batch> action of **file manager**.

Each of these batch-files consists of lines of four fields representing:

        arrival-time   cell-name   batch-size   Part-name

For example, the following line in a file of batch arrivals would indicate that a batch of 5 units of Part P is to arrive at ReceivingArea RAP at time 156.32:

        156.32 RAP 5 P

Only the first four fields on any line are read. Any line that begins with an asterisk ("*") is ignored. The lines in the file must be in chronological order -- that is, the time fields must form a non-decreasing sequence. Any line that is erroneous in any way (out of chronological order, non-existant cell-name or Part-name, improper batch-size) will be ignored (no warning given). The run will automatically stop when the file is exhausted.

F.5.2 Log Files

XCELL+ can generate log-files containing the history of unit withdrawals from unlimited-supply ReceivingAreas and unit acceptances at continuous-shipment ShippingAreas (see Sections B.4 and B.5). These files can then be analyzed externally to XCELL+ to determine the supply and demand characteristics of the model.

The default file names are XLPRALOG and XLPSALOG for, respectively, the receiving log and the shipping log. Other file names can be specified in the <set log/batch> action of **file manager**.

When a ReceivingArea is logging, each release of a unit to the factory from that ReceivingArea produces a line in the receiving-log-file consisting of four fields representing:

>   time-of-release ReceivingArea-name batch-size Part-name

When a ShippingArea is logging, each arrival of a unit from the factory to that ShippingArea produces a line in the shipping-log-file consisting of seven fields representing:

>   time-of-release ReceivingArea-name batch-size Part-name
>   "tag"-or-"notag" flowtime processing-time

Both flowtime and processing-time are 0 for an untagged unit.

Each log-file contains a header line (starting with "*") identifying the factory and the time of the run.

F.5.3 Files for Printed Output

XCELL+ can produce three different forms of printed output:

   1. <print description> in **change display** to print the equivalent of the
      <detail display> screens
   2. <print results> in **results** to print various types of run results

   3. key f9, at any time, to print the current screen image.

By default, all XCELL+ printed output is directed to printer-port LPT1. This specification can be changed in <set specs> in **change display**. Specifying a file name for the PRINTPORT (for example, XLP.OUT) will direct printed output to that file.

G

Examples of the Use of XCELL+

The use of XCELL+ continues to increase -- in education, research and industrial practice. Many courses, both in engineering and busiess, can now have hands-on laboratory exercises where before they could afford only descriptive and vicarious treatment of simulation. By drastically reducing the time required for students to become adequately competent with the tool many courses in production engineering and production management can now afford the time to actually make simulaton assignments. There can now be a more appropriate emphasis on the <u>results</u> rather than the <u>tool</u>, and there may even be time to address the difficult issues involved in proper conduct of an experimental investigation (see Section H).

XCELL+ is, of course, not alone in this campaign. Other simulation packages, with similar objectives, have appeared in the years since the original XCELL proved the possibility and utility of this approach. At the moment, SEE WHY and SIMFACTORY seem the best of the competition.

G.1 Use in Industry

It is still early to draw any definite conclusions about the impact of packages like XCELL+ on the industrial practice of simulation, but use is expanding -- especially now that XCELL+ has the full-scale professional support of Pritsker Corporation.

The "simulation industry" in general seems to be prospering, with increasing attendance at the major conferences. Of course, the increased cost/effectiveness of computing in general, and the graphics power of modern workstations deserve most of the credit, but the broadened user base made possible by packages like XCELL+ must have made some contribution.

Two different types of industrial usage seem to be emerging. First, there is "rough cut" modeling by simulation professionals who, in many cases, will then go on to program a conventional simulation model in one of the general-purpose simulation languages. For example, at WSC 86 the keynote speaker, Frank Babel of the EDS division of GM, showed a movie characterizing the practice of manufacturing simulation in EDS/GM. The movie showed the use of (an early version of) XCELL for "first stage" modeling, followed by detailed modeling in a general-purpose language.

For the most part, simulation professionals seem to regard packages such as XCELL+ as <u>complementing</u>, rather than competing directly with the general-purpose simulation programming systems. Initial modeling in XCELL+

helps screen out problems that are not ready for modeling, and identifies particular aspects of problems that need to be modeled in detail.

The second type of industrial use is by engineers and managers, on their own, independent of the simulation specialists. This was, of course, the original target audience for XCELL. The only fair statement is that the jury is still out on this type of usage. It is still not clear whether or not "do it yourself" simulation of manufacturing systems is possible, and if possible, whether or not it has yet been achieved. Many of the simulation specialists remain (predictably) skeptical, and stress the difficult aspects of the modeling task that are not eliminated by simplifying the construction of the model. There is general concern for the risks of putting a powerful tool in the hands of inexperienced users. One presumes that COBOL programmers in the MIS group felt the same way about spreadsheets, with some justification, but nevertheless the outcome of that development has been highly beneficial.

Primary usage of XCELL to date has been for the planning of new production facilities, and to evaluate proposed major changes in existing facilities, as one would expect. However, there is growing interest in the use of "fast model builders" as a communication tool between sales engineers and clients. If a model can be constructed quickly, it can facilitate understanding of both the problem and the proposed solution.

One common theme that has emerged in almost all of the industrial experience with XCELL+ is that elapsed time is a critical problem in simulation, often more important than the considerable cost and effort of conventional simulation studies. In all too many cases, the previous simulation tools have not been able to deliver answers in time for them to be useful. Many users seem quite ready to trade detail for response time, and to that audience in particular, packages like XCELL+ offer great promise.

G.2 A Classroom Case

The following mini-case-study has been used in a production and operations management course in the Johnson Graduate School of Management at Cornell. XCELL, rather than XCELL+, was actually used for the assignment, but none of the differences between the two systems is significant for this study. The students had no previous experience or instruction in simulation, and only a few minutes of classtime were spent preparing them for the use of XCELL.

A book of more substantial cases, involving use of XCELL or XCELL+, by Professors John O. McClain and L. Joseph Thomas of the Johnson School, has been published by the Scientific Press.

G.2.1 Study of a Gudgeon Production Line

The Problem

The Gudgeon Systems Manufacturing Company (GSM, Inc.) has redesigned its complete line of gudgeons and is planning a new manufacturing facility for this line. Through careful design, the new gudgeons can be produced with only two operations.

The second operation can be fully automated, and they propose using one of Yamazaki's new MAZAK Gudgeon Gougers -- the GG20 model. The GG20 has a nominal capacity of 20 gudgeons per hour. There is little variability in cycle time on the GG20 and the quality is essentially perfect. It will probably not even be necessary to inspect the output from the GG20. On the other hand, the GG20 is a very new and complex machine, and the Yamazaki engineers warn that GSM should expect random shutdowns after an average of 3 hours of run time. The maintenance crew will then have to replace the gouger module, which takes almost exactly 30 minutes.

The first operation represents quite a different situation. In spite of GSM's best engineering efforts, it is still highly variable in both cycle time and yield, due primarily to the inherent variability of the density of the silicon bronze castings. They expect to use Universal U14 Milerators for this operation. The U14 has an average processing time of 8 minutes per gudgeon, but tests have shown that any time between 5 and 11 minutes is equally likely to occur. However, the worst aspect of the operation is that fully 30% of the pieces will be defective after the first operation and will have to be discarded. On the good side, the U14 is a highly reliable machine and they do not expect it to suffer any breakdowns.

GSM envisions a production line with several U14s feeding a single GG20. Schematically it will look like the following:

The following questions need to be answered with regard to this production line:

(1) How many U14s are needed, operating in parallel, to match the performance of a single GG20?

(2) How much storage space should be provided for work-in-process inventory between the U14s and the GG20?

(3) What will the average effective production rate of this line be?

It has also been suggested that they use U16s instead of U14s. A U16 costs 50% more than a U14, but has a scrap rate of 15% and processing times that vary from 3 to 7 minutes per piece. Would this be a more effective machine for the first operation?

At some future time, assuming that GSM prospers and that the new design increases their share of the gudgeon market, they will need to increase the capacity beyond a single line. The obvious way to do this is to duplicate the initial line. However, assuming that there is only a single repair crew for the GG20s, two lines may not have quite twice the capacity of one line. How serious will this loss become as a third line is added and then a fourth, etc.? At what point should a second repair crew be added?

It has also been suggested that when the time comes to increase capacity they should not just duplicate the initial line, but rather should add a second GG20 and additional U14s to the existing line, all sharing a common storage area for work-in-process inventory. How much more (or less) effective would this plan be compared to duplicate lines?

G.2.2 A Student Solution to the Gudgeon Production Problem

The following analysis of the Gudgeon case was prepared by Rudy S. Chou and Douglas Salz, both students in the MBA program at the Johnson School. It is reproduced here, with their kind permission, essentially as they submitted it.

Report to: <u>Gudgeon Systems Manufacturing, Inc.</u>
by
Rudy S. Chou and Douglas Salz

EXECUTIVE SUMMARY

Our taskforce has studied the available options for the gudgeon manufacturing facility carefully, and we have come up with several conclusions regarding the facility. In analyzing the initial manufacturing line, we found that we will need four U14's to keep one GG20 running at full capacity. If U16's are used, only two of these machines will be needed. Comparing the two options reveals that choosing the U16 as the first machine in our line will be beneficial from both a cost and efficiency standpoint.

We also examined the scenario in which our market share for gudgeons increases substantially. The options available are to duplicate the existing line or use one buffer area and add additional U14's or U16's to accommodate additional GG20's. Our research indicates that one buffer area and additional machines to supply added GG20's will save buffer space and reduce the number of machines needed to keep the GG20's running at full capacity. Also a second repair crew should be added when the facility uses more than four GG20's.

ANALYSIS

Our first task in designing a new gudgeon manufacturing facility was to find out how many U14's are needed to match the capacity of one GG20. Statistically speaking, one GG20 working at full capacity would have a cumulative percentage time busy of 85.71%. This number was derived by taking the mean time between breakdowns (3 hours) and dividing this by the sum of the mean time between breakdowns and the repair time (.5 hours).

EXHIBIT A. Effects of Number of U14/U16's on GG20 Performance

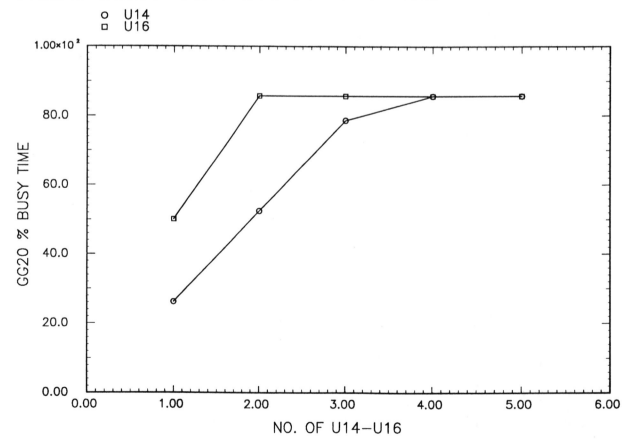

Once we knew that our task is to ensure an 85.71% GG20 busy time, we ran
simulations with one, two, three, and four U14's. The results are shown in
Exhibit A.   The simulation with four U14's was the first to produce an
85.71% busy time for the GG20. Since three U14's produced a percentage busy
time for the GG20 that was significantly lower than our target (78.5%
compared to 85.71%), we can conclude that it will take four U14's to run one
GG20 at full capacity. The average effective throughput for this line will
be 17.14 units per hour. In all the above simulations, the buffer was made
big enough (50 units) to ensure that it would not be a factor in the GG20
percent time busy.

Since our engineers envision a line with three U14's feeding one GG20, we
next examined the dynamics of this type of manufacturing line.   We have
already simulated a system exactly like this one when we explored how to run
one GG20 at full capacity. Consequently, we knew that the numbers we were
looking for were approximately 78.75% GG20 percentage busy time and 15.75
units for average throughput per hour. We ran this simulation for five
different buffer sizes, and the results are graphed on Exhibit B.   The
simulations for buffer sizes 50 and 20 resulted in the GG20 being run at
full capacity. We then tried buffer size 15, and it resulted in the GG20
being run at a lower capacity. After these simulations, we concluded that
the buffer size required to run one GG20 at full capacity with three U14's
is between 16 and 20 units. The exact number is insignificant due to the
following discussion on the U16's.

Our next task was to analyze a gudgeon manufacturing facility that used
U16's instead of U14's. The U16 costs fifty percent more but is more
production efficient. We want to determine if the U16 was a better choice
than the U14.

We knew from our U14 simulations that we were looking for approximately
85.71% busy time for the GG20 with an average throughput of approximately

EXHIBIT B. Effects of Buffer Capacity on GG20 Performance for Different Manufacturing Lines

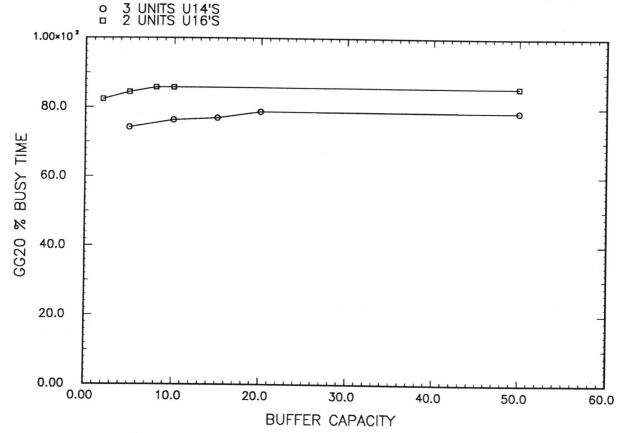

o   3 UNITS U14'S
□   2 UNITS U16'S

17.14 units per hour. We started by simulating one U16 with one GG20. This showed a GG20 percentage busy time and an average throughput well below our target numbers.   The next simulation contained two U16's and gave us the results we were looking for (see Exhibit A) and showed that it would take two U16's to keep one GG20 operating at full capacity. The buffer size was kept large enough in both the above simulations to ensure that it did not affect the GG20 percent busy time.

The correct buffer size was the next factor we examined for the U16 line. Simulations were run for five different buffer sizes. The results showed that the buffer size required to keep the GG20 at full capacity is an area that is between six and eight units large. Exhibit B shows the relationship between buffer size and GG20 capacity.

Our conclusion for our initial manufacturing line is that the best option is two U16's supplying one GG20 with a buffer size of approximately seven units. Since it would cost 50% more for a U16 than a U14, two U16's equal three U14's in cost. Comparing these two systems reveals that the U16's would require about one-half the buffer area while allowing the GG20 to run at full capacity. The U14's would inhibit GG20 percentage busy time by about 8%. In addition, more defective parts will be produced if U14's are chosen instead of U16's. This suggests additional cost disadvantage for U14's.

Our next analysis was addressed to facility expansion in case there is a significant increase in our gudgeon market share.   We first tried duplicating an original line of four U14's and one GG20. We could not duplicate the number of U14's because of the constraints of the software [NOTE: they were using the educational version which allows only a few processes] but we got around this by using an unlimited material input into

EXHIBIT C. Effects of Maintenance on Effective Total Throughput

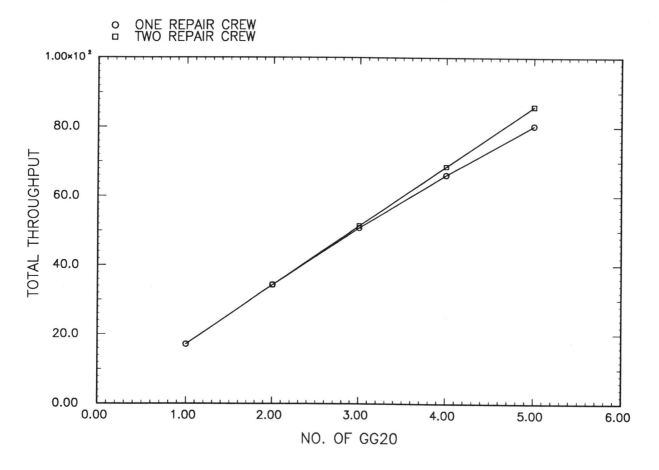

the buffer.   This simulates the actual situation because once the line is operating, the buffer will never be empty and throughput time is not affected by the U14's since they are always feeding enough into the buffer to keep the GG20 operating at full capacity.

We simulated 2 through 5 duplicate lines with one maintenance crew and discovered that the effect of only one maintenance crew was first felt at three lines.   The additional output units per hour in going from two to three lines is 99.7% of theoretical GG20 capacity (17.14 per hour); while going from three to four lines, the additional GG20 yields only 88% of its theoretical capacity.   Adding a second maintenance crew at four lines brings the GG20's back up to full capacity. The results from simulation are presented in Exhibit C.

The last situation we examined was the comparing of duplicating the initial line to meet increased capacity versus having one large buffer area servicing additional GG20's and U14's or U16's as needed.   We again could not simulate this on the computer [due to the limits of the educational version] but we were able to use some calculations with numbers already available.   One U14 can support one GG20 to run at approximately 26.25% of its full capacity (disregarding breakdowns).   This was calculated by taking the avarage acceptable production of one U14 per hour and dividing it by the full capacity per hour of one GG20 ((7.5 x 0.7)/20).   The same calculation can be done for the U16 and it can support one GG20 to run at approximately 51% of its full capacity.

The actual full capacity for one GG20 was determined previously to be approximately 85.71% busy time. Knowing these facts enables us to determine how many U14's and U16's will be needed to keep additional GG20's operating at full capacity. The results are graphed on Exhibit D and show that using

EXHIBIT D. Effects of Different Designs on the Minimum Number of U14/U16's Required

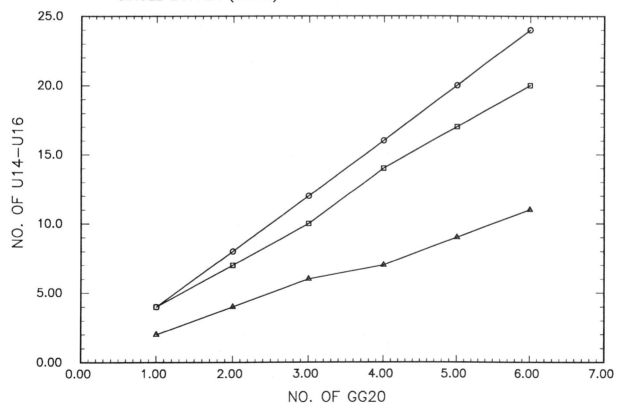

one large buffer area is a more effective way of increasing production than to duplicate the initial line.   For example, four GG20's would require sixteen U14's or eight U16's to keep the GG20 busy at all times if we duplicated the original line. If we choose the one buffer area alternative, only fourteen U14's or seven U16's will be needed.   The one buffer area option would reduce aggregate buffer space while at the same time use less machinery and this would increase efficiency and profits.

G.3 Research on the Role of Work-in-Process Inventory ___

This section describes an example of the use of XCELL+ to study <u>general issues</u> in manufacturing systems, as opposed to the study of one specific manufacturing problem.   The particular results described below represent the starting point of what has grown into a major investigation of the role of work-in-process inventory.

This has also been the topic of student assignments in both operations management and manufacturing engineering classes at Cornell. The assignment essentially coerces the students into discovering for themselves the relationship between throughput capacity and line length, and between throughput capacity and buffer size. Using XCELL+, this becomes a routine weekly exercise, rather than a massive term project.

The example described below concerns work-in-process inventory, but there are many other issues that could be comparably examined -- for example, maintenance policies, scheduling of shared machines, line balancing, alternate-routing schemes.

Inventory -- particularly work-in-process inventory -- is, of course, a timely topic. WIP used to be considered a useful mechanism for a variety of purposes:

        -- reduction in leadtime

        -- buffer between consecutive operations to cushion variability
             in processing times

        -- buffer against variability in process yield

        -- buffer against machine breakdown.

Recently, however, WIP has become the scapegoat in discussions of the many problems that beset American industry, and various knights are leading crusades to eliminate it. Curiously, like many theological debates, this one is innocent of any solid evidence regarding the issue -- in this case, quantitative information about the potential value of well-placed, well-managed work-in-process inventory.

Consequently, inventory is an appropriate and easily motivated topic for a student assignment, which might take the following form:

        Consider the role of work-in-process inventory in counteracting
        variability in processing time. Conduct a brief simulation study
        that will give some insight into the phenomenon.

One might procede as follows.

First, measure the "cost" of variability in terms of reduction in throughput of a production system. This can be done by comparing the throughput of production lines of different length. For example, consider four production lines that differ only in length, as shown in Figure G-1. Initially, assume that all the Buffers shown have zero capacity.   Assume that all the

Figure G-1

Comparison of four sequential production lines

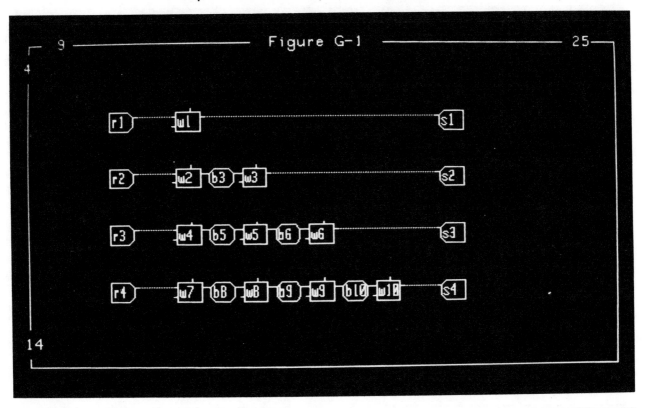

machines, in all the lines, are identical with respect to processing-times -- that is, each has the same probability distribution from which the individual processing-times are drawn.

Note that if there were no variability in processing-times, each of these four lines would then have exactly the same production rate. However, with variability there will be interference between adjacent machines. For example, consider the middle machine in the three-machine line in Figure G-1. When this machine finishes working on a particular unit, it cannot dispose of the finished unit until the next machine is ready to receive it -- that is, until the next machine has finished its current unit. Consequently, whenever by chance the middle machine has a shorter processing-time than the last machine, then the middle machine is temporarily "blocked" and must wait before disposing of its output.

Similarly, whenever the middle machine happens to have a shorter processing-time than the previous (first) machine, then the middle machine is temporarily "starved" and must wait for the first machine to finish its cycle. (The middle machine can, of course, be both blocked and starved at the same time.) The point is that <u>any</u> <u>time</u> <u>any</u> <u>machine</u> <u>spends</u> <u>either</u> <u>blocked</u> <u>or starved</u> is lost forever and causes a reduction in the throughput of the line. A typical situation during execution is shown in Figure G-2.

It would be reasonable to expect the amount of such stochastic interference to increase with the number of machines. In other words, the throughput should be a <u>decreasing</u> <u>function</u> <u>of</u> <u>the</u> <u>number</u> <u>of</u> <u>machines</u> in the line. The purpose of a simulation study might be to see <u>how</u> <u>fast</u> the throughput decreases with increases in line length.

In addition to the length of the line, the amount of stochastic interference will certainly depend on the particular distribution of processing-times.

Figure G-2

Sample state during execution of four line models

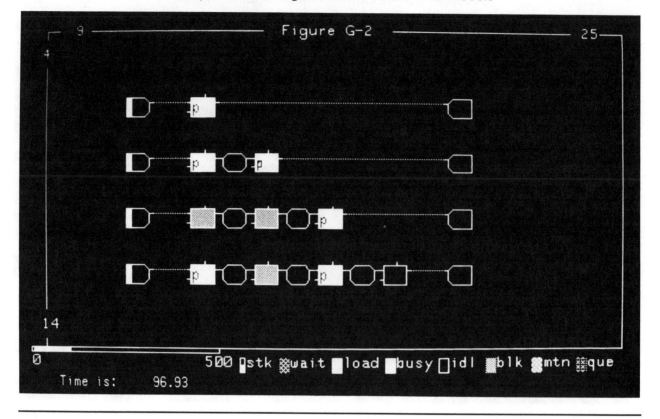

In this case, suppose we choose a uniform distribution over the interval from 5 to 15 -- that is, every processing-time between 5 and 15 is equally likely to occur. This situation, in which the minimum processing-time is 50% of the mean processing-time, and the maximum processing-time is 150% of the mean, is perhaps greater variability than should be observed in well-engineered operations. But it is nonetheless a reasonable place to start such a study, to see what the effect would be for such an extreme level of variability.

The model was run in the following way. Data for the first 500 timeunits (fifty times the mean processing-time) were discarded, to allow each line to approach steady-state operation. (See Section E.6.1.) Then a single run of 10,000 timeunits was made. The run actually included lines of eight and twelve machines, in addition to the four lines shown in Figure G-1. The results were the following:

number of machines in sequence	units completed in 10,000 timeunits
1	1017
2	854
3	812
4	784
8	766
12	754

These data are plotted in Figure G-3, in terms of performance relative to the throughput of the single-machine line.

Figure G-3

Throughput of unbuffered sequential production lines

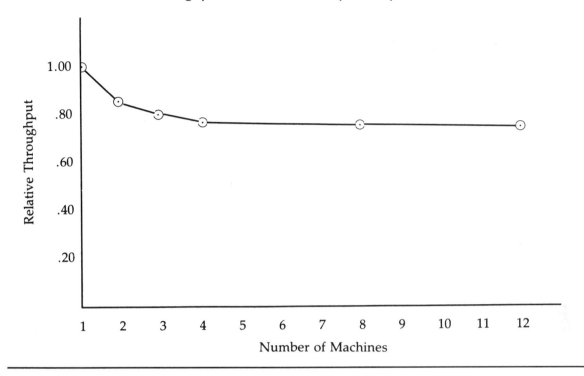

These results are quite surprising. Most people, when asked to predict the shape of this curve, expect a lower final asymptotic value, and much slower approach to that asymptote. Even though the processing-time distribution used in these tests has a higher degree of variability than would normally be encountered in well-engineering operations, the loss due to stochastic interference is very modest -- at most a reduction in throughput of 25 percent, even for very long lines. Moreover, almost all of the loss occurs in the first three machines of the line.

It would seem as if the behavior of such idealized production systems should be well-understood by every factory designer -- as a starting point in understanding the behavior of more complicated, and time-dependent systems.

The next question is the effect of the introduction of non-zero buffer inventory between the machines of such sequential lines. Consider the four-machine line in Figure G-1, as being long enough to be interesting, and short enough for convenient study. Now make a series of runs for different values of buffer capacity. In each run, the capacity of buffers B8, B9 and B10 is identical. Again, the results are based on a run of 10,000 timeunits, after discarding data for an initial 500 timeunit run-in. The results were the following:

capacity of buffers	units completed in 10,000 timeunits
0	784
1	925
2	948
4	972
8	990
16	998

These data are plotted in Figure G-4, in terms of performance relative to the throughput of an unbuffered, four-machine line.

These results are also surprising, both in the magnitude of the improvement achievable with small buffers, and the rapidly diminishing returns on increased buffer sizes.

They would suggest the following hypotheses, to be subjected to more elaborate testing:

1. Stochastic interference can be important between tightly-coupled (unbuffered) machines. However,

   a. the magnitude of the production loss is modest -- probably less than 25% unless the processing is wildly variable, and

   b. this is a short-line phenomenon, not increasing in proportion to line length.

2. Stochastic interference can be effectively eliminated by very small buffers between consecutive machines. Two units of buffering, or at most three, is all that can be justified for this purpose.

We have, in fact, pursued the matter considerably further, and these conclusions appear to be usefully robust -- that is, very similar results are obtained under a wide variety of conditions and assumptions.

There are many interesting variations of this problem. For example, consider the following questions:

--- **Figure G-4** ---

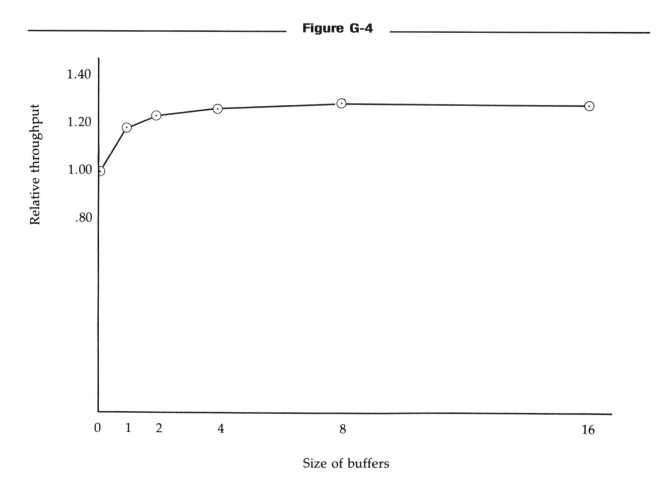

1. Suppose you were not constrained to have all buffers between machines have the same capacity. What would be the most effective allocation of a fixed total buffer capacity over the three possible locations (in a four-machine line)?

2. Suppose you could have only one buffer (in a four-machine line). Which of the three locations would be most effective?

3. Suppose the machine capacities were not perfectly balanced, as they were in this example. How would that affect the placement and effect of buffers?

4. Suppose you have three equal buffers of very large capacity in a four-machine line. How would the average contents of the three buffer compare?

5. Suppose there are two different parts being produced on the same four-machine line. That is, there are Processes for P and Q at each of the four WorkCenters, and stocks of P and Q at each of the three Buffers. How does Buffer capacity interact with Process switching to affect the throughput of the line?

There are also analogous studies to be made to evaluate the effect of buffers for other purposes.

Useful insight into an important problem can be obtained from the simple exercise described above -- yet the total "investigation" could be conducted by an experienced XCELL+ user in less than an hour, and even by a complete novice in less than two hours.

What is particularly intriguing is how the availability of a simple experimental tool -- e.g. XCELL+ -- has awakened interest in the experimental investigation of generic problems in manufacturing. In principle, the necessary models could have been programmed years ago; in practice, no one did so until the tools became easy to use.

H

The Conduct of a Simulation Study

Simulation "packages" like XCELL+ are revealing an underlying truth that has previously been obscured by the difficulty of constructing models, which is

> The process of effectively constructing a factory model, and using that model to learn something interesting about the factory is a challenging intellectual task. It requires a combination of competence, ingenuity and experience that is neither intuitively obvious nor trivially learned.

The risk inherent in packages like XCELL+ is that they place a sharp tool in the hands of inexperienced users. There is some prospect of accomplishing useful work, but also some danger of frustration, if not injury. You might consider this section the "possibly hazardous to your health" warning on the XCELL+ package.

While this User's Guide cannot really conduct a short course on the gentle art of simulation, it can at least warn you regarding some of the more common hazards in the undertaking. We have necessarily oversimplified the issues, but hope to at least provoke you to think about them. More complete and careful presentations are cited in the References.

H.1 Strategy, Tactics and Mechanics

The success of a simulation study depends upon decisions at three levels -- which we might separate as strategy, tactics and mechanics. Strategic issues are unquestionably more important than tactical issues, and tactics more important than mechanics. If you are studying the wrong questions, it doesn't greatly matter how you conduct the study, and if you conduct the study poorly, it matters little how you model the elements of the factory. But user's guides in general, and this one in particular, concentrate on the detailed mechanics of modeling and can thereby improperly suggest that these are the critical points.

Section H seeks to slightly redress that balance by mentioning some of the tactical issues in simulation, but unfortunately there seems to be little one can say in general about strategy.

One strategic issue that certainly should be clarified in each modeling exercise is whether the model itself is the goal of the process, or whether the model is constructed to yield useful information. Unless one is concerned with the model itself, it is hard to understand the effort that is sometimes expended building models that <u>look</u> like the real factory. It is even harder to understand the value of being able to rotate the model in three-dimensional space and view it from any angle. This issue is also related to scale and degree of detail, which are discussed in Section H.3.

Fundamentally, modeling is undertaken to <u>guide you in making changes</u> in the real factory, or in the design of a future factory. If a modeling exercise does not suggest some improvement that can be made in the real factory, it is more likely a failure in modeling than a testimonial to the perfection of the real thing. Once you understand this, you realize that the dominant virtues in a model are the <u>ease</u> <u>with</u> <u>which</u> <u>it</u> <u>can</u> <u>be</u> <u>changed</u>, and the reliability with which it <u>predicts</u> <u>the</u> <u>effect</u> <u>that</u> <u>change</u> <u>will</u> <u>have</u> on performance. It is much more important that the model predict the direction of performance change correctly than it is to reproduce the behavior of the existing factory. Relevant points are discussed in Sections H.3 and H.4.

The overriding goal of factory modeling is to obtain <u>insight</u> <u>into</u> <u>how</u> <u>the</u> <u>manufacturing</u> <u>process</u> <u>works</u> -- simply because this offers the best hope of stimulating ideas for changing it. There is currently some reaction to the interest in graphics and animation in simulation -- some critics say it is a fad and a gimmick, at best useful for debugging the model. They are simply wrong. The traditional statistical output of a simulation run may confirm that Workcenter 5 is blocked more often than it should be, but an interactive graphical system will be more effective in figuring out <u>why</u> it is blocking, and how that blocking can be alleviated. Animation alone is not adequate; there must be means of summarizing information as well. But a simulation system today without effective dynamic graphical displays is at a substantial disadvantage in the crucial task of making its users wiser.

H.2 The Design of Experiments _____

The "design of experiments" is a substantial and well-developed topic in the field of statistics. While we (long ago) had some training in the subject, we do not use the formal procedures of experimental design in our stimulation studies, and do not believe that the neglect of such procedures is a major problem in manufacturing. Consider the different conditions in our environment, compared to those in agriculture, biology, and psychology upon which the statistics of experimental design is based:

1. We exercise complete control over our experimental media. We can perfectly reproduce an "observation". We suffer drought and pestilence only of our own construction. We masochistically introduce variability, rather than spend our energy trying to overcome it.

2. We can experiment <u>sequentially</u>, examining each observation before planning the next, since we do not have a long germination or gestation period.

3. The magnitude of variability, relative to the effects we seek to measure, is probably an order-of-magnitude smaller.

4. The cost of our observations is relatively small.

In spite of these differences, there are probably ways the techniques of experimental design could be used to make our investigations more efficient, but this somehow does not seem to be as important as many other issues facing manufacturing simulation.

Undoubtedly, the topic in experimental design most relevant to simulation in manufacturing is the <u>exploration</u> <u>of</u> <u>response</u> <u>surfaces</u>, as used in chemical engineering. Assume that the yield Y of a manufacturing process is a function of the values assigned to a set of k control variables v1, v2, v3, ..., vk, as well as certain uncontrolled random phenomena. Ignoring variability, the values of Y represent a surface in k+1 dimensional space, and our task is to explore that surface and to discover the values of the control variables that result in a optimum value of Y.

The simulation model gives us an experimental means of exploring this space. Each run of the model, using a particular set of values of the k control variables, yields a single value of Y -- the elevation of one point on the response surface. Our experiment consists of crawling over this mountain in the dark, seeking to follow ascending gradients to higher and higher elevations.

Variability means that the surface is somewhat spongy, and one must take care to distinguish between lumps in a swamp and true uphill progress.

The shortcoming in this paradigm is that while chemical engineers are presumably interested in climbing natural mountains, manfacturing engineers are interested in building higher mountains (or, more precisely, higher models of mountains).

Our experiments are only partly involved in changes in parameters; changes in structure are at least as important. It is nonetheless useful to keep in mind that a simulation is fundamentally a device to obtain a measurement Y (or a variety of measurements Y1, Y2, ...) for a specific set of values for the control variables. The useful way to think about the process, and a useful way to present results, is to relate a particular measurement Yi to changes in a particular control variable vi -- that is, to vary the control variables one at a time. For example, consider the figures in Section G.

Most of the methodology literature in simulation is based on this underlying view. It is concerned with reducing the length of the run required to achieve a given quality of the measurement of Y, or conversely, to improve the quality of measurement of Y for a given length of run. Such matters are of more interest to professors than practitioners, the latter presumably understanding that terrain where such matters are critical is inherently unprofitable.

H.3 The Scale of the Model _____

The factory modeling world suffers from a curious malady, the origins of which are not clear: for some reason many people automatically assume that, to be useful, a simulation model of a manufacturing process has to be a full-scale model -- that is, a model with a one-to-one relationship between the elements of the model and those of the real factory. For example, if the factory consists of two hundred machines and if it produces five hundred different products over the course of a year, then the model ought to also have two hundred machines, and be run long enough to experience at least some production of each of the five hundred products. A simulation model of less than "full dimension" would generally be considered not adequately realistic.

For some reason, this malady of full-scale modeling seems less virulent among other types of designers. Many other fields routinely deal with scale models and partitioned models, particularly in the early stages of a design study. For example, naval architects perform tank tests on small-scale hull models, even though hydrodynamic phenomena are highly non-linear and prediction of full-scale behavior based on model performance is very complicated and potentially risky. Aircraft designers exploring airflow over a proposed airframe, will initially simulate airflow over separate subsystems -- wing-sections, weapons pods, etc. The point is that in many other fields full-scale and complete-system modeling is not automatically considered the only valid approach to simulation.

The situation is essentially the same for computer simulation of manufacturing systems. It is not always necessary to do full-scale, complete-system modeling, and even when you will eventually wind up with that type of model, it is often not the best way to start. There are obvious risks associated with studying a scale-model. There are less obvious, but nonetheless real, risks associated with "over-modeling": the model takes longer to build, longer to run, and is generally harder to understand.

Even problems that eventually will have to be subjected to full-scale modeling, should initially be attacked in sections, with scaled-down dimensions, and with many other radical simplifications. It is often the case that you don't really know what the problem is, or where the problem is, until after you have done some preliminary modeling. Packages like XCELL+ are uniquely appropriate for such initial studies, and even if it is later necessary to construct a model that is larger, or more detailed, in a general purpose modeling language, such as SLAM II, SEE WHY or SIMSCRIPT, the total cost of the two-phase study may well be less than that of a all-at-once, full dimension frontal assault.

In general, modeling is an example of what computer scientists describe as a "worse than linear" process. The work involved is more than proportional to the size of the model. In fact, it is probably close to a quadratic process -- when you double the size of the model, you quadruple the overall cost of the process. Moreover, this applies both to the construction of the model, and to the conduct of experiments using the model. This means that when you decide that your model must have one hundred elements, and cannot be approximated with fifty, you may well have committed yourself to a month's work rather than a week's work.

The general rule is that you should try to use the smallest model with the least amount of detail that will provide the required information, and not automatically assume that you must build a full-scale model with as much detail as your modeling tool will permit. For example, just because XCELL+ has facilities with which you can model machine breakdown, this does not mean that every model you build has to reflect the reality of breakdowns. Although presumably all machines have some probability of breakdown, in many studies this may not be a relevant or significant part of the problem and should therefore be omitted from the model.

Try to remember that the KISS principle applies: do everything you can to

"Keep It Small and Simple".

H.3.1 Partitioning and Scaling

There are basically two ways to keep a model small: partitioning and scaling. Partitioning simply means studying sections of the factory separately, rather than trying to do it all at once. There are both parallel and serial partitioning strategies.

Serial partitioning means to study successive stages in the manufacturing process separately. Look for "natural fault-lines" along which to partition the model into stages. Presumably, everyone recognizes the obvious partitions by geography or organizational boundaries. But there are also partitioning opportunities within what is apparently an integrated manufacturing process. For example, a large buffer that can be assumed to always have some material, but never be filled to capacity, is a potential partition point. The processing upstream of the buffer constitutes one model, with the buffer represented by a Shipping Area. The downstream processing constitutes a second model with the buffer represented by a Receiving Area. A bottleneck machine can also provide a useful point-of-partition.

Parallel partitioning is simply recognition that many factories consist of replications of a basic production unit -- there are two or more copies of essentially the same production unit, operating in parallel to achieve the required volume. Unless these parallel units interact in a significant way -- by sharing maintenance facilities, for example -- it may be adequate to build a model with only one unit. This may seem obvious, but we wouldn't mention it if we hadn't seen the opportunity for partitioning of this type so often ignored. For example, suppose you are studying the performance of an automatic storage and retrieval system for a warehousing operation. If the relevant issue is the relationship between the bin assignment algorithm and the average pick-time, does your model have to have twelve parallel bays -- just because the real warehouse will have twelve bays?

Scaling is more subtle, and often takes more ingenuity and courage. For example, suppose you are concerned with the capacity of a multi-station assembly line that produces batches of different products. Say the issues are such things as inter-station buffer capacity, treatment of rework, provision of parallel stations where reliability is a problem, and the effect of batch size on time lost in setup. Assume the real factory will consist of a hundred stations and will produce several hundred products. We would nevertheless start with a model of, say, a ten-station line producing five different products. We would experiment extensively with this model, and try to understand its behavior thoroughly, before even considering building a bigger model. There are three possible outcomes of this preliminary study:

1. The problem proves so difficult you cannot understand it, or find improvements, even on the scale-model. It is very unlikely that you will do better on a larger model, so you might as well give up on this approach.

2. You come up with such an ingenious modification that it will have obvious benefit for lines of any length, or any mix -- so it is not necessary to build a full-scale model.

3. You come up with a proposal that needs to be tested on a larger, or more detailed model.

With the first two outcomes, you avoid full-scale modeling altogether. Even in the case of the third outcome, you begin construction of a larger model with much better understanding of what is important and how the model is going to be used.

Scaling is applicable in many different ways. For example, suppose the real process you are modeling deals with units in fixed batches or lots -- say with a lot-size of 100. You can use the various batching and triggering mechanisms to represent this quite realistically. However, the first question you should ask is whether it would be possible to let each XCELL+ "unit" represent a lot of 100 real units. This would probably reduce your effort in constructing the model, and it will certainly result in a drastic reduction in the time required to run the model.

H.4 Tests of Validity

It seems patently obvious that a factory model must be "valid" in order to be useful, but it is surprisingly difficult to come up with a clear and precise definition of validity in this context. Unfortunately, what it often means is that, as a preliminary exercise to establish the validity of the model, you must attempt to reproduce some period of performance of the real factory. This necessarily involves you in both full-scale modeling and real-data collection, so if you are inescapably pledged to the validity check ritual you are probably also doomed to run a large model on real data. Conversely, if you can manage to avoid either one-to-one representation or real-data collection you can probably also avoid the formal validity check.

The basic problem with the typical validity check is that it really isn't much of a confirmation of validity. In order to produce results that are recognizably similar to those of the target system you will probably have to "adjust" either the structure of the model or the way in which it is run, or both, to an extent that should give you trouble with your conscience if not your supervisor.

An additional shortcoming of the validity check is that even if it were, it would be largely irrelevant. The purpose of the simulation study is presumably to predict the performance of variations of the factory that do not now exist. While it is to some degree reassuring to be able to recognizably model the factory as it does exist, this provides no guarantee that the altered model truly predicts the performance of the factory that might some day exist. This prediction is still a matter of judgment and faith. The validity check ritual that presumably strengthens that faith also consumes a scarce resource -- time and cost -- that could often be better invested.

All of these issues -- dimension, data and validity -- arise in a fundamental misunderstanding of the purpose of a simulation study, and the nature of the potential result of such a study. The value of a model lies in what it does for the modeler, and not in what the model itself can do. The model should help the modeler understand how a system works and yield insight as to what the critical aspects are. In some cases, much of this "education" occurs in the process of constructing the model, and it is almost irrelevant whether or not the model runs at all -- much less whether it can reproduce actual performance.

The usual way a model performs this magic is by showing direction -- that is, by indicating that if you make a certain type of change, performance will get better or get worse. By doing this repeatedly, you get a sense of the shape of the "response surface" of system performance and some idea of how sharp the peaks and precipices are in that surface. All this depends upon differences in performance between two versions of the model, and the credibility of such differences is not tremendously enhanced by spending a great deal of time trying to reproduce actual history.

H.5 The Use of "Real" Data

It is not always possible to base a simulation study on "real data", and not always necessary, even when it is possible. It is, however, always painful, slow and costly to use such data. Therefore, you should resist the temptation, or the instructions, to collect real data with all the ingenuity you can muster. The collection process is much more difficult than you can imagine, and the result is much less valuable than you might think. Even in the real (that is, non-academic) world, there is life without real data. We offer the following assertions and suggestions:

1. It is often possible to obtain useful and practical results from a simulation study with no real data whatever.

2. To the extent that you must collect real data, postpone doing so until you have exhausted every possible trick for avoidance. The collection of real data should be a desperate last step in the study, rather than a mandatory preparatory phase (as so often seems to be the practice). At least postpone collection until after the model is built, so you can experimentally determine what data are necessary, and what degree of quality is required.

3. When you are finally forced to start collecting, collect as little data as you can get away with, from the easiest source available. The utility of the final results of the study depends so little on either the quality or quantity of the data that you should waste as little time as possible in its pursuit.

4. Understand that the collection of real data has more to do with giving the impression of reality to those inexperienced with simulation, than with enhancing the utility of the results.

For example, consider the data regarding processing times for a particular
operation P. The real issues are the following:

1. Does the processing time vary significantly from one repetition of
   the operation to the next? That is, is it a <u>constant</u> or a
   <u>random</u> <u>variable</u>? Use some common sense in answering even this
   question. For example, if your model involves both machine-paced
   and manual operations, it may be adequate to represent the time
   for a machine-paced operation as a constant, since even if there
   is in fact some variability (say, due to material hardness) it is
   probably negligible compared to the variability of the manual
   operations in the model.

2. What is the magnitude of variability, relative to the mean value?

3. What is the relative frequency of "short times", "average times",
   and "long times"?

Suppose you construct the model, and make preliminary runs with different
assumed values for the processing times of operation P.   Suppose these
runs indicate that varying the mean processing time of P from 3 minutes to
10 minutes has no apparent effect on the overall throughput of the line
(although it will affect the utilization statistics for the Workcenter on
which P is performed). How much time are you willing to spend to collect
data to establish that the processing time of P is approximately normally
distributed with a mean of 6.932 minutes and a standard deviation of 1.704
minutes?

Suppose you know that the mean processing time is 7 minutes and the issue
is the relative degree of variability. Try making one run with processing
times uniformly distributed between 1 and 13, and another run with times
uniformly distributed between 5 and 9. Depending upon the effect this has
on the property being measured, decide how much effort is appropriate to
determine the "true" distribution.

A similar approach can be taken to the form of the distribution. It is
easy to make runs with uniform and exponential distributions (having the
same mean).   If you cannot distinguish between the results using these
extreme choices of distributions, how much effort is justified to
determine whether the real data are Weibull, Erlang or Exponential?

The general (Ramberg-Schmeiser) distribution available in XCELL+ is
primarily an argument-ender rather than a useful facility.   For cases
where the form of the distribution is really significant, or for users who
are skeptical of sensitivity arguments, like those given above, the
general distribution will surely suffice, but we suspect it is rarely
needed.

But suppose, for one reason or another, you have to collect some
processing time data.   Few people who have not had the misfortune of
trying to collect real data in a manufacturing shop can believe how
difficult the process is. First you start with the hope that someone else
has already collected the appropriate data and you have only to discover
where the data are. It would seem that since processing time represents
money, surely the cost accountants would have the data you need. But
remember that "distribution" and "variance" have another meaning to
accountants, and that their data have been selected, adjusted, aggregated
and otherwise massaged to serve purposes of their own.   You could easily
end up with data that are undeniably "real", but essentially worthless for
your purposes. Borrowing "production control" data will prove to be only
slightly less frustrating.

So finally, in desperation, you get a stopwatch and go out to collect data
of your own -- always assuming that this is an existing process and not a

prospective one.   You should eventually be   able to accumulate a pile of
data that are about as real as data can be.   But you might pause to wonder
whether the operator you observed is representative of all operators,
whether the ambient temperature affects the times, whether the frequency
of bent leads that had to be straigtened was typical, etc. In other
words, you now have a real sample from which you can infer information
about the characteristics of the underlying distribution.   Just because
your sample is real doesn't mean it is typical or useful. Nonetheless,
you now have some real data, and naive listeners can sometimes be
encouraged to believe that your simulation results are more valid because
encouraged to believe that your simulation results are more valid because
of its presence.

In general, whenever you are driven to collect "raw" data -- either by
direct observation, or by extraction from existing databases -- you will
find that it must be "edited" before it can be used. Editing is some
combination of selection, filtering, or otherwise "cleaning it up".   It is
a highly subjective process in which you impose your conception of
reasonableness upon what was ostensibly real.   Consequently, as a
practical matter, "reality" is more a question of degree of editing or
abstraction, than an absolute property. Once you understand this you tend
be a bit more liberal in your data collection practices.

The alternative to real data is presumably "artificial" data, generated
from "standard" distributions.   But even when data are synthesized in this
way, presumably the parameters of the distribution are chosen to reflect
properties of the real system. Hence the difference between edited real
data, and artificial data from distributions with realistic parameters is
more one of degree than of absolute principal. The proper way to pose the
question is "What degree of reality?" do you need in your data.

One useful way to reduce your data collection task is to invert the sense
of the problem. For example, suppose your task is to determine whether
one or two repairmen is required to service a certain group of machines.
The answer obviously depends on the mean-time-between-failure of the
machines. The obvious way to proceed is to collect data to determine that
the mean is approximately M, and then run your model to learn that for M,
the best number of repairmen is, say, one.   Alternatively, before you
collect any data at all, use your model to determine the transition value
M' between the one-repairman region and the two-repairman region.   That
is, find M' such that for all values of M less than M', the answer is one
repairman. It may then take much less careful data collection to learn
whether the actual value of M is greater than or less than M'.

Finally, be wary of using the exponential or other highly skewed
distributions for anything except breakdowns in simulation of a
manufacturing process. True, there is evidence suggesting that this is a
fundamental distribution in nature. If you are studying the arrival of bees
at a hive, or time between telephone calls, it is reasonable to assume that
times are exponentially distributed. On the other hand, in manufacturing
there are presumably industrial engineers whose job it is to make sure that
processing times are not exponentially distributed.   (In a crude model, the
rare long times in an exponential distribution might be considered to
represent rework or breakdown, but there are more realistic ways in XCELL+
to represent those phenomena.) The exponential distribution is beloved of
queuing theorists for the same reason that mathematical programmers like
linear cost functions -- it makes their life much easier, whether or not it
is the best approximation of reality.

H.6 Data Collection and Analysis _____

The funniest part of many simulation studies is the solemn announcement that the result is "statistically significant at the 5% (or whatever) level". There are a few situations where such reassurance is appropriate, but more situations when it is pretentious and confusing. For example, suppose you have conducted a careful comparison of designs X and Y, and have discovered that only under special and unlikely conditions is X marginally better than Y. Unless you are writing a thesis you surely don't want to report that

> "We have established that X is significantly better than Y (at the 5% level)."

The important result is that

> "We have determined that Y is effectively as good as X under all conditions, and is better under the conditions most likely to be encountered."

However, this is not meant to excuse you from understanding the meaning of statistical significance, or to entirely relieve you of the burden of assuring your readers that you have not been deceived by variability. As an absolute minimum, you must replicate your principal runs -- repeat the runs using a different seed in the random number generator. This will give you some idea of the inherent variability of your measurement process. Unless the difference between alternative X and alternative Y is large compared to the difference between alternative X with seed 1 and alternative X with seed 2, you probably haven't learned anything worth reporting.

In general, the formal acceptance or rejection of a statisical hypothesis has little place in a simulation study. Suppose, for example, that you are comparing the results Ra and Rb of two variations, A and B, of some model. Assuming that the structural difference between A and B is non-trivial and worth testing, you know, a priori, that there is some difference in behavior between the two systems -- perhaps miniscule, but nonetheless real. If, therefore, you fail to reject the hypothesis of difference between Ra and Rb, you are simply reporting that either the experimental conditions or the run lengths were inadequate to detect the difference. On the other hand, if you do reject the hypothesis of difference, there is either a big difference, or you have a marvelously precise measurement tool -- and the reader gets to guess which is the case.

In conclusion, we offer several variations of the infamous Conway-Maxwell Axiom of Significance in Simulation:

> If you need a formal test of statistical significance to establish the importance of your result, you are doing research and not manufacturing engineering.

> The inherent approximation in your model is at least as great as the statistical variability, so if you need formal statistics to prove your result, don't believe it.

> If you can't see it with the naked eye, forget it.

APPENDIX 1

Dimensional Limits

There are two different sizes of XCELL+, with different limits on the number of each type of element that can be included in the model. The limits are the following:

	Production Version defaults	Educational Version limits	XLPSPECS code	Element size (bytes)
Factory floor:				
rows	40	40		
columns	60	60		
WorkCenters	60	16	WK	262
Processes	240	64	PC	154
links (input and output to Processes)	600	600	LK	8
Buffers	80	80	BF	80
stock (particular Part at a Buffer)	300	300	ST	62
Requests/Deliveries	500	500	RQ	8
Parts	240	16	PT	12
units (tagged, and in ordered Buffers)	800	800	UN	32
ReceivingAreas	50	50	RA	122
ShippingAreas	50	50	SA	136
MaintenanceCenters	25	25	MF	70
AuxiliaryResources	25	25	AX	54
ControlPoints	99	32	CP	136
Destinations	800	800	DN	6
PathSegments	800	800	PS	30
Carriers	100	100	CR	64
Zones	100	100		
Entities*	800	800	ENT	

Entities are the total number of WorkCenters, Buffers, ReceivingAreas, ShippingAreas, Processes, stocks, MaintenanceCenters, AuxiliaryResources, ControlPoints and PathSegments.

When any of these limits is reached, you are automatically placed in **file manager** menu so you can store the current version of the model. The XCELL+ session then terminates. You must restart the system, and then retrieve the model you stored -- presumably to simplify it so you can stay within the dimensional limits.

These dimensional limits on the Production Version (but not the Educational
Version) can be changed by providing an XLPSPECS file. This is a file named
XLPSPECS that resides in the same directory as the XLP program (the XLP.EXE
file). This file consists of lines that begin with an XLPSPECS code (given
in table above) and the number of elements of that type. For example, a
file consisting of the following lines:

        WK 100
        PC 300
        CP 0
        CR 0

would increase the limits on WorkCenters and Processes by using the memory
space that would normally be used for ControlPoints and Carriers.   The
XLPSPECS file allows you to reallocate the available memory to better match
the requirements of your particular model.   Element types not referenced in
the XLPSPECS file use the default dimensions. The total space (size times
limit) for any single element type cannot exceed 64K. Any line that begins
with an asterisk ("*") in the XLPSPECS file is ignored.

The current model limits can be viewed by pressing the <see/set specs> key
in the change display menu.

The XLPSPECS file can also be used to set the "device" to receive all
printed output and the type of printer to be used. The device is set by a
line in the file of the form:

        PRINTPORT <device>

where "<device>" is either the name of a "port" (to which a real printer is
attached) or a file (when output is to go to a file rather than a real
printer). The default value of PRINTPORT is LPT1. For example, to direct
all printed output to a file named XLP.OUT the XLPSPECS line would be:

        PRINTPORT XLP.OUT

The type of printer can be specified by an XLPSPECS line of the form:

        PRINTTYPE <printer>

where "<printer>" is replaced by one of the following:

        HP-LASERJET   IBM-PROPRINTER
        HP-THINKJET   IBM-GRAPHICS
        HP-QUIETJET   EPSON-FX85/185
        HP-82905B

        OKIDATA-ML84   DIABLO-34LQ
        OKIDATA-ML92/93   NEC-P6/P7
        OKIDATA-ML182/183   TOSHIBA-P351C

The file XLPPRINT.CFG (supplied with XCELL+) contains tables describing
these printers. XLPPRINT.CFG must be present in the same directory as the
XLP.EXE and XLPSPECS files.

APPENDIX 2

Summary of Menus

This Appendix describes, in outline form, the XCELL+ menu-tree. Each line corresponds to an action key, and represents another menu if there are lines indented underneath it. In each menu the keys are listed as they appear in left to right order (corresponding to keys F1 to F8). In some cases, a particular key can have several different actions, depending upon the current state of the model and the run controls. In such cases, all the alternatives are listed, with the alternatives after the first marked with a "/". For example, in **change display** menu, key F7 is <reduced scale> if the display is currently in normal scale, and <normal scale> if the display is currently in reduced scale.

Not all of the options listed below are always available. For example, when there is no current model in the workspace, the **analysis**, **design**, and **run** modes are not accessible. The labels for the corresponding keys do not appear on the screen, and the keys are ineffective.

The **HELP** menu, accessible from many points in the menu-tree, is not shown in this outline. Its role is obvious, and it only returns to the menu from which it was entered. Similarly, the <return> action always associated with key F8 is omitted from the outline.

Main session control

    change display
        refresh display (clear the screen and re-draw the model)
        display detail (display single cell in detail)
        change view (shift the origin of the display window)
        change Areas (specify Floor Areas)
        print description (print the contents of all detail displays)
        see/set specs (display system dimensions; change factory name)
        reduced scale (change from normal to reduced scale display)
        /normal scale (change from reduced to normal scale display)

    analysis
        structural check
        flow analysis
        bottleneck analysis

    new factory (clear the workspace and prepare a new factory model)

```
design
    cell-cursor on an occupied cell:
        refresh display (clear and re-draw the model)
        display detail (display single cell in detail)
        change all ... (enter Tabular Editor)
            print table
            change all in factory (for column selected)
            change all shown (for column selected)
            change one (single element, single value)
        copy cell (create a new element like the cell-cursor element)
        remove cell (clear the cell)
        move cell (move the cell-cursor element to another cell)
        change cell (enter design sub-menu for particular element,
                except when positioned on PathSegment)
            change PathSegment
                detail display
                change (entire) Path
                    suppress draw (omit symbols for entire Path)
                    /resume draw (draw symbols for entire Path)
                    change traverse-time for Path
                    change travel direction
                    make Path automatically reversible
                change transit-time (single Segment)
                change cost (all Segments of all Paths)
                change Carrier (if Carrier present)
                    change speed
                    change relative speed of all empty Carriers
                    change cost (of all Carriers)
                add/remove Carrier

    cell-cursor on an unoccupied cell:
        add WorkCenter (WorkCenter design)
            detail display
            options
                suppress draw (omit symbol for this element)
                /resume draw (draw symbol for this element)
                change name
                change capital cost
                change operating cost
            maintenance
                assign MaintenanceCenter
                random failures
                    change to scheduled maintenance
                    no maintenance
                    exponential failure-rate
                    general failure-rate
                    exponential repair-times
                    constant repair-times
                    general repair-times
                scheduled maintenance
                    change to random failures
                    assign MaintenanceCenter
                    no maintenance
                    set maintenance interval
                    exponential service-times
                    constant service-times
                    general service-times
            remove Process
            add/copy Process; change Process (Process design)
                display detail
                AuxiliaryResources
                    assign resource 1
                    assign resource 2
                processing-times
```

```
                    uniform distribution
                    exponential distribution
                    finite-normal distribution
                    constant times
                    general distribution
                    change parameters
                    setup-times
                            group code
                            major-setup
                            minor-setup
                input
                        X-input
                        Y-input
                output
                        multiple units
                                single unit
                                change number
                        reject-output
                                scrap rejects
                                recycle rejects
                                rework rejects
                                change % rejects
                                drift
                                        initial %
                                        rate of change
                                        reset limit
                        normal-output
                switching control
                        trigger-high
                        trigger-low
                        batch-size
                        priority

    add Buffer (Buffer design)
        detail display
        options
                suppress draw (omit symbol for this element)
                /resume draw (draw symbol for this element)
                change name
                change capital cost
                change operating cost
        request, delivery, order, capacity
                specify request
                        change level
                        change Part
                        assign source
                        assign destination
                specify delivery
                        change level
                        change Part
                        assign source
                        assign destination
                CONVEYOR
                /minimum holding-time
                FIFO order
                LIFO order
                capacity
            delete stock
            create stock
            initial stock

    add ReceivingArea (ReceivingArea design)
        detail display
        options
                suppress draw (omit symbol for this element)
                /resume draw (draw symbol for this element)
```

```
            change name
            change capital cost
            change operating cost
      change Part
      tagging
            sampling frequency
            tagging on/off
      arrivals
            regular-batch ON/OFF
            manual-batch ON/OFF
            file-batch ON/OFF
            batch-size distribution
            time between batches
            storage-capacity
            logging ON/OFF

add ShippingArea (ShippingArea design)
      detail display
      options
            suppress draw (omit symbol for this element)
            /resume draw (draw symbol for this element)
            change name
            change capital cost
            change operating cost
      assign/change Part
      shipments
            regular-batch ON/OFF
            manual-batch ON/OFF
            file-batch ON/OFF
            batch-size distribution
            time between batches
            storage-capacity
            logging ON/OFF

add MaintenanceCenter (MaintenanceCenter design)
      detail display
      options
            suppress draw (omit symbol for this element)
            /resume draw (draw symbol for this element)
            change name
            change capital cost
            change operating cost
      number of teams

add ControlPoint (ControlPoint design)
      detail display
      options
            change zone
            change limit (limit on Carriers in zone)
            Holding (make this a HoldingPoint)
            Charging
                  time to charge (charging-time)
                  run time (full-charge run-time)
                  reserve time (reserve run-time)
                  charging ON/OFF (make this a ChargingPoint)
            change capital cost
            change operating cost
      pickup/dropoff connections
      change Paths
            add new Path
                  add ControlPoint to terminate Path
                  back up 1 Segment
                  abort Path
            remove top Path
            remove right Path
```

```
                              remove bottom Path
                              remove left Path
                              change Path
                                     change top
                                     change right
                                     change bottom
                                     change left
                        traffic-control
                              detail display
                              rules for loaded Carriers
                                     wait/not wait for dropoff
                                     set destination sequence
                                     balance load by destination ON/OFF
                                     route Carriers by Part
                              rules for empty Carriers
                                     wait/not wait for pickup
                                     skip N empties
                                     set destination sequence
                              manual/automatic traffic-control
                              change Carrier speed
                                     change all transit-times
                                     change relative speed of empty Carriers
                                     change Carrier cost
                              change transit-time
                        add/remove Carrier

                  add AuxiliaryResource (AuxiliaryResource design)
                        detail display
                        options
                              suppress draw (omit symbol for this element)
                              /resume draw (draw symbol for this element)
                              change name
                              change capital cost
                              change operating cost
                        number of resources

      file manager
            merge factory
            assign disk (designate one disk drive as "current" for models)
            erase file (erase one file containing a factory model)
            list files (list all files containing factory models)
            retrieve factory (copy model from disk file to workspace)
            store factory (copy model from workspace to disk file)

      run
            paused:
                  tagging (turn on tagging of sample units)
                  /stop tagging (turn off tagging of sample units)
                  display detail (display single cell in detail)
                  controls
                        audible alarms
                              alarm on WorkCenter blocked
                              alarm on Buffer full
                              alarm on ReceivingArea empty
                              alarm on ShippingArea full
                              alarm on MaintenanceCenter queued
                              no alarms
                              all alarms
                        re-start results (clear results; leave state)
                        re-start run (clear results and state)
                        new random-number seed (supply new seed)
                        display options
                              trace display
                              chart display
                              plot display
```

```
        change view (shift the origin of the display window)
        period length (change the length of the run period)
modify state (manually change state individual elements)

results
        print results (dump display to printer)
        costs
        thruput
        work-in-process inventory
        utilization
                AuxiliaryResource utilization
                WorkCenter utilization
                MaintenanceCenter utilization
                Carrier utilization
        flowtime
begin run
/resume run

running:
        suspend draw (let model run without updating display)
        /resume draw (resuming updating display)
        one step (advance run by all events at this point in time)
        slower (insert an artificial delay between display updates)
        faster (remove an artificial delay between display updates)
        auto run (run procedes automatically)
```

APPENDIX 3

Summary of Changes in Release 4

Release 4 of XCELL+ (XCELL+4) is a major new release with many new features. In particular, XCELL+4 enhances the productivity and conveniece of XCELL+ for experienced users and larger models, without in any way eroding the ease-of-initial-entry for neophyte users. This Appendix summarizes these changes relative to the previous Release (3.1).

System Size
Although the size of the XCELL+4 program is substantially larger, a major revision of the overlay structure has <u>reduced</u> the program memory requirement. This means that even though the size of the data-structure for most entities (see Appendix 1) has increased, XCELL+4 can, in general, accommodate slightly larger models. (The new overlay structure can be further exploited, so future releases can make additional improvements in this regard.)

Files
XCELL+4 uses a DOS file-suffix of "XL4" (rather than "XLP" as in previous releases). XLP factory-files cannot be retrieved directly by XCELL+4, but a separate XLP-to-XL4 conversion program is available. See Section F.4.

Model Compatibility
XCELL+4 is <u>almost</u> fully upward-compatible with previous releases. The only difficulties are the following:
   1. The change in the method of assigning random-numbers to different entities (see item 7 below) means that <u>results</u> from runs will, in general, not be identical.
   2. A ControlPoint serving as a HoldingPoint ("empty-HOLD" in previous terminology) in XCELL+4 cannot also have a pickup-link, a dropoff-link, an empty-WAIT option, an empty-SKIP option, or a full-WAIT option. The file conversion routine will automatically delete such links and options from a ControlPoint with the empty-HOLD option.

Major New Facilities

1. The Tabular Editor
   In design, many entities of a particular type can be viewed at one time, in a tabular (spreadsheet) form, and changed with a "full-screen editor". See Section B.1.1.

2. Default Attributes
   You now have the option of changing many of the default attributes (the values assigned to newly-created entities). See Section B.1.1.1.

3. Floor Areas
    You can now identify (with background colors) different sections
    of the factory model, and place identifying labels on these
    sections. See Section A.7.

4. File-Merge
    You can now merge a factory model from disk with the model already
    in the workspace (rather than necessarily replacing the workspace
    model). See Section F.2.1.

5. Materials Handling Zones
    The materials handling network (ControlPoints and Paths) is now
    partitioned into "zones", each of which has a limited capacity of
    Carriers. See Section B.9.5.

6. Materials Handling Battery-charging Facilities
    A ControlPoint can be designated as a "ChargingPoint", and Carriers
    can have a limited run-time between rechargings. See Section B.9.6.

Additional Features
    7. Separate Random-number Sequences
        Each entity requiring randon-numbers now has its own sequence -- a
        change that should permit a substantial reduction of the variability
        of results. See Section E.6.2.

    8. Process Creation
        A new Process can now be made by copying an existing Process at the
        same WorkCenter. See Section B.2.1.

    9. Initial Stock in Buffers
        The initial stock-level in a Buffer can now be specified during
        design (in addition to the option of setting it manually at the
        beginning of each run).

    10. Minimum Stock in Buffers
        The system now keeps track of the minimum (as well as the maximum
        and average) stock of each Part in each Buffer.

    11. Stock-levels in ReceivingAreas and ShippingAreas
        The system now keeps track of the minimum, maximum and average
        stock in each (batch-mode) ReceivingArea and ShippingArea.

    12. Blocking Statistics
        The amount of time each WorkCenter spends in the "blocked" state
        is now recorded and reported separately.

    13. The CONVEYOR Option for Buffers
        There is now a CONVEYOR option (functionally equivalent to a
        FIFO order with minimum-holding-time) with a distinctive display
        symbol for Buffers.

Changes in Terminology and Presentation
    14. The various menus are now called "menus" (rather than "modes").

    15. "Maintenance Facilities" are now called "MaintenanceCenters".
        There is no change in the way they are used.

    16. All of the entity-types are now spelled without blanks: "Receiving
        Area" is now "ReceivingArea", "Control Point" is now "ControlPoint",
        etc.

    17. What was a "hold-only Control Point" is now a "HoldingPoint". A
        HoldingPoint is now dedicated to that purpose -- it can no longer

also have pickup or dropoff-links, or the empty-SKIP, empty-WAIT, or full-WAIT options.

18. Displays now show only the option-in-effect at the moment.
    For example,
                "empty Cars <WAIT> for pickup"
                        rather than
                "empty Cars <WAIT><not wait> for pickup"
    In general, user-changable parameters are shown on displays in capital letters, enclosed in "< >", as <WAIT> above.

19. The number of loaded Carriers enroute to a ControlPoint now includes a loaded Carrier at that ControlPoint.

20. Most of the 3-line, yellow-background detail overlays have been redesigned and reformatted.

21. Most of the error messages have been revised for greater consistency. (In general, consistency in abbreviations, capitalization and punctuation has been improved.)

22. The detailed-display and results-displays have been drastically reformatted (to reduce the amount of vertical screen-scrolling required, and condense the volume of paper required when these screens are printed).

23. The <change symbol> key in each sub-menu of design is now <options>.

24. Results regarding the flowtime of tagged units have been moved from <thruput results> to a separate key and screen.

25. All of the HELP screens have been updated, and HELP is now available in many more menus.

APPENDIX 4

Computer Hardware Requirements
and Startup Instructions

<u>Required Hardware:</u>

A machine compatible with an IBM PC/AT with at least 640K of memory
Hard disk
Enhanced Graphics Adaptor (EGA) with at least 256K of memory
EGA-compatible color monitor
5.25" or 3.5" floppy-disk drive
MSDOS 2.1 or later

<u>Loading XCELL+ into the computer:</u>

For 3.5" diskettes:
        Insert the disk labeled "XCELL+ Release 4.0" into the drive
        Type   A:INSTALL
        Follow the screen instructions in the installation program

For 5.25" diskettes:
        Insert the disk labeled "Diskette A XCELL+ Release 4.0"into
            the drive
        Type   A:INSTALL
        Follow the screen instructions in the installation program
            (i.e., for using diskettes A and B)

<u>Running XCELL+:</u>

Set the default disk-drive to be the hard disk drive, and make "XLP"
the current directory. Then type XLP

To load one of the demonstration factories (from the main menu):

        type: f6   (to change to the file manager menu)
                f5   (to list the factory models available)
                f6   (to retrieve one of the models)
                name ENTER (one of the model names listed on the screen)

<u>To simulate (execute) the demonstration model:</u>

        type: f8   (to leave the file manager menu)
                f7   (to enter the run menu)
                f7   (to prepare to run)
                f7   (to actually begin automatic execution)

At this point you can speed-up or slow-down the execution, using keys f5 (slower) or f6 (faster). After a specified time period the execution will pause. You can either continue the execution (by again typing f7) or examine results, as described below.

To examine simulation results:

At any point during a simulation run, you can pause and examine results up to that point by:

```
type:   f8              (to pause the execution)
        f6              (to switch to the results menu)
           f2           (to display a cost summary)
           f3           (to display a throughput summary)
           f4           (to display a work-in-process summary)
           f5           (to display various types of utilization)
           f6           (to display a summary of unit flowtime)
           f8           (to leave results menu and return to run menu)
```

To build a new model:

Follow the keyscript instructions given in Section A.5 of the User's Guide.

To exit XCELL+ at any point:

Press key f8 repeatedly until the prompt for key f7 reads "REALLY QUIT"; then press key f7. This returns control to the MSDOS operating system.

APPENDIX 5

A General Probability Distribution
(Ramberg-Schmeiser)

A general probability distribution is provided for situations in which none of the standard, built-in distributions (Uniform, Exponential, Finite-Normal and Constant) provides an adequate representation. The general distribution can be used as a source of random times for:

    1. processing times for Processes (see Section B.2.1.3)

    2. time between failures for Maintenance (see Section B.2.2)

    3. time to repair in Maintenance (see Section B.2.2)

The Ramberg-Schmeiser distribution is used. This distribution was developed specifically for use in simulation studies, with concern for both the efficiency of generating random observations on a computer, and the generality of the distribution forms available.

Special cases of the R-S distribution give exact representations of the Uniform and Constant distributions. Appropriate R-S parameter choices give very good approximations to the following types of distribution:

Exponential	Normal	Lognormal	Student's T
Weibull	Gamma	Beta	

    Even U-shaped distributions can be obtained by appropriate choices
        of parameters.

    Most distributions of empirical data can also be approximated by a
        suitable Ramberg-Schmeiser distribution.

The particular form of R-S distribution is specified graphically. The density function is displayed, showing possible values and their relative frequencies. The values of the mean, variance, minimum and maximum of the distribution, as well as the current values of the four R-S parameters ("Parm 1", "Parm 2", "Parm 3" and "Parm 4") are also shown. (These four parameters determine the shape of the R-S density function.)

You can alter the shape of the R-S density function either by changing the value of the parameters directly, or by "re-shaping" the distribution by "shifting", "scaling", "skewing", etc. You must judge the suitability of a particular R-S distribution from the appearance of the density function, and the values of the mean, variance, minimum and maximum. There is no provision to formally "fit" a R-S distribution to a given set of data.

<u>Characteristics of the Ramberg-Schmeiser Distribution</u>

The R-S distribution is defined on the finite interval (Min,Max) where Min>=0. There are four parameters:

Parm1   A <u>location</u> parameter that positions the distribution, but does not alter its shape or width.

Parm2   A <u>scale</u> parameter that sets the width (Max-Min).

Parm3, Parm4   <u>Shape</u> parameters that control the skewness and kurtosis (tail intensity).

The R-S distribution is <u>symmetric</u> when Parm3 = Parm4.

The correspondence between the R-S distribution and other standard distributions is the following:

R-S parameters:

	Parm1	Parm2	Parm3	Parm4
Uniform	mean	1/(mean-Min)	1.0	1.0
Exponential	0	-.00058/mean	0	-.00058
Finite Normal	mean	1/(mean-Min)	.1349	.1349
Constant	mean	mean/2	0	0

The values of Min and Max depend on the values of all four parameters. Also, when you change the other parameters there are some automatic adjustments made to Parm1 to ensure the Min is non-negative. The Min and MAx values are determined as follows:

Parm3	Parm4	Min	Max
>0	>0	Parm1-1/Parm2	Parm1+1/Parm2
=0	>0	Parm1	Parm1+1/Parm2
>0	=0	Parm1-1/Parm2	Parm1
=0	=0	Parm1	Parm1

There are three different approaches to specifying a particular R-S distribution:

1. automatic specification of an R-S distribution "like" one of the standard distributions

2. direct assignment of values to the four parameters

3. "reshape" operations that alter the parameters indirectly.

At each stage in specification, the current R-S density function is displayed, along with the values of the four parameters, and the resulting values of Min, Max, mean and variance.

The details of this process are the following:

If P is the random variable of the R-S distribution, and U is a uniformly distributed random number [0,1], then

P = Parm1 + (U^Parm3 - (1-U)^Parm4)/Parm2

where ^ means exponentiation.

The mean of P is

Pmean = Parm1 + (1/(1+Parm3) - 1/(1+Parm4))/Parm2

The variance of P is

Pvar = (C - A^2)/Parm2^2

where A = 1/(1+Parm3) - 1/(1+Parm4)

C = 1/(1+2Parm3) + 1/(1+2Parm4) - 2B(1+Parm3,1+Parm4)

where B(x,y) is the Beta function.

B(x,y) = (G(x)G(y))/G(x+y)

where G(z) is the Gamma function. The Gamma function is evaluated recursively on the interval 0<=z<=1, and then G(z+1), for 0<=z<=1, is approximated by the formula in Abramawitz and Stegun.

References:

Ramberg, J. S., and B. W. Schmeiser, "An Approximate Method for Generating Asymmetric Random Variables", <u>Communications</u> <u>of</u> <u>the</u> <u>ACM</u>, Vol. 17, pp. 78-82

Abramowitz, M, and I. A. Stegun, <u>Handbook</u> <u>of</u> <u>Mathematical</u> <u>Functions</u>, National Bureau of Standards Aplied Mathematics Series 55, June 1964

APPENDIX 6

Summary of Differences
Between XCELL+ and XCELL

The original version of this modeling system was called XCELL, and this is still in use in some places (XCELL needs less memory than XCELL+ and uses only CGA graphics). For the benefit of anyone who might be upgrading to XCELL+ from XCELL, this Appendix from the first edition of the XCELL+ User's Guide is reproduced here. (The spelling used here is that of XCELL, rather than XCELL+.)

Functionally, XCELL+ is a superset of XCELL. Everything in XCELL is carried over into XCELL+ and, with a single exception, has the same meaning in both packages. The exception is the precise definition of when a Process having both X-input and Y-input is "startable". In XCELL a Process is startable if either the X-input or Y-input is available; in XCELL+ a Process is startable only if both X-input and Y-input are available (unless they come from the same source element). See the explanation in Section B.2.1.5.3.

There has been some minor renaming of features and rearrangement of menus and modes, but in general, someone familiar with XCELL will find XCELL+ familiar and convenient.

Although the basic idea is the same, the graphical displays in XCELL+ have been significantly revised, in part to take advantage of the color and increased resolution available with the EGA board, but also reflecting better ideas on how to pack more usable information onto a small display screen.

Considerably more information is available, and more is presented graphically. For example, you can now distinguish between different types of arrival mechanisms at a Receiving Area by the position of the link-attachment stub (see Section B.4). However, the stub-position code is not something you must commit to memory, since the full textual description of a element is still available in <display detail>.

In many situations in design, where more detail is required than can be shown graphically, XCELL automatically flashes the <display detail> screen. In place of this, XCELL+ uses a 3-line overlay window, showing only the information appropriate to the particular context. This relies on an overlay window facility built into XCELL+, rather than on some general purpose "windowing package".

Overall, as a result of the redesign of the graphical displays, there are almost twice as many rows and twice as many columns in the portion of the factory floor that can be seen at one time in normal-scale display -- even though more information is presented for each element. There is also a significant increase in the number of rows and columns in "reduced-scale

display", and reduced-scale display is now available in all modes -- it can
be used in **run** mode as well as **design**.

The functional enhancements in XCELL+, relative to XCELL, are listed below,
with references to the appropriate sections in the User's Guide.

Unit tagging (Sections B.4.1, E.2.1.3, E.3, E.4)
    The identity of individual elements can optionally be preserved.
    Sample units are tagged, as they are released from the Receiving Area.
    The progress of a tagged unit can be observed in tracing and charting
    (with units color-coded by the Receiving Area of origin), and average
    flow-time, total processing time, and total waiting time is computed
    for tagged units.

More flexible Buffers (Sections B.6.2, B.6.3, C.2.3, C.3.1)
    Buffers have new options:
        1. Zero-capacity is allowed, useful to pool input and distribute
           output of a Process.
        2. Ordering can be first-in-first-out (FIFO) or last-in-first-out
           (LIFO).
        3. LIFO Buffers can have a minimum holding-time for units.

Cost Computations (Sections B.7, E.4)
    Each element has two separate cost coefficients:
        1. A fixed, or "capital" cost -- the cost of having this element
           in the model, regardless of what work it does.
        2. A variable, or "operating" cost -- the cost per unit of thruput
           of work the element does.
    These costs are automatically summarized on the <cost results> display.
    (In many cases, this summary makes it unnecessary to transfer the
    simulation results to a separate spreadsheet for analysis.)

Thruput counts
    The number of units moving through each element is counted and
    reported.

Commitment of Receiving Areas and Shipping Areas to a particular part
    (Sections B.4.2, B.5.1) Receiving Areas must be, and Shipping Areas
    can be associated with one type of part.

File-batch mode for Receiving Areas and Shipping Areas (Sections B.4, B.5)
    The batch schedule of arrivals and shipments can be drawn from an
    auxiliary file. (The effect is like manual-batch, but is of course,
    more convenient for repeated runs.)

Logging of supply and demand (Section B.4, B.5)
    The pattern with which units are drawn from Receiving Areas and
    accepted by Shipping Areas can be recorded in an auxiliary file for
    external analysis.

Sequence-dependent setup time (Section B.2.1.4)
    There are major and minor setups, depending upon whether or not the
    previous Process was in the same "group" as the new Process.

Drift of percent reject (Section B.2.1.2.2)
    The percentage of units rejected by a Process can gradually change,
    and be automatically reset when a limiting value is reached.

Multiple-unit output (Section B.2.1.2.3)
    The normal-output of a Process can be partitioned into multiple units.

Renaming Process output (Section B.2.1.2)
    The output of a Process can be a part whose name is different from the
    Process itself. The implication is that there can be **two** or more
    different Processes on the same Workcenter that all produce the same
    part.

<u>Null-input</u> and <u>Null-output</u> <u>Processes</u> (Sections B.2.1.1.1, B.2.1.2.4)
Processes with neither X nor Y-input links specified are assummed to not need input, and are startable without input. Similarly, Processes without specification of a normal-output links are assumed to have no concern for disposition of normal-output and are never blocked on completion of a good unit.

<u>Total-content</u> <u>Buffer</u> <u>Triggers</u> (Section B.2.1.5.2)

<u>Generalized</u> <u>Gantt</u> <u>Chart</u> (Section E.2.1.3)
Maintenance Facilities, as well as Workcenters are now included on the Gantt Chart. As new Workcenters and Maintenance Facilities are added to the model, they are automatically included in the Gantt Chart, if there are free lines in the Chart. You now have complete control over which Workcenters and Maintenance Facilities are included in the Chart, and how they are assigned to individual lines of the Chart.

<u>Overlay</u> <u>Buffer</u> <u>Plotting</u> (Section E.2.1.2)
The plot of Buffers contents -- a separate display mode in XCELL -- is now an overlay on the tracing display. Three-quarters of the tracing display is still visible, so that tracing and plotting can be viewed at the same time. There is also now the option of showing the <u>maximum</u> stock, in a multi-stock Buffer, rather than the level of a specific stock.

<u>Complete</u> <u>hard-copy</u> <u>of</u> <u>model</u> <u>specifications</u> (Section E.4.2)
There is a single-key command to print the contents of all the detailed display screens. The dump-to-printer of the graphical display of the factory floor is also builtin.

<u>Result</u> <u>output</u> <u>to</u> <u>a</u> <u>file</u> (Section E.4.3)
Result output can be directed to a standard data file, so it can be analyzed external to XCELL+ (by a spreadsheet package, for example).

<u>Suppress</u> <u>display</u> for all types of elements (Section A.6.1)
Any drawing of any element, regardless of type, can be suppressed.

<u>Jump</u> <u>to</u> design (Section A.2)
A special "direct jump" to design mode has been assigned to (unlabeled) function key F10. This is a convenient short-cut for the most frequently travelled path for experienced users.

<u>Auxiliary</u> <u>Resources</u> (Sections B.2.1.6, B.8)
Each Process can optionally require one or two Auxiliary Resources (in addition to availability of Workcenter). This can represent an operator, or just a means of limiting the number of Processes that can be active simultaneously.

<u>Asynchronous</u> <u>Materials</u> <u>Handling</u> <u>Facilities</u> (Section B.9)
Networks of Paths and Control Points, linked for pick-up and drop-off to Receiving Areas, Buffers, Workcenters and Shipping Areas. Carriers bear unit loads over the networks.

APPENDIX 7

Sample Models

Several examples of factory models are included on the XCELL+ distribution disk. These are described below.

Example: Semi-Automatic Machines

      Model filename: SEMIAUTO

A semi-automatic machine is a machine which requires an operator at the start and end of a cycle, but not during the bulk of processing. An example would be a machine that operates automatically but requires an operator for loading and unloading.

In this example, each automatic machine is represented by a WorkCenter and a Buffer. Each WorkCenter has 3 Processes: PLD (load operation), PPC (actual processing), and PUL (unload). Process descriptions are as follows: (where k is the WorkCenter number -- i.e. for W2, K = 2)

        PLD   processing-time = 1
                setup-time = 0
                input is Part PLD from Buffer B1
                output is Part PLD to Buffer Bk
                trigger-low on 0 parts in Buffer Bk
                1 unit of AuxiliaryResource A1 required

        PPC   processing-time = 1
                setup-time = 0
                input is Part PLD from Buffer Bk
                output is Part PPC to Buffer Bk

        PUL   processing-time = 1
                setup-time = 0
                input is Part PPC from Buffer Bk
                output is Part PUL to ShippingArea S1
                1 unit of AuxiliaryResource A1 required

  Note that the processing-times may be specified as any constant, or from a distribution. The operator for the loading and unloading is represented by AuxiliaryResource A1.

Example: Indexing Conveyor

      Model filename: INDEX

An indexing conveyor is a transfer device with a fixed capacity which simultaneously moves each position a set distance. Empty positions are preserved, meaning that parts will not advance forward to fill an empty position before the indexing time.

One solution is to model each of the four positions on the conveyor as a WorkCenter. Because an indexing conveyor   is   non-accumulating, each WorkCenter must have two Processes -- one representing the Process for the actual part, and the other representing a Process for an empty position. This prevents parts on the previous position from "accumulating" into the next position.

Output from the four WorkCenters flows to a Buffer B2. When the fourth part arrives at the Buffer the conveyor is ready to index, and Process X at WorkCenter IDX is triggered. This releases four parts to Buffer B5. An assembly Process at WorkCenter NXT, combined with the triggered Process at WorkCenter IDX, forces the indexing operation to take place at all conveyor positions simultaneously. Additionally, NXT renames the parts to correspond to the next Buffer position and moves them to Buffer B6. When a part completes processing at the last station, it flows off the conveyor to Buffer B3.

Example: Electronic Assembly Area

> Model filename: ELECASSY

In this example, electronic parts are first loaded onto the conveyor, then assembled in five consecutive operations (10, 20, 30, 40, 50), and then unloaded from the conveyor. There is one station each for loading, for operation 10, for operation 20 and for unloading. There are three stations each for operations 30, 40, and 50 -- because those operations have long processing-times. Each individual part will go through one sequence of operation 30, 40, and 50 (bypassing the other 30, 40, 50 sequences).

Additionally, a pallet is required to process and move a part on the conveyor.

operation	processing-time (per unit, in seconds)
LOAD	9.0
10	8.5
20	8.6
30	26.5 average (range is 25 - 28)
40	26.5 average (range is 25 - 28)
50	26.5 average (range is 25 - 28)
UNLOAD	8.5

conveyor speed = 1 foot/second
pallet length = 1 foot

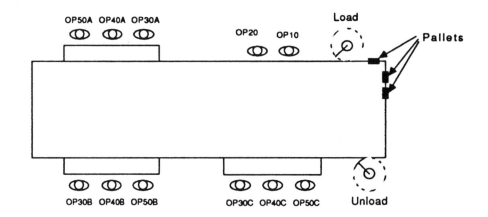

Example: Sheet Mill

        Model filenames: MILL and MILL_MH

Annealed steel coils arrive at a holding area where they cool for 2 - 3
days.   After cooling they are moved via overhead crane onto a roller
conveyor (with capacity of 10 coils). It takes at least 10 minutes for the
conveyor to move a coil to the next processing station -- the temper mill.
Tempering takes 20 - 30 minutes depending on coil size, and requires an
operator. Coils move off the temper mill to an "out space" with capacity
for a single coil. There the crane picks the coil up and moves it to the
packaging/shipping area, where it is prepared for shipment to the customer.
A single maintenance crew is responsible for both crane and temper mill
failures.

Sheet Mill-Post Annealing

Two different versions of an XCELL+ model for this facility are provided.
The model in file MILL represents the overhead crane with WorkCenters. The
model in file MILL_MH uses the specialized materials handling elements to
represent the crane.

XCELL+ Model of Sheet Mill

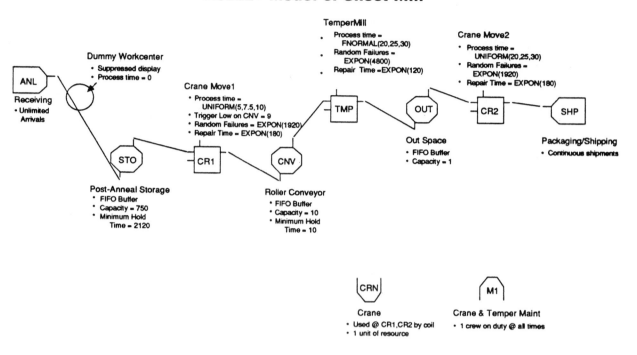

XCELL+ Model of Sheet Mill with Material Handling Constructs

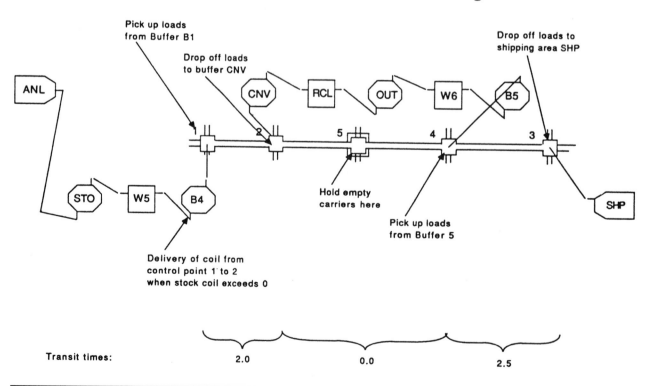

Example: Conveyor System

       Model filename: CEXAMPLE

This model represents an assembly operation for two similar parts, P1 and P2. An unlimited supply of raw material is assumed. Upon arrival at the system each part is loaded onto a pallet and six manual operations are performed on it: OP10, OP20, OP30, OP40, OP50, and OP60. Processing takes place on a dedicated conveyor loop (a separate loop for each part type). When a part reaches the end of its loop it is unloaded from its pallet and transferred to a belt conveyor. The belt conveyor is represented by a first-in-first-out Buffer with a minimum holding-time of 10 seconds. At the end of the belt conveyor the part is picked up by one of two robots and transferred onto another pallet on a common conveyor for both part types.

Conveyor System Example

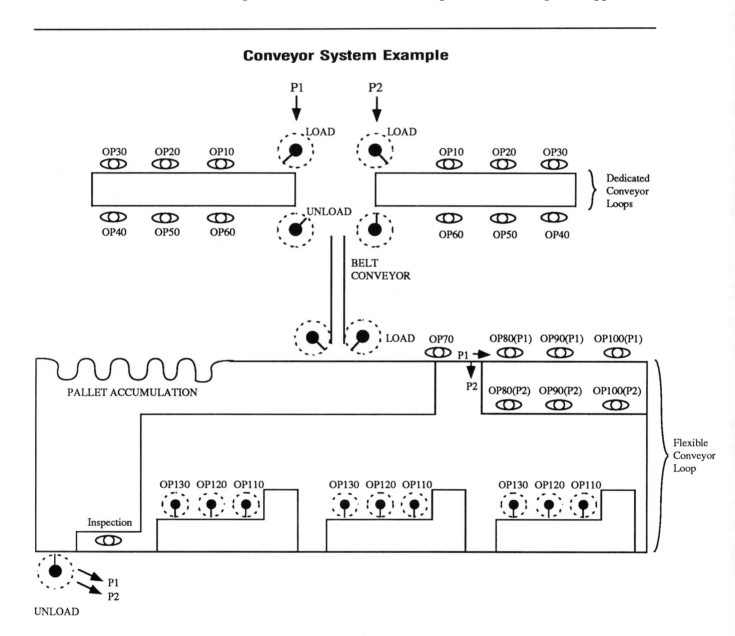

The first operation on this final conveyor loop, OP70, is required for both part types. Parts are next routed by type such that a specialized set of three operations (OP80, OP90, and OP100) are performed on each type. (P1's stay on the upper portion of the loop for these operations; P2's take the lower portion.) The final three processing operations (OP110, OP120, and OP130) are the same for both part types and are performed at one of three groups of three robotic workstations. The conveyor is controlled so that the same number of pallets to routed to each of the three robot groups.

Parts are then inspected. 15% of the parts fail this inspection and are routed back to OP80, OP90 and OP100 for reprocessing. 20% of the reprocessed parts fail a second inspection and are scrapped. Acceptable parts are routed to the unload station.

All the robots are subject to periodic failure. There are two repair crews, one dedicated to the load/unload robots, and the other dedicated to the nine robots performing operations OP110, OP120, and OP130.

For example, this model might be useful for:
> -- estimating the number of pallets required for maximum throughput
> -- identifying the bottleneck that limits throughput
> -- determining repair crew staffing
> -- determining the sensitivity of throughput to robot downtime characteristics.

Index—Glossary

(citations are to Sections in the User's Guide)

accept: the movement of material into a ShippingArea -- B.5

analysis: examination of the factory model for inconsistencies, omissions, rough estimation of capacity -- D

animation: dynamic display of events; tracing -- E.2.1.1

Area: (Floor Area) a portion of the factory floor designated by a distinctive background color -- A.7

arrivals: material arriving at a ReceivingArea -- B.4

assembly: action that occurs when a Process has two (or more) inputs -- B.2.1.1, C.2.3

audible alarm: optional tone issued when disruption of flow occurs -- E.2.2

automatic run: running the model continuously (as opposed to manual "one-step") -- E.1

automatic switch: switching between Processes at a WorkCenter automatically, (as opposed to manual switching) -- B.2.1.5

AuxiliaryResource: home site for a number of Resources of a particular type needed by specified Processes -- B.2.1.6, B.8

backlogging demand: technique to avoid losing unsatisfied demand at ShippingAreas -- C.6.2

batch-mode: an arrival mechanism at a ReceivingArea -- B.4
: a shipment mechanism at a ShippingArea -- B.5

batch-size in processing: number of consecutive units that must be produced before a Process switch is allowed -- B.2.1.5

blocking: state that occurs when a Process cannot dispose of its output -- E.2.1.1, E.2.1.3, E.2.2
: state when a Carrier cannot move because another Carrier is present in the "next" cell -- E.2.1.1

bottleneck: an element limiting the throughput capacity of a factory model; detected by Analysis -- D.4

173

breakdown: event when a WorkCenter requires (unscheduled) Maintenance -- B.2.2

Buffer: cell in which to store work-in-process inventory between two consecutive Processes -- B.6

capacity: number of units a Buffer can hold -- B.6
      : number of units a batch-mode ReceivingArea can hold -- B.4
      : number of units a batch-mode ShippingArea can hold -- B.5

capital cost: fixed cost of including element in model -- B.7

Carrier: a movable element to transport material over Paths -- B.9.3

cell: one position on the factory floor; can accommodate a single element -- A.3

cell-cursor: underscore on screen identifying one particular cell -- A.3
      dotted cell-cursor can be moved for cell selection
      corner-only cell-cursor indicated cell has been selected

changeover: switch of a WorkCenter from one Process to another -- B.2.1.4

charging-time: the time a Carrier spends at a ChargingPoint have its batteries recharged -- B.9.6

ChargingPoint: a special type of ControlPoint where Carrier batteries are recharged -- B.9.6

charting: display option during run -- E.2.1.3

checking: consistency checking in model Analysis -- D.2

composite element: a factory element modeled by two or more model elements -- C.2

ControlPoint: intersection of Paths in a materials handling network -- B.9

conversion: a supporting package to convert model files to Release 4 format from previous release format -- F.4

conveyor: mechanism to move material between cells; represented by Process input and output -- B.2.1.1, B.2.1.2, C.3.1

copy: action during design to duplicate an existing element into an empty cell -- B.1

cost summary: summary of capital and operating costs of the model -- B.7, E.4

cumulative results: results from the beginning of the run -- E.4.1

cursor: underscore on screen identifying one particular cell -- A.3
      dotted cursor can be moved for cell selection
      corner-only cursor indicates a cell has been selected

deadlock: situation when no further progress in the run is possible -- E.1.1

default: the value supplied, or action taken automatically if you don't specify otherwise; many default values can be changed using the Tabular Editor -- B.1.1.1

delivery: method of dynamic Carrier dispatch -- Section B.6.5

design: the menu during which the structure of the model is changed, accessible from **main session control** -- B

destination: ControlPoint to which a routed Carrier is headed -- B.9.4

destination list: a list of ControlPoint numbers associated with a particular ControlPoint -- B.9.4

display detail: expansion of scale of display so entire screen is devoted to a single element

dis-assembly: partitioning the output of a Process -- B.2.1.2.3, C.2.4

drift: change in percent of reject-output -- B.2.1.2.2

dropoff connection: link from a ControlPoint for Carrier discharge -- B.9.1

dropoff-time: time for Carrier to make a dropoff at a ControlPoint -- B.9.1

dummy Process: a secondary Process in a composite WorkCenter, usually with 0 processing-time, used to expand the capability of the standard Process -- C.2

echelon stock: the term (in inventory theory) for the total stock in the system of a particular part -- C.7

empirical distribution: a statistical distribution based on actual observations; modeled in XCELL+ by a Ramberg-Schmeiser distribution -- B.2.1.3, B.2.2, Appendix 5

empty Carrier: Carrier not currently bearing any part -- E.2.1.1

engagement: Carrier making dropoff to a WorkCenter retained during Processing of unit -- B.9.1.1

event: an action during running a model that changes the state of some element

exponential distribution: optional distribution for processing-times and maintenance -- B.2.1.3, B.2.2

FIFO Buffer: optional first-in-first-out ordering of units in a Buffer -- B.6.2

file: a block of data in disk storage -- F

file-batch: optional batch-mode for ReceivingArea or ShippingArea where batch specification is given in a file -- B.4, B.5, F.5

file manager: menu in which you can store a factory model on disk, or retrieve a model previously stored -- F

finite-normal distribution: optional distribution for processing-times -- B.2.1.3

Floor Area: a portion of the factory floor designated by a distinctive background color -- A.7

flow: throughput capacity of model -- D.3

flow-time: time for a unit to pass through the factory, from release from ReceivingArea to acceptance at ShippingArea -- B.4.1, E.4

frequency of tagging: the sampling rate for tagging units on release from ReceivingArea -- B.4.1

full-charge run-time: the time that a Carrier can run when its batteries are fully-charged -- B.9.6

function key: one of the special numbered keys on the keyboard whose role is described by labels on the display screen -- A.2

general distribution: optional facility for modeling arbitrary or empirical distribution of processing-times and maintenance activity -- B.2.1.4, B.2.2, Appendix 5

Gantt charting: display option during run -- E.2.1.3

group code: means of specifying similarity between Processes to control amount of setup-time -- B.2.1.4

high-trigger: Process switch invoked by a stock increasing to a specified level -- B.2.1.5.2

holding-time: an option on a FIFO Buffer giving the minimum time a unit must remain in the Buffer -- B.6.2, C.3.1.1

HoldingPoint: a ControlPoint at which empty Carriers are pre-positioned for release by request -- B.9.4.3

idle: state of a WorkCenter when no input material is available -- B.2

input: to overall system at ReceivingArea -- B.4
  : to Process -- B.2.1.1
  : to Buffer -- B.6
  : to ShippingArea -- B.5

inventory results: the results regarding work-in-process inventory from running the model; for each Buffer, batch-mode ReceivingArea and batch-mode ShippingArea -- E.4

jump to design: a special menu change assigned to function key F10 -- A.2

kurtosis: characteristic of shape of a statistical distribution -- Appendix 5

LIFO Buffer: option last-in-first-out ordering of units in a Buffer -- B.6.2

limits: capacity limit of Buffer -- B.6
  : capacity limit of batch-mode ReceivingArea -- B.4
  : capacity limit of batch-mode ShippingArea -- B.5

line balancing: shifting work between adjacent Processes to equalize the unit processing-times -- C.5.5

link: general term for connection between two elements for material flow -- A.4

loaded Carrier: Carrier currently bearing one unit of particular Part -- E.2.1.1

logging: optional recording in a log file of releases from a ReceivingArea or acceptances by a ShippingArea -- B.4, B.5, F.6

low-trigger: Process switch invoked by a stock decreasing to a specified level -- B.2.1.5.2

macro facility: the ability to define "higher level" constructs (larger than a single element) for repeated use -- F.2.1

main: "main XCELL+ session control" -- the bottom level of the menu-tree -- A

MaintenanceCenter: mechanism for repairing and providing scheduled
          maintenance for WorkCenters -- B.3, B.2.2

major-setup: the setup-time required when the group of the Process being
          setup is different from the group of the previous
          Process -- B.2.1.4

manual batch: optional delivery to ReceivingArea -- B.4
          : optional shipment from ShippingArea -- B.5
          each batch is specified individually as it occurs

materials handling: the movement of units between elements -- C.3

menu: the current situation in the session; a position in the menu-tree;
          a particular set of actions assigned to the function
          keys -- A.2, Appendix 2

merge factories: the merger of a factory model (from disk) with the
          model currently in the workspace -- F.2.1

minimum batch-size: the batch-size for a Process below which the
          WorkCenter will become oversaturated with setup-time
          -- D.3.9

minimum holding-time: an option on a FIFO Buffer giving the minimum time
          a unit must remain in the Buffer -- B.6.2, C.3.1.1

minor-setup: the setup-time required when the group of the Process being
          setup is the same as the group of the previous Process
          -- B.2.1.4

move: action during design to relocate an existing element to a different
          cell -- B.1

multiple units: optional partition of normal-output into multiple units
          -- B.2.1.2.3

names: identification assigned to an individual element. Names are 10
          or fewer characters, and must be unique -- A.4
          Only first 3 characters are shown on normal-scale
          display. Elements can be referenced by full name
          as an alternative to moving the cell-cursor.

new factory: action accessible from **main** session control to clear workspace
          to begin construction of a new factory model;
          destroys current model in the workspace

normal distribution: optional distribution for processing-times -- B.2.1.3

normal-output: the "good" (non-rejected) output of a Process -- B.2.1.2
          shown attached to the right-side stub of Process

null-input Process: Process with neither X nor Y-input -- B.2.1.1.1

null-output Process: Process without normal-output link -- B.2.1.2.4

operating cost: the cost, per unit of thruput, of running a particular
          element -- B.7, E.4

operation: the basic task of the model, which is performed on a part by a
          Process at a WorkCenter -- B.2.1

operator (for a Process): modeled by AuxiliaryResource -- B.2.1.6

ordered Buffer: optional form of Buffer in which order of individual units
          is significant -- B.6.2

output: from overall system at ShippingArea -- B.5
      : from Process -- B.2.1.2
      : from Buffer -- B.6
      : from ReceivingArea -- B.4

palletizer: a material handling device for batching units -- C.3.3

panning: the act of shifting the viewing window on the factory floor
(also called "scrolling") -- A.6

parking area: a ControlPoint at which empty Carriers are held -- B.9.4.3

Part: name of a particular product that flows through system; each Process
is associated with some Part, and the output of the
Process bears that name -- B.2.1

Path: a connected sequence of Segments between ControlPoints -- B.9.2

pause: status in **run mode** when model is not actually running -- E.1

period: result collection interval during run -- E.4.1

pickup connection: link to a ControlPoint over which Carrier picks-up
a load -- B.9.1

pickup-time: time for Carrier to make a pick-up at a ControlPoint -- B.9.1

plotting: display option during run; displays stock in a Buffer -- E.2.1.2

pre-positioning Point: a ControlPoint at which empty Carriers are held
-- B.9.4.3

printing: -- E.4.2, E.4.3, Appendix 1

priority: tie-breaking value for selecting Processes on a WorkCenter --
B.2.1.5

Process: the activity of processing a particular Part at a particular
WorkCenter -- B.2.1

processing-time: time required for a Process to perform one cycle, that is
to produce one unit of its Part -- B.2.1.3
      : also total of all processing-times for a tagged unit
-- B.4.1, E.4

pull-production: scheme in which Processes are invoked by stock at
a downstream cell falling to a critical value
-- B.2.1.5.2

push-production: scheme in which Processes are invoked by stock at an
upstream cell increasing to a critical value
-- B.2.1.5.2

queue: WorkCenters waiting for available service team at Maintenance
Center -- B.2.2, B.3

QUIT: the command (F8 in **main**) that returns you from XCELL+ to the MSDOS
operating system

Ramberg-Schmeiser distribution: an optional distribution used to model
processing-times and maintenance activity,
-- B.2.1.3, B.2.2, Appendix 5

random number: an observation from a probability distribution, used for
processing-times, breakdown and repair events, and
Process yield -- B.2.1.2.1, B.2.1.3, B.2.2, E.6.2

ReceivingArea: source of input to factory model -- B.4

recycle: repeat operation when output is rejected; the default disposition
of rejected-output of a Process; shown as link from
top stub of Process to left side of same Process
-- B.2.1.2.1

reduced scale: optional display form in which cell size in reduced, hence a
larger segment of the factory floor is visible at one
time -- A.6

regular-batch: optional delivery to ReceivingArea -- B.4
: optional shipment from ShippingArea -- B.5

reject: defective output from Process -- B.2.1.2.1
shown attached to the top stub of Process
: batch-arrival turned away from ReceivingArea -- B.4

release: the movement of material from a ReceivingArea into the factory
-- B.4

remaining-run-time: the length of time a Carrier can continue to run
before its battery is discharged -- B.9.6

remove: action during design to delete an existing element -- B.1

rename output: an option in which the output of a Process can be given
a name different from that of the Process itself
-- B.2.1.2

repair: the period during which a WorkCenter is undergoing service by a
MaintenanceCenter -- B.2.2

request: a mechanism for dynamic dispatch of Carriers -- B.6.4

request-only ControlPoint: a ControlPoint where pickups are made only
in response to requests or deliveries -- B.9.4.3

reserve run-time: the level of remaining-run-time at which an emtpy
unrouted Carrier is directed to a ChargingPoint --
B.9.6

reset limit: the value of drifting percent of rejects at a Process that
causes the percent to be reset to its original value
-- B.2.1.2.2

results: the data produced by running the model; a menu in which these
data are summarized -- E.4

return: move "down" the menu tree to previous menu; the action assigned to
function key 8 -- A.2

reversible Path: an optional form of Path for which direction is dynamically
reversible -- B.9.2.1

rework: rejected output from a Process directed to a Buffer -- B.2.1.2.1
link shown from top stub of Process

routed Carrier: a Carrier headed for a predetermined destination -- B.9.4

routing: the sequence of operations to be performed on a particular Part,
hence the path Part follows from one Process/WorkCenter
to another -- B.2

run: menu during which the factory model is operated; reached from main
session control -- A.2, E

run-in: the early portion of a run, from which results are discarded
-- E.6.1

schedule: of arriving material at ReceivingArea -- B.4
: of shipments from ShippingArea -- B.5
: of Processes at a WorkCenter -- B.2.1.5

scheduled maintenance: optional maintenance service at regular intervals --
B.2.2

scrap: rejected output from a Process directed to a ShippingArea --
-- B.2.1.2.1; link shown from top stub of Process

scrolling: act of repositioning the display window -- A.5

Segment: single cell component of a Path between ControlPoints -- B.9.2

service-team: the resource at a MaintenanceCenter that provides
scheduled maintenance or repair service to
WorkCenters -- B.3

setup-time: time required to prepare a WorkCenter for a Process after
another Process has been running -- B.2.1.4

shift view: the act of repositioning the viewing window on the factory
floor -- A.6

shipments: release of finished product from factory model to outside World
-- B.5

ShippingArea: a location from which shipments are made -- B.5

shortage: batch-shipments not satisifed by stock on hand -- B.5

single-step: executing all events at one particular time under manual
control during tracing -- E.2.1.1

skewness: characteristic of shape of a statistical distribution
-- Appendix 5

startable: a Process having all required material available -- B.2.1.5.3

stock: the quantity of a particular Part at a particular Buffer -- B.6

structure: The permanent characteristics of the factory model, specified
during **design** -- B

structural check: an examination of the model for consistency and
continuity performed by the Analysis option -- D.2

suppress display: option of suppressing the display of the symbol for an
individual element -- A.6.1

switch: change from one Process to another at a WorkCenter -- B.2.1.5

Tabular Editor: facility with which to change many attributes of all
elements of a particular type;
also used to change default values -- B.1.1

tagging: identification of individual units as they are released from a
ReceivingArea -- B.4.1, E.3

thruput: the number of distinct units passing through an element; the basis
of operating cost summary -- B.7, E.4

timeunits: means of synchronizing activity in the model (undimensioned) --
B.2.1.3

tracing: display option during run -- E.2.1.1

traffic-control: the rules that control the direction a departing Carrier takes from a ControlPoint -- B.9.4

transit-time: time for a Carrier to cross a single Segment or ControlPoint -- B.9.1, B.9.2.2

traverse-time: time for a Carrier to traverse an entire Path -- B.9.2.2 a sum of individual transit-times

trigger: stock level that invokes a Process-switch -- B.2.1.5.2

trigger-high: Process-switch invoked by a stock increasing to a specified level -- B.2.1.5.2

trigger-low: Process-switch invoked by a stock decreasing to a specified level -- B.2.1.5.2

uniform distribution: optional distribution of processing-times -- B.2.1.3
: optional distribution of batch-arrivals -- B.4
: optional distribution of arrival intervals -- B.4
: optional distribution of shipment sizes -- B.5
: optional distribution of shipment intervals -- B.5
: optional distribution of maintenance intervals -- B.2.2
: optional distribution of service-times -- B.2.2

unit: the increment of material movement in the model

unit tagging: the identification of individual units as they are released from a ReceivingArea -- B.4.1, E.3

unordered Buffer: the default Buffer in which the order of individual units is immaterial -- B.6.1

utilization: the fraction of time that a WorkCenter, MaintenanceCenter AuxiliaryResource or Carrier is busy -- D.3.7, E.4

variance: characteristic of shape of a statistical distribution -- Appendix 5

wait: retaining a Carrier at a ControlPoint for pickup or dropoff -- B.9.4

waiting-time: the time between release from ReceivingArea and acceptance at a ShippingArea when unit is not being processed; difference between flowtime and processing-time -- B.4.1, E.4

window: the portion of the factory floor visible on the display screen -- A.6

WorkCenter: active element of a model; site where Processes are performed -- B.2

workspace: the portion of computer memory where the current model resides; holds only one model -- F

work-in-process inventory: units in the factory; in particular, units in Buffers, ReceivingAreas or ShippingAreas not being processed -- E.4

X-input: arbitrary name for one input to Process (top stub on left) -- B.2.1.1

Y-input: arbitrary name for one input to Process (lower stub on left) -- B.2.1.1

yield: fraction of good units produced by a Process -- B.2.1.2.1

zero-capacity Buffer: a Buffer with zero storage-capacity used to aggregate or distribute material flow -- B.6.3

zone: a portion of the network of ControlPoints and Paths with a limited number of Carriers; every ControlPoint belongs to some zone -- B.9.5

zoom: the act of changing from normal to reduced scale, or reduced to normal scale -- see A.6

References

1. General references on simulation are:

   Shannon, Robert E., _Systems Simulation: the art and science_, Prentice-Hall, Englewood Cliffs, NJ, 1975

   Law, Averill M., and W. David Kelton, _Simulation Modeling and Analysis_, McGraw-Hill, New York, NY, 1982

   Gordon, Geoffrey, _System Simulation_ 2nd edition, Prentice Hall, Englewood Cliffs, NJ, 1978

2. Two classic (i.e. ancient, but still sometimes quoted) position papers on simulation methodology are:

   Conway, R. W., B. M. Johnson, and W. L. Maxwell, "Some Problems of Digital Systems Simulation", _Management Science_, Vol. 6, October 1959

   Conway, R. W., "Some Tactical Problems in Digital Simulation", _Management Science_, Vol. 10, October 1963

   More recent references on methodology and measurement are:

   Duersch, R. R., and L. W. Schruben, "An Interative Run Length Control for Simulation on PCs", _Proceedings of the 1986 Winter Simulation Conference_, Washington, DC, December 8, 1986

   Schruben, L., "Simulation Modeling with Event Graphics", _Communications of the ACM_, Vol. 26, No. 11, November 1983

   Schruben, L., "Control of Initialization Bias in Multivariate Simulation Response", _Communications of the ACM_, Vol. 24, No. 4, April 1981

   Schruben, L., "Confidence Interval Estimation Using Standardized Time Series", _Operations Research_, Vol. 31, No. 6, November 1983

3. References for some of the major general-purpose simulation languages are:

   GPSS, GPSS/H
      Gordon, G., _System Simulation_, 2nd ed., Prentice-Hall, Englewood Cliffs, NJ, 1978
      Wolverine Software Corp. 7630 Little River Turnpike, Suite 208 Annandale, VA 22003

SIMSCRIPT
    Kiviat, P. J., R. Villanueva, and H. M. Markowitz,
        The SIMSCRIPT II Programming Language, Prentice-Hall,
        Englewood Cliffs, NJ, 1968
    Russell, E. C., Simulation and SIMCRIPT II.5, CACI Inc.,
        Los Angeles, CA, 1976

SLAM II
    Pritsker, A. A. B., Introduction to Simulation and SLAM II,
        3rd Edition, Systems Publishing, West Lafayette,
        Indiana, 1986

SIMAN
    Pegden, C. D., Introduction to SIMAN, Systems Modeling
        Corporation, State College, Pa., 1982

SEE WHY
    SEE WHY Visual Interative Simulation Reference Manual, Istel Inc,
        83 Cambridge Street, Burlington, MA 01803

TESS
    Pritsker Corporation, P.O.Box 2413, West Lafayette, IN 47906

4. References for some recent simulation systems with graphical interfaces,
   presumably oriented to manufacturing applications are listed below. (This
   list is far from exhaustive, and inclusion on the list does not imply any
   value judgment or endorsement on our part.)

SLAMSYSTEM
SLAMSYSTEM Extended Modeling Option - Packaging Lines
    Pritsker Corporation, P.O. Box 2413, West Lafayette, IN 47906

MAP/1
    Miner, R.J., and L. J. Rolston, MAP/1 User's Manual, Pritsker
    Corporation, P.O. Box 2413, West Lafayette, IN 47906

GPSS/PC
Minuteman Software, Stow, MA

WITNESS   (an application package, based on SEE WHY)
    Introduction to WITNESS - User Manual,
    Istel Inc., 83 Cambridge Street, Burlington, MA 01803

AUTO MOD
    Auto Simulations Inc., Bountiful, Utah

Modelmaster II
    Factory Automation Division, General Electric Co.,
    Charlottesville, VA

SIMFACTORY (an application package, based on SIMSCRIPT)
    CACI Inc., 3344 North Torrey Pines Court, La Jolla, CA 92037

SIMPLE_1
    SIMPLE_1 User's Guide and Reference Manual, Sierra Simulations and
    Software, 303 Esther Avenue, Campbell, CA 95008

PCModel, PCModel/GAF
    Simulation Software Systems, 2470 Lone Oak Drive, San Jose,
    CA 95121

MicroSAINT
    Micro Analysis and Design, Inc., 9132 Thunderhead Drive,
    Boulder, CO 80302

MAST
> CMS Research, Inc., 600 S. Main St., Brooklyn Center, Oshkosh,
> WI 54901

IDSS
> IDSS Prototype (2.0), Version 4, User's Reference Manual,
> Pritsker Corporation, P.O. Box 2413, West Lafayette, IN 47906

PAW
> Melamed, B., and R. J. T. Morris, "Visual Simulation: The
> Performance Analysis Workstation", IEEE Computer, August
> 1985
> Information Research Associates, 911 West 29th Street, Austin,
> TX 78705

CINEMA (a graphical interface to SIMAN)
> Systems Modeling Corp., PO Box 10074, State College, PA 16805

5. The reference for the general probability distribution:

> Ramberg, J. S., and B. W. Schmeiser, "An Approximate Method for
> Generating Asymmetric Random Variables",
> Communications of the ACM, Vol. 17 (1974)

6. References regarding the generation of pseudo-random numbers:

> Knuth, D. E., The Art of Computer Programming, Vol 2, Addison-
> Wesley, Reading, Mass., 1969

> Marsaglia, G., "Random Numbers Fall Mainly in the Planes",
> National Academic of Science Procedings, 61:25-28, 1968

> Ahrens, J. H., and U. Dieter, "Computer Methods for Sampling from the
> Exponential and Normal Distributions",
> Communications of the ACM, Vol. 15 (1972)

> Ahrens, J. H., and U. Dieter, "Computer Methods for Sampling from the
> Gamma, Beta, Poisson and Binomial Distributions",
> Computing, Vol. 12 (1974)

7. Two recent surveys of the status of manufacturing theory and practice
are:

> Vollmann, Thomas E., William L. Berry and D. Clay Whybark,
> Manufacturing Planning and Control Systems, 2nd edition,
> Irwin, Homewood, Illinois 1984

> Johnson, Lynwood A., and Douglas C. Montgomery, Operations Research
> in Production Planning, Scheduling, and Inventory Control,
> Wiley, New York, NY 1974

8. The classic reference on factory scheduling is, of course:

> Conway, R. W., W. L. Maxwell and L. W. Miller, Theory of Scheduling,
> Addison Wesley, Reading, Mass., 1967

9. A book of cases suitable for operations management classes:

> Thomas, L. Joseph, and David Edwards, Cases in Operations Management
> using the XCELL Factory Modeling System, Scientific Press,
> Palo Alto, CA 1987

Other case material involving XCELL is available from the Harvard
Graduate School of Business.